WITHDRAWN

ULTIMATE BOOK OF BUSINESS FORMS

Second Edition

D1417927

Use These Tabs to Navigate This Book

All the forms found in this book along with many others are available for download from the Web site that supports this book. Go to **www.entrepreneur.com/formnet** to learn more.

ULTIMATE BOOK OF BUSINESS FORMS

Second Edition

KAREN THOMAS

Entrepreneur® Press

Publisher: Jere Calmes
Cover Design: Beth Hanson-Winter
Composition: CWL Publishing Enterprises, Inc., Madison, Wisconsin, www.cwlpub.com

This publication is designed to provide accurate and authoritative information in regard to the subject matter covered. It is sold with the understanding that the publisher is not engaged in rendering legal, accounting, or other professional services. If legal advice or other expert assistance is required, the services of a competent professional person should be sought.

—From a Declaration of Principles jointly adopted by a
Committee of the American Bar Association and
a Committee of Publishers and Associations

ISBN 13: 978-1-59918-389-5
     10: 1-59918-398-7

Library of Congress Cataloging-in-Publication Data

Thomas, Karen (Karen M.), 1979-
    Ultimate book of business forms / by Karen Thomas.
  —2nd ed.
    p. cm.
  Rev. ed. of: Ultimate book of business forms.
  ISBN-13: 978-1-59918-389-3 (alk. paper)
  ISBN-10: 1-59918-389-7
    1. New business enterprises—Law and legislation—United States—Forms.
  I. Thomas, Karen (Karen M.), 1979—Ultimate book of business forms. II. Title. III. Series.

  KF1355.A65T48 2010b
  346.73'0650269—dc22

                                                    2010016454

14 13 12 11 10   10 9 8 7 6 5 4 3 2 1

Contents

Preface

The Ultimate Book of Business Forms, Second Edition delivers the must-have forms—and then some—that small business owners need to operate whether in the office, offsite, at home, or online. Since the original title was published, the small business owner has evolved in conjunction with technology, the working environment, and economy. The new edition is structured to support a business owner's progression and is organized in a in a logical fashion that is consistent with the natural evolution of a small business.

The second edition is the forms book for the modern entrepreneur who's just started his or her business or is adapting existing operations to succeed in a highly digital and regulated world. Each chapter serves a distinct purpose in terms of providing the essential forms business owners can use to operate more efficiently and resourcefully, ultimately saving time and money.

Supporting Web Site

Every small business is unique. Therefore it's essential to have business forms that are customizable depending on your business's needs. The forms included in this book can be found online at **www.entrepreneur.com/formnet**. Forms will be available in the following formats: Word, Excel, and PDF and can be completely customized to match your business' brand, processes, and culture.

This book can be used as your reference guide as you work with each customizable form. Refer to the book to understand when and how to use the forms. Balance your budgets, file for tax rebates, and even determine if your Twitter and Facebook accounts are impacting your bottom line. There are hundreds of forms at your disposal, and each one serves a specific purpose that will help streamline business processes and maximize time.

Finding the forms online is easy. Simply visit the site, **www.entrepreneur.com/formnet**, select the appropriate forms category, and download as many forms as you need from each. There's no cost or special code required to access and customize these forms for your business.

About the Author

Karen Thomas is an accomplished writer who has much experience in business and technical writing. Thomas reported for the Orange County Register, published business and startup books with Entrepreneur Press, and continues to produce technical and consumer-friendly articles for several online properties. In addition to authoring business books, Thomas is the creative director at Affnet, Inc., an Orange County-based marketing and technological firm.

Acknowledgments

I would like to thank Jere Calmes and the team at Entrepreneur Press for allowing me this opportunity to revise the *Ultimate Book of Business Forms*. Their innate understanding of a small business owner's needs is proven in each Entrepreneur Press publication including the *Ultimate Book of Business Forms*, Second Edition, which provides a whole new slew of business forms for the modern-day businessman or woman.

CHAPTER 1

Name Your Business

OW IMPORTANT IS ESTABLISHING A name for your business? Before the marketing team can qualify the importance of a business's nomenclature, the legal department (or person in charge of the business' compliance) should understand why it's first necessary to establish a DBA.

The United States government's official online business resource (**www.business.gov**) outlines the DBA need and processes as follows:

> The legal name of a business is the name of the person or entity that owns a business. If you are the sole owner of your business, its legal name is your full name. If your business is a partnership, the legal name is the name given in your partnership agreement or the last names of the partners. For limited liability corporations (LLCs) and corporations, the business' legal name is the one that was registered with the state government.

Your business' legal name is required on all government forms and applications, including your application for employer tax IDs, licenses, and permits. However, if you want to open a shop or sell your products under a different name, then you may have to file a "fictitious name" registration form with your government agency.

A fictitious name (or assumed name, trade name, or DBA name is a business name that is different than your personal name, the names of your partners, or the officially registered name of your LLC or corporation.

This chapter includes several state-specific forms that business owners can use to file their DBA. The following state-specific DBA forms are included in this chapter: Alaska, Arkansas, Delaware, Louisiana, Iowa, Ohio, and Washington.

While it's essential to file a DBA to maintain legal compliance, a DBA is also a central component of your business brand. When selecting your DBA consider where it will appear, how it will sound, and so on. A DBA can differentiate your business from competitors. Also, once you select a DBA, make sure to check registered and unregistered trademarks to ensure you're not infringing on businesses of the same moniker.

It's best to check with your state or local agencies within your county to determine what DBA forms are required. Doing so before any business is transacted is recommended, as well.

While it's up to each individual state to decide how a business has to file its DBA, a majority either require businesses to file by mail or online. The information required online and each form differs, as well. This chapter includes several samples of forms required by states that mandate businesses mail hard copies. Many states allow business owners to file a DBA completely online.

1. Alaska Doing Business As Form

**Department of Commerce, Community, and Economic Development
Division of Corporations, Business, and Professional Licensing
Corporations Section
PO Box 110808
Juneau AK 99811-0808**

BUSINESS NAME
REGISTRATION APPLICATION

Check if this is a renewal application ☐

FULL BUSINESS NAME:

"Assumed Names" or "Fictitious Names" are referred to in Alaska as DBA Names. If the owner is a corporate entity, and is registering the name as a DBA name, list the name and principal office address of the entity.

NAME AND ADDRESS OF BUSINESS OWNER:

Name	
Mailing Address	
City, State, Zip	

NAME AND ADDRESS OF THE BUSINESS:

Name	
Mailing Address	
City, State, Zip	

ADDITIONAL PERSONS THAT HAVE AN INTEREST IN THE BUSINESS:

Name	
Mailing Address	
City, State, Zip	

The nature of the business is:

The signer acknowledges that the business is in operation. **Pursuant to AS 12.70.020 for the privilege of engaging in a business in the state, a person must first obtain a business license.**

Business License Number	

The signer must be an owner of the business, or an authorized person of the DBA entity.

Signature	**Title**

Date	**Contact Name and Phone Number** (to resolve questions with this filing)

Mail the completed form and the $25.00 non-refundable filing fee in U.S. Funds to:

**State of Alaska
Corporations Section
PO Box 110808, Juneau, AK 99811-0808**

08-575 (Rev. 12/07)

2. Arkansas Fictitious Name Form

Arkansas Secretary of State

Charlie Daniels

State Capitol • Little Rock, Arkansas 72201-1094
501-682-3409 • www.sos.arkansas.gov

Business & Commercial Services, 250 Victory Building, 1401 W. Capitol, Little Rock

INSTRUCTIONS: File with the Secretary of State's Office, Business Services Division, State Capitol, Little Rock, Arkansas 72201-1094. A copy will be returned to the entity and must be filed with the County Clerk in the county in which the entity registered office is located (unless registered office is in Pulaski County).

APPLICATION FOR FICTITIOUS NAME

Select entity type:
[ ] For-Profit Corporation ($25.00 fee)   [ ] Nonprofit Corporation ($25.00 fee)
[ ] General Partnership ($15.00 fee)   [ ] Limited Partnership ($15.00 fee)
[ ] LLC ($25.00 fee)   [ ] LLP ($15.00 fee)
[ ] LLLP ($15.00 fee)

    Pursuant to the provisions of Arkansas law, the undersigned entity hereby applies for the use of a fictitious name and submits herewith the following statement:

1.   The fictitious name under which the business is being, or will be, conducted by this entity is:

_____

2.   The character of the business being, or to be, conducted under such fictitious name is:

_____

3.   a) The entity name of the applicant and its date of qualification in Arkansas: _____

_____

b) The entity is [ ] domestic   [ ] foreign (state of domestic registration) _____

c) The location (city and street address) of the registered office of the applicant entity in Arkansas is:

_____
Street   City   State   ZIP Code

I understand that knowingly signing a false document with the intent to file with the Arkansas Secretary of State is a Class C misdemeanor and is punishable by a fine up to $100.00 and/or imprisonment up to 30 days.

Authorizing Officer _____
(Type or Print)

Authorized Signature: _____
(Chairman, Partner or other authorized person)

Address: _____

Fee: see top of page. Make payable to Arkansas Secretary of State.   DN-18/F-18/Rev. 4/06

3. Delaware Procedure for Filing Fictitious Name Certificate

PROCEDURE FOR FILING FICTITIOUS NAME CERTIFICATE

1. This certificate is being filed in accordance with Title 6 <u>Del. C.</u> Chapter 31. The applicant must bear primary responsibility for determining whether there is in existence any other business or organization utilizing the same fictitious name. The acceptance and recording of a fictitious name certificate in the Prothonotary's Office shall in no way be deemed a warranty of the applicant's right to operate under the name registered.

2. Make sure the form is complete and the information is accurate.

3. After the form is completed, please return it to the cashier for processing. If you are returning it by mail, be sure that it is notarized. Please enclose a stamped, self-addressed envelope so that we may send you a certified copy as proof of filing for your records. To register in New Castle County, mail the completed form to:

    New Castle County Prothonotary
    500 N. King Street
    Suite 500, Lower Level 1
    Wilmington, DE 19801-3746

4. The filing fee is $25.00. Your check or money order should be made payable to the "Prothonotary".

5. If you sell, change the name, or in any other way change the status of the business, you should notify this office.

6. The filing of the document covers only New Castle County. Pursuant to Title 6 <u>Del. C.</u> Chapter 31, § 3101 and § 3103, if you are going to do business in Kent or Sussex County, you will need to register with the respective Prothonotary's Office in each county.

Kent County Prothonotary	Sussex County Prothonotary
38 The Green	1 The Circle, Suite 2
Dover, DE 19901	Georgetown, DE 19947
(302) 739-3184	(302) 856-5742

7. This registration of a Trade (fictitious) name with this office has no connection with the need for a license to do business in Delaware. Applications for a Delaware Business License are available at the Division of Revenue, State of Delaware, Carvel State Building, 8th & French Streets, Wilmington, DE 19801 (302) 577-5800.

http://courts.state.de.us/superior
302-255-0825

4. Louisiana Trade Name Application

Jay Dardenne **Secretary of State** 	**APPLICATION TO REGISTER TRADE NAME** **TRADEMARK OR SERVICE MARK** (Pursuant to R.S. Of 1950, Title 51, Chapter 1, Part VI as amended)

Enclose $50 filing fee **Make remittance payable to** **Secretary of State** ***Do Not Send Cash***	Return to: **Commercial Division** **P. O. Box 94125** **Baton Rouge, LA 70804-9125** **Phone (225) 925-4704** **Web Site: www.sos.louisiana.gov**

STATE OF _____

PARISH/COUNTY OF _____

Check One: ( ) Trade Name ( ) Trademark ( ) Service Mark

Check One: ( ) Original Filing ( ) Renewal

1. Name of person(s), Corporation, Limited Liability Company or Partnership applying for registration: _____
_____

2. If applicant is a corporation, list state of incorporation: _____
_____

3. Full street address and P. O. Box address, city, state, and zip of applicant: _____
_____

4. Name of trade name, trademark or service mark to be registered. If logo is included, please describe. If the LOGO of your trade name, trademark or service mark is part of your registration, attach 3 copies of design.
_____
_____

5. Type of business or list of goods or services to which the trade name, trademark or service mark is applied:
_____

6. Enter class(es) in which trademark or service mark is registered: _____
(Class list on reverse side. There is a $50 registration fee for each class number registered.)
_____

7. Date trade name, trademark or service mark first used by applicant _____
Month, Day, Year

8. Date trade name, trademark or service mark first used in Louisiana_____
Month, Day, Year

I, the applicant, am the owner of the trade name, trademark or service mark sought to be registered and no other person, firm, association, union or corporation has the right to such use in such class, either in the identical form hereinabove described, or in any such resemblance thereto as may be calculated to deceive, and the facsimiles or counterparts herein filed are true and correct.

Sworn to and subscribed before me, the undersigned Notary Public, on this date: _____

The below named person swears that he is the applicant, or an authorized representative of the applicant, named in the foregoing application, and that the facts alleged in said application are true.
NOTARY NAME MUST BE TYPED OR PRINTED WITH NOTARY #

_____
Applicant or Authorized Representative

_____   _____
Notary Signature   Title

SS309 Rev. 10/06   (see instructions on back)

5. Iowa Application for Reservation of Name

MICHAEL A. MAURO
Secretary of State
State of Iowa

APPLICATION FOR RESERVATION OF NAME

TO THE SECRETARY OF STATE OF THE STATE OF IOWA:

The undersigned applies to reserve exclusive use of a business organization name, pursuant to the: (check one)

☐ Iowa Business Corporation Act (*profit corporations*)

☐ Revised Iowa Nonprofit Corporation Act (*nonprofit corporations*)

☐ Iowa Limited Liability Companies Act

☐ Iowa Uniform Limited Partnership Act - The new applicant is: (check one)

    ☐ A person intending to organize a limited partnership under this chapter and to adopt the name.

    ☐ A limited partnership or a foreign limited partnership authorized to transact business in this state intending to adopt the name.

    ☐ A foreign limited partnership intending to obtain a certificate of authority to transact business in this state and adopt the name.

    ☐ A person intending to organize a foreign limited partnership and intending to have it obtain a certificate of authority to transact business in this state and adopt the name.

    ☐ A foreign limited partnership formed under the name.

    ☐ A foreign limited partnership formed under a name that does not comply with section 488.108, subsection 2 or 3.

☐ Iowa Cooperative Associations Act (Iowa Code Ch. 501A)

1. The name to be reserved is _____

2. The name and address of the applicant is

    Name _____

    Address _____

    City, State, Zip _____

Signature _____

Type or print name & title _____

Date _____

NOTES:

1. The filing fee is $10.00. Make checks payable to SECRETARY OF STATE.
2. The information you provide will be open to public inspection under *Iowa Code* chapter 22.11.

SECRETARY OF STATE
Business Services Division
Lucas Building, 1st Floor
Des Moines, Iowa 50319

Phone: (515) 281-5204
FAX: (515) 242-5953 or (515) 281-7142
Website: www.sos.state.ia.us

635_0051
rev 03/07

6. Ohio Name Registration

Form 534A Prescribed by the:
Ohio Secretary of State

Central Ohio: (614) 466-3910
Toll Free: (877) SOS-FILE (767-3453)

www.sos.state.oh.us
Busserv@sos.state.oh.us

	Expedite this form: (select one) Mail form to **one** of the following:
Expedite	PO Box 1390 Columbus, OH 43216
	*** Requires an additional fee of $100 ***
Non Expedite	PO Box 670 Columbus, OH 43216

NAME REGISTRATION
Filing Fee $50

(CHECK ONLY ONE (1) BOX)

Trade Name (167-RNO) Date of first use: _____	Fictitious Name (169-NFO)

Name being registered or reported: _____

Name of the Registrant: _____

NOTE: If the registrant is a foreign corporation licensed in Ohio under an assumed name, provide the assumed name and the name as registered in its jurisdiction of formation.

The Registrant is a(n): (Check only one (1) box)

Individual

Partnership
Registration # , if any _____

Limited Partnership
Registration # _____

If foreign, Jurisdiction of Formation _____

Limited Liability Partnership
Registration # _____

If foreign, Jurisdiction of Formation _____

Limited Liability Company
Registration # _____

If foreign, Jurisdiction of Formation _____

Ohio Corporation
Charter # _____

Foreign Corporation
Ohio license # _____

Jurisdiction of Formation _____

Unincorporated Association

Professional Association

Other

Form 534A   Last Revised: 12/01/08

All registrants must complete the information in this section

Business address:

_____
Mailing Address

_____   _____   _____
City   State   Zip Code

The general nature of the business conducted by the registrant:

_____

_____

Complete the information in this section if registrant is a partnership not registered in Ohio

Provide the name and address of at least one general partner:

Name   Address

_____   _____

_____   _____

_____   _____

NOTE: Pursuant to OAG 89-081, if a general partner is a foreign corporation, it must be licensed to transact business in Ohio; if a general partner is a foreign corporation licensed in Ohio under an assumed name, please provide the assumed name and the name as registered in its jurisdiction of formation.

By signing and submitting this form to the Ohio Secretary of State, the undersigned hereby certifies that he or she has the requisite authority to execute this document.

REQUIRED
Must be authenticated
(signed) by the registrant or
an authorized
representative

_____   _____
Signature   Date

_____
Print Name

_____   _____
Signature   Date

_____
Print Name

7. Washington Master Business Application

Master License Service
Department of Licensing
PO Box 9034
Olympia WA 98507-9034
Telephone: (360) 664-1400
www.dol.wa.gov

Information provided may be subject to disclosure
under the public disclosure law (RCW 42.56)

Legal Entity/Owner Name

Unified Business Identifier (UBI)

Federal Employer Identification Number (FEIN)

For Validation - Office Use Only

01P-400-925-0003

Master Business Application
For faster service - Apply online @
www.dol.wa.gov
or print in dark ink and mail to Master License Service

1. Purpose of Application
Please check all boxes that apply.

☐ Open/Reopen Business
complete sections 2, 3, 4, (5 if hiring employees) and 6

☐ Open Additional Location
complete sections 2, 3, 4, (5 if hiring employees) and 6

☐ Change Ownership
complete sections 2, 3, 4, (5 if you have employees) and 6

☐ Register Trade Name
complete sections 2, 3, 4 and 6

☐ Change Trade Name - *complete sections 2, 3, 4 and 6*

Indicate name to be ***cancelled***: _____

☐ Change Location - *complete sections 2, 3, 4 and 6*

Indicate old address to be closed: _____

☐ Add License/Registration to Existing Location
complete sections 2, 3, 4, and 6

☐ Business Has or Will Have Employees
*complete **all** sections*

☐ Business Has or Will Have Employees Under Age 18
*complete **all** sections*

☐ Hire Persons to Work In or Around Your Home
*complete **all** sections*

☐ Other - *complete all sections* _____

2. Licenses and Fees
Use the License Fee Sheet for the information needed to complete this list.

Indicate Registrations Needed:	Fees Due
☐ Tax Registration – Do you want a separate tax return for each business? ☐ Yes ☐ No	**No Fee**
☐ Industrial Insurance (Workers' Compensation) – *Required if you will have employees.*	**No Fee**
☐ Unemployment Insurance – *Required if you will have employees.*	**No Fee**
☐ Minor Work Permit – *Required if you will have employees under age 18.*	**No Fee**
☐ New Trade Name (Doing Business As):	**$ 5.00**

Indicate Additional Trade Names (*$5 each name*) **or Other Licenses** (*such as Lottery Retailer*):

➤	$
➤	$
➤	$
➤	$
➤	$
➤	$

Enclose check for **total amount due**, including the Processing Fee, which MUST be submitted with this form.

Make check payable to the WASHINGTON STATE TREASURER.

Processing Fee	$	**15.00**
Total Amount Due	$	

BLS-700-028 (R/01/09) Page 1 of 4

The Department of Licensing has a policy of providing equal access to its services.
If you need special accommodation, call (360) 664-1400 or TTY (360) 664-8885.

3. Owner Information

Sole Proprietor

a. *Select only one ownership structure:*

☐ Sole Proprietor
If married, should spouse's name appear on license? ☐ Yes ☐ No *(If you answer No, you must still enter the spouse information in section "3f" below.)*

Partnership / Corp.

☐ Corporation* ☐ Non Profit Corporation* *(educational, religious, charitable)* ☐ Limited Liability Company*
☐ Partnership (# of partners:_____) ☐ Limited Partnership* ☐ Limited Liability Partnership* ☐ Joint Venture
These ownership structures must contact the Secretary of State office for additional filing requirements.

_____
Name of Corporation, LLC, Partnership, LLP, or Joint Venture Name (examples: ABC, Inc. OR Fir Trees Unlimited LLC)

State incorporated/formed: _____ Year incorporated/formed: _____

Other

☐ Association ☐ Trust ☐ Municipality ☐ Tribal Government Other_____

_____
Name of Organization (example: Anderson Family Trust)

b. Indicate this ownership structure's first date of business at this location. _____ / _____ **(Required.** If unknown, please estimate.)
Out-of-state businesses should use the first date of operation in WA.   MM   YY

c. _____
Doing Business As *(DBA)*/Trade Name

d. _____
Business Mailing Address *(Street & Suite No. or PO Box, do not use building name)*   City   State   Zip code

e. (____) _____ (____) _____ _____
Business Telephone Number   Fax Number   Internet/E-Mail Address

f. *List all owners & spouses:* Sole proprietor, partners, officers, or LLC members. *(Attach additional pages if needed.)*

Governing Persons

➤ _____
Name *(Last, First, Middle)*   Date of Birth   Social Security Number*   % Owned

_____
Home Address *(Street or PO Box)*   City   State   Zip code

_____ (____) _____   Are you married? ☐ Yes ☐ No If yes, enter spouse information below.
Title   Home Telephone Number

_____
Spouse Name (Last, First, Middle)   Spouse Date of Birth   Spouse Social Security Number*

➤ _____
Name *(Last, First, Middle)*   Date of Birth   Social Security Number*   % Owned

_____
Home Address *(Street or PO Box)*   City   State   Zip code

_____ (____) _____   Are you married? ☐ Yes ☐ No If yes, enter spouse information below.
Title   Home Telephone Number

_____
Spouse Name (Last, First, Middle)   Spouse Date of Birth   Spouse Social Security Number*

➤ _____
Name *(Last, First, Middle)*   Date of Birth   Social Security Number*   % Owned

_____
Home Address *(Street or PO Box)*   City   State   Zip code

_____ (____) _____   Are you married? ☐ Yes ☐ No If yes, enter spouse information below.
Title   Home Telephone Number

_____
Spouse Name (Last, First, Middle)   Spouse Date of Birth   Spouse Social Security Number*

*The Social Security Number is required for all sole proprietors. It is also required for all partners, officers, and LLC members of businesses that will have employees, and all owners and spouses of businesses that will have liquor, lottery or private investigator licenses. Not fully completing section "f" will result in application delays. (RCW 26.23.150, RCW 50.12.070)

BLS-700-028 (R/01/09) Page 2 of 4

4. Location / Business Information

Check the appropriate box and provide the corresponding physical address on line 4.b. below.

a. ☐ This application is for a Washington location *(provide the Washington address)*

      Is this Location inside city limits?   ☐ Yes ☐ No

    ☐ This Business has **No** Washington location *(provide the primary business address)*

b. _____   _____   _____   _____
    Business Street Address *(Do not use a PO Box or PMB Address)*   City   State   Zip code

c. If the address above is out-of-state and you have employees or representatives working in Washington, please provide **one** of their Washington addresses (we will not use this address for mailing purposes):

    _____   _____   _____   _____
    Business Street Address *(Do not use a PO Box or PMB Address)*   City   State   Zip code

d. Provide the **estimated** gross annual income in Washington *(check the one box that applies to your business)*:

    ☐ $0 - $12,000   ☐ $12,001 - $28,000   ☐ $28,001 - $60,000   ☐ $60,001 - $100,000   ☐ $100,001 and above

e. Indicate the business activities in Washington State *(check all that apply)*:

    ☐ Wholesale   ☐ Retail   ☐ Manufacturing   ☐ Services

f. Describe in detail the principal products or services you provide in Washington State *(failure to provide this information will cause delay in processing your application)*:

    _____

    _____

g. Did you buy, lease, or acquire all or part of an existing business?   ☐ No   ☐ All   ☐ Part

    Date bought/leased/acquired:_____ / _____ / _____   _____
                      MM   DD   YY   Prior Business Name

    _____   (____)_____
    Prior Owner's Name   Telephone Number

h. Did you purchase/lease any fixtures or equipment on which you have not paid sales or use tax?   ☐ Yes   ☐ No

    If yes, indicate purchase or lease price: **$** _____

i. If this business is owned by, controlled by, or affiliated with any other business entity, please indicate that business entity's name:

    _____

j. If you are changing your business structure *(such as changing from sole proprietorship to corporation)* and want the

    old account closed, please indicate the UBI number to be closed:_____

    Do you wish to cancel all the trade names registered under the old UBI number?   ☐ Yes   ☐ No
    (You must re-register all trade names you use under the new business structure.)

k. If you have ever owned another business, please provide: _____   _____
                                                   Business Name   UBI Number

l. Provide your bank's name: _____   Branch:_____

If you plan to have employees or wish to register for elective coverage for owners or excluded employees, complete Section 5.
(For information see the Industrial Insurance or Unemployment Insurance sections on the License Fee Sheet.)

BLS-700-028 (R/01/09) Page 3 of 4

5. Employment / Elective Coverage

Employment accounts cannot be established unless you plan to employ persons within the **next 90 days**. If accounts are established, employment tax returns will be required quarterly **even if you have not hired.**

a. Date of first employment or planned employment at this location: ___ / ___ / ___   First date wages paid: ___ / ___ / ___
MM DD YY   MM DD YY

b. Number of persons you employ or plan to employ at this location *(do not include owners)*: _____

c. Estimate the number of persons under age 18 (minors) you will employ in the next 12 months and duties they will perform:

	Number	Duties to be performed by minors (Check www.teenworkers.lni.wa.gov)
Ages 16-17:	_____	_____
Ages 14-15:	_____	_____
Under age 14:	_____	_____

d. Please check the **ONE** box which best describes the major operation of your business.

☐ (01) Construction-Wood Framing only   ☐ (05) Shipbuilding   ☐ (09) Mfg. - Food Products   ☐ (13) Retail/Wholesale Trade
☐ (02) Construction - All other   ☐ (06) Mining/Quarrying/Sand & Gravel   ☐ (10) Miscellaneous Mfg.   ☐ (14) Services/Maint./Restaurants
☐ (03) Logging/Forestry/Trucking   ☐ (07) Mfg. - Wood/Metal/Stone Products   ☐ (11) Machine Shops/Auto Repair   ☐ (15) Communications
☐ (04) Temp. Help Co./Employee Leasing   ☐ (08) Mfg. - Chemicals   ☐ (12) Agricultural/Farming   ☐ (16) Clerical/Professional Occup.

e. Describe in detail the activities of your workers. Then estimate the total workers' hours for a 3-month period. (One full-time worker = 480 total hours for 3 months.)

	3-Month Estimate	
	Number of Workers	Workers' Hours (Include Minors)
Example: *Office Staff - reception, accounting, data entry*	2	960
➢ _____		
➢ _____		
➢ _____		

f. If you have more than one Washington location, how do you wish to receive the following quarterly reports?

Unemployment Insurance: ☐ All locations combined   ☐ Each location separately (multiple reports)
Workers' Compensation: ☐ All locations combined   ☐ Each location separately (multiple reports)

Additional Coverage is available as noted below. *(See License Fee Sheet for more information.)*

Note: Starting January 2009, profit corporations with employees must cover corporate officers that provide services in Washington with Unemployment Insurance. If you choose to exempt some or all officers from this coverage, you must submit the Exemption Form. Visit www.esd.wa.gov/uitax/whatsnew/index.php for the form and more information.

g. If your profit corporation doesn't have employees, do you want unemployment insurance coverage for corporate officers?
☐ **Yes** – Prior to coverage, Form 5203 is required. This form will be sent to you by Employment Security Dept.

h. Do you want workers' compensation coverage for owners (sole proprietor, partners, corporate officers, LLC members/ managers)? *(In an LLC with managers, you may elect to cover those persons who are both members (owners) and managers. In an LLC with members only, you may elect to cover those members.)*
☐ **Yes** – Prior to coverage, Form F213-042-000 is required. This form will be sent to you by the Dept. of Labor & Industries.
☐ **No**

i. Do you want elective workers' compensation coverage for excluded employment? *(See License Fee Sheet for descriptions.)*
☐ **Yes** – Prior to coverage, Form F213-112-000 is required. This form will be sent to you by the Dept. of Labor & Industries.
☐ **No**

6. Signature *Signature of sole proprietor or spouse, partner, corporate officer, or limited liability member/manager.*

I, the undersigned, declare under the penalties of perjury and/or the revocation of any license granted, that I am the applicant or authorized representative of the firm making this application and that the answers contained, including any accompanying information, have been examined by me and that the matters and things set forth are true, correct and complete.

X _____   ___ / ___ / ___
Signature Required   Date

_____   _____   (___) _____   ___ / ___ / ___
Application Prepared By *(Please Print)*   Title   Telephone No.   Date

_____   (___) _____   ___ / ___ / ___
UBI Agency Representative   Telephone No.   Date

BLS-700-028 (R/01/09) Page 4 of 4

CHAPTER 2

Forms for the Sole Proprietor

THE GOOD NEWS ABOUT STARTING A BUSI-ness solo is that there are only a few forms you need to file to get started. Simply put, the sole proprietorship is essentially the simplest form of business. The definition of a sole proprietorship is that it's an operation of one person in business for profit. The distinction between the sole proprietor and the business itself is that there is no distinction. This means that the sole proprietor's personal assets are at risk for the debts, obligations, and judgments of the business.

To get your sole proprietorship off and running, the first thing to do is name your business and file a *Fictitious Business Name Statement* by registering the name of your business in the county where you do business. Refer to Chapter 1 to review the forms required to properly file the name of your organization.

This chapter provides a sample form *SS-4*, which provides a sole proprietor with an Employer Identification Number (EIN). Regardless of the number of businesses operated, a sole proprietor should file only one Form SS-4 and needs only one EIN. Once you receive your EIN, you can put it to use immediately. As a sole proprietor, an EIN enables you to open a bank account, apply for business licenses, and file your tax return.

When it comes time to pay taxes, sole proprietors use form 1040 just as one would to file personal income taxes. Refer to the *Sample Form 1040* to view the information required by this form. In addition to Form 1040, we included *Sample Form 1040 Schedule C*, which must be filed to report income or loss from a business operated by a sole proprietor.

8. IRS Form SS-4, Application for Employer Identification Number

Form **SS-4** (Rev. January 2010) Department of the Treasury Internal Revenue Service	**Application for Employer Identification Number** (For use by employers, corporations, partnerships, trusts, estates, churches, government agencies, Indian tribal entities, certain individuals, and others.) ▶ See separate instructions for each line.　▶ Keep a copy for your records.	OMB No. 1545-0003 EIN

	1 Legal name of entity (or individual) for whom the EIN is being requested	

Type or print clearly.

2 Trade name of business (if different from name on line 1)	**3** Executor, administrator, trustee, "care of" name
4a Mailing address (room, apt., suite no. and street, or P.O. box)	**5a** Street address (if different) (Do not enter a P.O. box.)
4b City, state, and ZIP code (if foreign, see instructions)	**5b** City, state, and ZIP code (if foreign, see instructions)

6 County and state where principal business is located	

7a Name of responsible party	**7b** SSN, ITIN, or EIN

8a Is this application for a limited liability company (LLC) (or a foreign equivalent)? . . . . ☐ **Yes** ☐ **No**	**8b** If 8a is "Yes," enter the number of LLC members . . . . . ▶

8c If 8a is "Yes," was the LLC organized in the United States? . . . . ☐ **Yes** ☐ **No**

9a **Type of entity** (check only one box). **Caution.** If 8a is "Yes," see the instructions for the correct box to check.

☐ Sole proprietor (SSN) _____	☐ Estate (SSN of decedent) _____
☐ Partnership	☐ Plan administrator (TIN) _____
☐ Corporation (enter form number to be filed) ▶_____	☐ Trust (TIN of grantor) _____
☐ Personal service corporation	☐ National Guard　☐ State/local government
☐ Church or church-controlled organization	☐ Farmers' cooperative　☐ Federal government/military
☐ Other nonprofit organization (specify) ▶_____	☐ REMIC　☐ Indian tribal governments/enterprises
☐ Other (specify) ▶	Group Exemption Number (GEN) if any ▶

9b If a corporation, name the state or foreign country (if applicable) where incorporated	State	Foreign country

10 **Reason for applying** (check only one box)

☐ Started new business (specify type) ▶ _____ ☐ Hired employees (Check the box and see line 13.) ☐ Compliance with IRS withholding regulations ☐ Other (specify) ▶	☐ Banking purpose (specify purpose) ▶ _____ ☐ Changed type of organization (specify new type) ▶ _____ ☐ Purchased going business ☐ Created a trust (specify type) ▶ _____ ☐ Created a pension plan (specify type) ▶ _____

11 Date business started or acquired (month, day, year). See instructions.	**12** Closing month of accounting year

13 Highest number of employees expected in the next 12 months (enter -0- if none). If no employees expected, skip line 14.	**14** If you expect your employment tax liability to be $1,000 or less in a full calendar year **and** want to file Form 944 annually instead of Forms 941 quarterly, check here. (Your employment tax liability generally will be $1,000 or less if you expect to pay $4,000 or less in total wages.) If you do not check this box, you must file Form 941 for every quarter. ☐
Agricultural　｜　Household　｜　Other	

15 First date wages or annuities were paid (month, day, year). **Note.** If applicant is a withholding agent, enter date income will first be paid to
nonresident alien (month, day, year) . . . . ▶

16 Check **one** box that best describes the principal activity of your business.
☐ Health care & social assistance　☐ Wholesale-agent/broker
☐ Construction　☐ Rental & leasing　☐ Transportation & warehousing　☐ Accommodation & food service　☐ Wholesale-other　☐ Retail
☐ Real estate　☐ Manufacturing　☐ Finance & insurance　☐ Other (specify)

17 Indicate principal line of merchandise sold, specific construction work done, products produced, or services provided.

18 Has the applicant entity shown on line 1 ever applied for and received an EIN? ☐ **Yes** ☐ **No**
If "Yes," write previous EIN here ▶

Third Party Designee	Complete this section **only** if you want to authorize the named individual to receive the entity's EIN and answer questions about the completion of this form.	
	Designee's name	Designee's telephone number (include area code) (　)
	Address and ZIP code	Designee's fax number (include area code) (　)

Under penalties of perjury, I declare that I have examined this application, and to the best of my knowledge and belief, it is true, correct, and complete.

Name and title (type or print clearly) ▶	Applicant's telephone number (include area code) (　)
Signature ▶ 　　　　　　　　　　　　Date ▶	Applicant's fax number (include area code) (　)

For Privacy Act and Paperwork Reduction Act Notice, see separate instructions.　　Cat. No. 16055N　　Form **SS-4** (Rev. 1-2010)

9. IRS Form 1040, U.S. Individual Tax Return

Form 1040

Department of the Treasury—Internal Revenue Service
U.S. Individual Income Tax Return **2009** (99) IRS Use Only—Do not write or staple in this space.

For the year Jan. 1–Dec. 31, 2009, or other tax year beginning _____ , 2009, ending _____ , 20 ___ | OMB No. 1545-0074

Label

(See instructions on page 14.)
Use the IRS label.
Otherwise, please print or type.

Presidential Election Campaign

L A B E L — H E R E

Your first name and initial | Last name | **Your social security number**

If a joint return, spouse's first name and initial | Last name | **Spouse's social security number**

Home address (number and street). If you have a P.O. box, see page 14. | Apt. no. | ▲ You **must** enter your SSN(s) above. ▲

City, town or post office, state, and ZIP code. If you have a foreign address, see page 14. | Checking a box below will not change your tax or refund.

► Check here if you, or your spouse if filing jointly, want $3 to go to this fund (see page 14) ► ☐ You ☐ Spouse

Filing Status

Check only one box.

1 ☐ Single
2 ☐ Married filing jointly (even if only one had income)
3 ☐ Married filing separately. Enter spouse's SSN above and full name here. ►
4 ☐ Head of household (with qualifying person). (See page 15.) If the qualifying person is a child but not your dependent, enter this child's name here. ►
5 ☐ Qualifying widow(er) with dependent child (see page 16)

Exemptions

6a ☐ **Yourself.** If someone can claim you as a dependent, **do not** check box 6a . . . . .
b ☐ **Spouse** . . . .
c Dependents:

(1) First name Last name	(2) Dependent's social security number	(3) Dependent's relationship to you	(4) ✓ if qualifying child for child tax credit (see page 17)
			☐
			☐
			☐
			☐

If more than four dependents, see page 17 and check here ► ☐

d Total number of exemptions claimed . . . .

Boxes checked on 6a and 6b ___
No. of children on 6c who:
• lived with you ___
• did not live with you due to divorce or separation (see page 18) ___
Dependents on 6c not entered above ___
Add numbers on lines above ► ___

Income

Attach Form(s) W-2 here. Also attach Forms W-2G and 1099-R if tax was withheld.

If you did not get a W-2, see page 22.

Enclose, but do not attach, any payment. Also, please use Form 1040-V.

7 Wages, salaries, tips, etc. Attach Form(s) W-2 . . . . | 7 |
8a **Taxable** interest. Attach Schedule B if required . . . . | 8a |
b **Tax-exempt** interest. **Do not** include on line 8a . . . | 8b | |
9a Ordinary dividends. Attach Schedule B if required . . . . | 9a |
b Qualified dividends (see page 22) . . . . . | 9b | |
10 Taxable refunds, credits, or offsets of state and local income taxes (see page 23) . . | 10 |
11 Alimony received . . . . | 11 |
12 Business income or (loss). Attach Schedule C or C-EZ . . . . | 12 |
13 Capital gain or (loss). Attach Schedule D if required. If not required, check here ► ☐ | 13 |
14 Other gains or (losses). Attach Form 4797 . . . . | 14 |
15a IRA distributions . | 15a | | b Taxable amount (see page 24) | 15b |
16a Pensions and annuities | 16a | | b Taxable amount (see page 25) | 16b |
17 Rental real estate, royalties, partnerships, S corporations, trusts, etc. Attach Schedule E | 17 |
18 Farm income or (loss). Attach Schedule F . . . . | 18 |
19 Unemployment compensation in excess of $2,400 per recipient (see page 27) . . . | 19 |
20a Social security benefits | 20a | | b Taxable amount (see page 27) | 20b |
21 Other income. List type and amount (see page 29) _____ | 21 |
22 Add the amounts in the far right column for lines 7 through 21. This is your **total income** ► | 22 |

Adjusted Gross Income

23 Educator expenses (see page 29) . . . . | 23 | |
24 Certain business expenses of reservists, performing artists, and fee-basis government officials. Attach Form 2106 or 2106-EZ | 24 | |
25 Health savings account deduction. Attach Form 8889 . | 25 | |
26 Moving expenses. Attach Form 3903 . . . . . | 26 | |
27 One-half of self-employment tax. Attach Schedule SE . | 27 | |
28 Self-employed SEP, SIMPLE, and qualified plans . | 28 | |
29 Self-employed health insurance deduction (see page 30) | 29 | |
30 Penalty on early withdrawal of savings . . . . . | 30 | |
31a Alimony paid **b** Recipient's SSN ► ___ | 31a | |
32 IRA deduction (see page 31) . . . . | 32 | |
33 Student loan interest deduction (see page 34) . . . | 33 | |
34 Tuition and fees deduction. Attach Form 8917 . . . | 34 | |
35 Domestic production activities deduction. Attach Form 8903 | 35 | |
36 Add lines 23 through 31a and 32 through 35 . . . . | 36 |
37 Subtract line 36 from line 22. This is your **adjusted gross income** . . . . . ► | 37 |

For Disclosure, Privacy Act, and Paperwork Reduction Act Notice, see page 97. | Cat. No. 11320B | Form **1040** (2009)

Form 1040 (2009)

Page **2**

Tax and Credits	**38**	Amount from line 37 (adjusted gross income)		**38**
	39a	Check { **You** were born before January 2, 1945, ☐ Blind. } **Total boxes**		
		if: { **Spouse** was born before January 2, 1945, ☐ Blind. } checked ▶ **39a**		
Standard Deduction for—	**b**	If your spouse itemizes on a separate return or you were a dual-status alien, see page 35 and check here▶ **39b**☐		
	40a	**Itemized deductions** (from Schedule A) **or** your **standard deduction** (see left margin) . .		**40a**
• People who check any box on line 39a, 39b, or 40b **or** who can be claimed as a dependent, see page 35.	**b**	If you are increasing your standard deduction by certain real estate taxes, new motor vehicle taxes, or a net disaster loss, attach Schedule L and check here (see page 35) . ▶ **40b**☐		
	41	Subtract line 40a from line 38		**41**
	42	**Exemptions.** If line 38 is $125,100 or less and you did not provide housing to a Midwestern displaced individual, multiply $3,650 by the number on line 6d. Otherwise, see page 37 . .		**42**
• All others:	**43**	**Taxable income.** Subtract line 42 from line 41. If line 42 is more than line 41, enter -0- . .		**43**
Single or Married filing separately, $5,700	**44**	**Tax** (see page 37). Check if any tax is from: **a** ☐ Form(s) 8814 **b** ☐ Form 4972 .		**44**
	45	**Alternative minimum tax** (see page 40). Attach Form 6251		**45**
Married filing jointly or Qualifying widow(er), $11,400	**46**	Add lines 44 and 45 . . . . ▶		**46**
	47	Foreign tax credit. Attach Form 1116 if required . .	**47**	
	48	Credit for child and dependent care expenses. Attach Form 2441	**48**	
Head of household, $8,350	**49**	Education credits from Form 8863, line 29	**49**	
	50	Retirement savings contributions credit. Attach Form 8880	**50**	
	51	Child tax credit (see page 42)	**51**	
	52	Credits from Form: **a** ☐ 8396 **b** ☐ 8839 **c** ☐ 5695	**52**	
	53	Other credits from Form: **a** ☐ 3800 **b** ☐ 8801 **c** ☐	**53**	
	54	Add lines 47 through 53. These are your **total credits**		**54**
	55	Subtract line 54 from line 46. If line 54 is more than line 46, enter -0- . . . . ▶		**55**
Other Taxes	**56**	Self-employment tax. Attach Schedule SE		**56**
	57	Unreported social security and Medicare tax from Form: **a** ☐ 4137 **b** ☐ 8919 . .		**57**
	58	Additional tax on IRAs, other qualified retirement plans, etc. Attach Form 5329 if required . .		**58**
	59	Additional taxes: **a** ☐ AEIC payments **b** ☐ Household employment taxes. Attach Schedule H		**59**
	60	Add lines 55 through 59. This is your **total tax** . . . . ▶		**60**
Payments	**61**	Federal income tax withheld from Forms W-2 and 1099 . .	**61**	
	62	2009 estimated tax payments and amount applied from 2008 return	**62**	
	63	Making work pay and government retiree credits. Attach Schedule M	**63**	
If you have a qualifying child, attach Schedule EIC.	**64a**	**Earned income credit (EIC)**	**64a**	
	b	Nontaxable combat pay election **64b**		
	65	Additional child tax credit. Attach Form 8812	**65**	
	66	Refundable education credit from Form 8863, line 16 . . .	**66**	
	67	First-time homebuyer credit. Attach Form 5405	**67**	
	68	Amount paid with request for extension to file (see page 72) .	**68**	
	69	Excess social security and tier 1 RRTA tax withheld (see page 72)	**69**	
	70	Credits from Form: **a** ☐ 2439 **b** ☐ 4136 **c** ☐ 8801 **d** ☐ 8885	**70**	
	71	Add lines 61, 62, 63, 64a, and 65 through 70. These are your **total payments** . . . . . ▶		**71**
Refund	**72**	If line 71 is more than line 60, subtract line 60 from line 71. This is the amount you **overpaid**		**72**
Direct deposit? See page 73 and fill in 73b, 73c, and 73d, or Form 8888.	**73a**	Amount of line 72 you want **refunded to you.** If Form 8888 is attached, check here . ▶ ☐		**73a**
	▶ **b**	Routing number [ ] ▶ **c** Type: ☐ Checking ☐ Savings		
	▶ **d**	Account number [ ]		
	74	Amount of line 72 you want **applied to your 2010 estimated tax** ▶	**74**	
Amount You Owe	**75**	**Amount you owe.** Subtract line 71 from line 60. For details on how to pay, see page 74 . ▶		**75**
	76	Estimated tax penalty (see page 74)	**76**	

Third Party Designee

Do you want to allow another person to discuss this return with the IRS (see page 75)? ☐ **Yes.** Complete the following. ☐ **No**

Designee's name ▶	Phone no. ▶	Personal identification number (PIN) ▶ [ ]

Sign Here

Under penalties of perjury, I declare that I have examined this return and accompanying schedules and statements, and to the best of my knowledge and belief, they are true, correct, and complete. Declaration of preparer (other than taxpayer) is based on all information of which preparer has any knowledge.

Joint return? See page 15. Keep a copy for your records.

Your signature	Date	Your occupation	Daytime phone number
Spouse's signature. If a joint return, **both** must sign.	Date	Spouse's occupation	

Paid Preparer's Use Only

Preparer's signature ▶	Date	Check if self-employed ☐	Preparer's SSN or PTIN
Firm's name (or yours if self-employed), address, and ZIP code ▶		EIN	
		Phone no.	

Form **1040** (2009)

10. IRS Form 1040 Schedule C, Profit or Loss from Business

SCHEDULE C
(Form 1040)

Department of the Treasury
Internal Revenue Service (99)

Profit or Loss From Business
(Sole Proprietorship)

▶ **Partnerships, joint ventures, etc., generally must file Form 1065 or 1065-B.**
▶ **Attach to Form 1040, 1040NR, or 1041.** ▶ **See Instructions for Schedule C (Form 1040).**

OMB No. 1545-0074

2009

Attachment
Sequence No. **09**

Name of proprietor

Social security number (SSN)

A	Principal business or profession, including product or service (see page C-2 of the instructions)	**B** Enter code from pages C-9, 10, & 11 ▶
C	Business name. If no separate business name, leave blank.	**D** Employer ID number (EIN), if any

E Business address (including suite or room no.) ▶
City, town or post office, state, and ZIP code

F Accounting method: **(1)** ☐ Cash **(2)** ☐ Accrual **(3)** ☐ Other (specify) ▶

G Did you "materially participate" in the operation of this business during 2009? If "No," see page C-3 for limit on losses ☐ Yes ☐ No

H If you started or acquired this business during 2009, check here . . . . ▶ ☐

Part I Income

1	Gross receipts or sales. **Caution.** See page C-4 and check the box if:		
	• This income was reported to you on Form W-2 and the "Statutory employee" box on that form was checked, or	▶ ☐	
	• You are a member of a qualified joint venture reporting only rental real estate income not subject to self-employment tax. Also see page C-3 for limit on losses.		**1**
2	Returns and allowances		**2**
3	Subtract line 2 from line 1		**3**
4	Cost of goods sold (from line 42 on page 2)		**4**
5	**Gross profit.** Subtract line 4 from line 3		**5**
6	Other income, including federal and state gasoline or fuel tax credit or refund (see page C-4)		**6**
7	**Gross income.** Add lines 5 and 6 . . . . ▶		**7**

Part II Expenses. Enter expenses for business use of your home **only** on line 30.

8	Advertising	**8**		**18**	Office expense	**18**
9	Car and truck expenses (see page C-4)	**9**		**19**	Pension and profit-sharing plans .	**19**
10	Commissions and fees .	**10**		**20**	Rent or lease (see page C-6):	
11	Contract labor (see page C-4)	**11**		**a**	Vehicles, machinery, and equipment	**20a**
12	Depletion	**12**		**b**	Other business property . .	**20b**
13	Depreciation and section 179 expense deduction (not included in Part III) (see page C-5)	**13**		**21**	Repairs and maintenance . . .	**21**
				22	Supplies (not included in Part III) .	**22**
				23	Taxes and licenses	**23**
				24	Travel, meals, and entertainment:	
				a	Travel	**24a**
14	Employee benefit programs (other than on line 19) . .	**14**		**b**	Deductible meals and entertainment (see page C-6) . .	**24b**
15	Insurance (other than health)	**15**		**25**	Utilities	**25**
16	Interest:			**26**	Wages (less employment credits) .	**26**
a	Mortgage (paid to banks, etc.)	**16a**		**27**	Other expenses (from line 48 on page 2)	**27**
b	Other	**16b**				
17	Legal and professional services	**17**				

28	**Total expenses** before expenses for business use of home. Add lines 8 through 27 . . . . . ▶	**28**	
29	Tentative profit or (loss). Subtract line 28 from line 7	**29**	
30	Expenses for business use of your home. Attach **Form 8829**	**30**	
31	**Net profit or (loss).** Subtract line 30 from line 29.		
	• If a profit, enter on both **Form 1040, line 12,** and **Schedule SE, line 2,** or on **Form 1040NR, line 13** (if you checked the box on line 1, see page C-7). Estates and trusts, enter on **Form 1041, line 3.**	**31**	
	• If a loss, you **must** go to line 32.		
32	If you have a loss, check the box that describes your investment in this activity (see page C-7).		
	• If you checked 32a, enter the loss on both **Form 1040, line 12,** and **Schedule SE, line 2,** or on **Form 1040NR, line 13** (if you checked the box on line 1, see the line 31 instructions on page C-7). Estates and trusts, enter on **Form 1041, line 3.**	**32a** ☐ All investment is at risk. **32b** ☐ Some investment is not at risk.	
	• If you checked 32b, you **must** attach **Form 6198.** Your loss may be limited.		

For Paperwork Reduction Act Notice, see page C-9 of the instructions.   Cat. No. 11334P   Schedule C (Form 1040) 2009

Schedule C (Form 1040) 2009   Page **2**

Part III   **Cost of Goods Sold** (see page C-8)

33   Method(s) used to value closing inventory: **a** ☐ Cost   **b** ☐ Lower of cost or market   **c** ☐ Other (attach explanation)

34   Was there any change in determining quantities, costs, or valuations between opening and closing inventory? If "Yes," attach explanation . . . . ☐ **Yes**   ☐ **No**

35 Inventory at beginning of year. If different from last year's closing inventory, attach explanation . . .	**35**	
36 Purchases less cost of items withdrawn for personal use	**36**	
37 Cost of labor. Do not include any amounts paid to yourself	**37**	
38 Materials and supplies	**38**	
39 Other costs	**39**	
40 Add lines 35 through 39	**40**	
41 Inventory at end of year	**41**	
42 **Cost of goods sold.** Subtract line 41 from line 40. Enter the result here and on page 1, line 4 . . .	**42**	

Part IV   **Information on Your Vehicle.** Complete this part **only** if you are claiming car or truck expenses on line 9 and are not required to file Form 4562 for this business. See the instructions for line 13 on page C-5 to find out if you must file Form 4562.

43   When did you place your vehicle in service for business purposes? (month, day, year)   ▶ _____ / _____ / _____

44   Of the total number of miles you drove your vehicle during 2009, enter the number of miles you used your vehicle for:

a Business _____   **b** Commuting (see instructions) _____   **c** Other _____

45   Was your vehicle available for personal use during off-duty hours? . . . . ☐ **Yes**   ☐ **No**

46   Do you (or your spouse) have another vehicle available for personal use? . . . . ☐ **Yes**   ☐ **No**

47a   Do you have evidence to support your deduction? . . . . ☐ **Yes**   ☐ **No**

b   If "Yes," is the evidence written? . . . . ☐ **Yes**   ☐ **No**

Part V   **Other Expenses.** List below business expenses not included on lines 8–26 or line 30.

--	
--	
--	
--	
--	
--	
--	
--	
48 **Total other expenses.** Enter here and on page 1, line 27	**48**	

Schedule C (Form 1040) 2009

CHAPTER 3

Forms for LLCs

THE *LLC-1, CALIFORNIA LLC ARTICLES OF Organization* is the form required in the State of California to organize and register a limited liability company. Each state requires a different form. The *Sample Letter to Secretary of State Accompanying Articles of Organization* is a simple cover letter that you should include when submitting LLC papers to the Secretary of State.

A *registered agent* is a person or entity authorized and obligated to receive legal papers on behalf of an LLC. *The Sample Letter to Registered Agent Accompanying Articles of Organization* is a simple cover letter that you should deliver to your registered agent upon the organization of your LLC. Keep in mind that your state of organization may use a different term than "registered agent." Typical equivalents include "agent for service of process," "local agent," and "registered agent."

The next group of forms includes different types of LLC operating agreements and deserves some comment. LLCs are managed in one of two ways, either "member-managed" or "manager-managed." Member-managed LLCs are governed by the LLC's owners (members) equally, like a standard partnership. Manager-managed LLCs are governed by one or more appointed managers who often need not be members of the LLC. This manner of management by appointment is called "representative management." Manager-managed LLCs are managed much like corporations—with an appointed body of persons other than the company's ownership. The body of managers that undertakes governing responsibilities can come in the form of a board of managers or a committee of managers. Thus, the *Short-Form Operating Agreement for Member-Managed LLC* and the *Long-Form Agreement for Member-Managed LLC* are the short and long versions of operating agreements for member-managed LLCs. Similarly the *Short-Form Operating Agreement for Manager-Managed LLC* and the *Long-Form*

Operating Agreement for Manager-Managed LLC are short and long versions of operating agreements for manager-managed LLCs.

The *Membership Ledger* is a written table showing the owners of an LLC. The ledger must also indicate the percentage held by each owner. As new members are added to the LLC through the sale of membership interests, their ownership is recorded on the ledger. The membership ledger should also show transfers of members' ownership interest, as when a member passes away and transfers his or her interest through his or her will. The importance of the membership ledger cannot be overstated, and it should be diligently maintained. The membership ledger is akin to the deed for a piece of real estate. The ledger is the primary evidence of ownership in an LLC, and carries a great degree of weight when presented in court. LLC owners should insist on receiving updated copies of the membership ledger periodically.

Each member admitted to the LLC should execute the *Investment Representation Letter*. The investment representation letter offers some measure of protection to the entity because the member being admitted to the LLC makes certain representations regarding his qualifications and fitness to serve as a member of the LLC. Also, in the investment representation letter the member makes certain representations regarding his or her investment objectives, which are necessary in order to comply with state and federal securities laws.

The *Appointment of Proxy for Member's Meeting* is an authorization by one member giving another person the right to vote the owner's shares in a company, in this case an LLC. The term *proxy* also refers to the document granting such authority. Proxy rules are typically outlined in state law and an LLC's operating agreement. Often proxies are granted when members don't wish to attend member meetings, but they want their vote to be counted. They can thus grant their proxy to another person to attend the meeting and vote their shares on their behalf.

The *Call for Meeting of Members* is an instruction by LLC members to the managers that the members want to call a meeting of members. This serves as official notice to the managers. This call is only required by manager-managed LLCs; if a member in a member-managed LLC wants to call a meeting of members, he or she would skip the call, and simply send a notice of meeting of members to all other members. The next form in this chapter is a notice of meeting of members.

The *Notice of Meeting of LLC Members* is an LLC's announcement to its members that a meeting of members has been called.

While LLC members and managers enjoy far fewer corporate formalities than corporation owners, an LLC must still maintain records of its meetings. When an LLC's members meet to formally vote on any matter, the results of that vote should be committed to written minutes called the *Minutes of Meeting of LLC Members*.

In the real world, most LLC votes are taken by written consent in a document called an *Action by Written Consent of LLC Members* rather than by notice and meeting and an in-person vote. Use the written consent form when you wish to take a company action in writing, rather than by a noticed meeting. Keep in mind, however, that your operating agreement and articles may require more than a simple majority to pass certain actions. Written consents are important company records and should be maintained in the record books.

The *Written Consent of Members Approving a Certificate of Amendment of Articles of Organization Changing an LLC's Name* is a specific example of a written consent. In this case, the written consent authorizes a change to the LLC's charter to change the LLC's legal name.

11. LLC-1, California LLC Articles of Organization

Secretary of State
Business Programs Division

1500 11ᵗʰ Street, 3ʳᵈ Floor
Sacramento, CA 95814

Business Entities
(916) 657-5448

LIMITED LIABILITY COMPANIES

California Tax Information

Registration of a limited liability company (LLC) with the California Secretary of State (SOS) will obligate an LLC that is not taxed as a corporation to pay to the Franchise Tax Board (FTB) an annual minimum tax of $800.00 and a fee based on the annual total income of the entity. The tax and fee are required to be paid for the taxable year of registration and each taxable year, or part thereof, until a Certificate of Cancellation is filed with the SOS. (Rev. and Tax. Code §§ 17941 and 17942.) An LLC is not subject to the taxes and fees imposed by Revenue and Taxation Code sections 17941 and 17942 if the LLC did no business in California during the taxable year and the taxable year was 15 days or less. (Rev. and Tax. Code § 17946.)

An LLC that is taxed as a corporation generally determines its California income under the Corporation Tax Law commencing with Revenue and Taxation Code section 23001.

PLEASE NOTE: A domestic nonprofit LLC is a taxable entity and subject to the tax requirements stated above unless the LLC has applied for tax-exempt status and the FTB determines the LLC qualifies for tax-exempt status. Therefore, until such a determination is made, a nonprofit LLC must file a return and pay the associated tax (and, if applicable, the fee) every year until the LLC is formally cancelled. If the LLC intends to seek tax exempt status:

- At the time of filing its Articles of Organization with the SOS, the LLC must include, in an attachment to that document, additional statements as required by the law under which the LLC is seeking exemption. Please refer to the FTB's Exemption Application Booklet (FTB 3500 Booklet) for information regarding the required statements and for suggested language.

- After filing its Articles of Organization with the SOS, the LLC may apply for tax-exempt status by mailing an Exemption Application (Form FTB 3500), along with an endorsed copy of the Articles of Organization and all other required supporting documentation, to the FTB, P.O. Box 942857, Sacramento, California 94257-4041.

- The FTB 3500 Booklet and Form FTB 3500 can be accessed from the FTB's website at www.ftb.ca.gov or can be requested by calling the FTB at 1-800-338-0505. For further information regarding franchise tax exemption, refer to the FTB's website or call the FTB at (916) 845-4171.

For further information regarding franchise tax requirements, please contact the FTB at:

From within the United States (toll free) ....(800) 852-5711
From outside the United States (not toll free) ....(916) 845-6500
Automated Toll Free Phone Service ....(800) 338-0505

Professional Services Information

A domestic or foreign LLC may not render professional services. (Corp. Code § 17375.) "Professional services" are defined in California Corporations Code sections 13401(a) and 13401.3 as:

> Any type of professional services that may be lawfully rendered only pursuant to a license, certification, or registration authorized by the Business and Professions Code, the Chiropractic Act, the Osteopathic Act or the Yacht and Ship Brokers Act.

If your business is required to be licensed, registered or certified, it is recommended that you contact the appropriate licensing authority before filing with the SOS's office in order to determine whether your services are considered professional.

LLC Info (REV 04/2007)

INSTRUCTIONS FOR COMPLETING THE ARTICLES OF ORGANIZATION (FORM LLC-1)

For easier completion, this form is available on the Secretary of State's website at http://www.sos.ca.gov/business/ and can be viewed, filled in and printed from your computer. The completed form along with the applicable fees can be mailed to Secretary of State, Document Filing Support Unit, P.O. Box 944228, Sacramento, CA 94244-2280 or delivered in person to the Sacramento office, 1500 11th Street, 3rd Floor, Sacramento, CA 95814. If you are not completing this form online, please type or legibly print in black or blue ink. This form is filed only in the Sacramento office.

Statutory filing requirements are found in California Corporations Code sections 17051 and 17052. All statutory references are to the California Corporations Code, unless otherwise stated.

FEES: The fee for filing Form LLC-1 is $70.00. There is an additional $15.00 special handling fee for processing a document delivered in person to the Sacramento office. The special handling fee must be remitted by separate check for each submittal and will be retained whether the document is filed and/or rejected. The preclearance and/or expedited filing of a document within a guaranteed time frame can be requested for an additional fee (in lieu of the special handling fee). Please refer to the Secretary of State's website at http://www.sos.ca.gov/business/precexp.htm for detailed information regarding preclearance and expedited filing services. The special handling fee or preclearance and expedited filing services are not applicable to documents submitted by mail. Check(s) should be made payable to the Secretary of State.

COPIES: The Secretary of State will certify two copies of the filed document(s) without charge, provided that the copies are submitted to the Secretary of State with the document(s) to be filed. Any additional copies submitted will be certified upon request and payment of the $8.00 per copy certification fee.

Pursuant to Section 17375, a domestic limited liability company may not render professional services, as defined in Sections 13401(a) and 13401.3. Professional services are defined as any type of professional services that may be lawfully rendered only pursuant to a license, certification, or registration authorized by the Business and Professions Code, the Chiropractic Act, the Osteopathic Act or the Yacht and Ship Brokers Act. If your business is required to be licensed, certified or registered, it is recommended that you contact the appropriate licensing authority before filing with the Secretary of State's office in order to determine whether your services are considered professional.

Filing this document shall obligate most limited liability companies to pay an annual minimum tax of $800.00 to the Franchise Tax Board pursuant to Revenue and Taxation Code section 17941.

Complete the Articles of Organization (Form LLC-1) as follows:

Item 1. Enter the name of the limited liability company. The name must end with the words "Limited Liability Company," or the abbreviations "LLC" or "L.L.C." The words "Limited" and "Company" may be abbreviated to "Ltd." and "Co.," respectively. The name of the limited liability company may not contain the words "bank," "trust," "trustee," "incorporated," "inc.," "corporation," or "corp.," and must not contain the words "insurer" or "insurance company" or any other words suggesting that it is in the business of issuing policies of insurance and assuming insurance risks.

Item 2. This statement is required by statute and should not be altered. Provisions limiting or restricting the business of the limited liability company may be included as an attachment.

Items 3 & 4 Enter the name of the agent for service of process in California. An agent is an individual, whether or not affiliated with the limited liability company, who resides in California or a corporation designated to accept service of process if the company is sued. The agent should agree to accept service of process on behalf of the limited liability company prior to designation.

If a corporation is designated as agent, that corporation must have previously filed with the Secretary of State, a certificate pursuant to Corporations Code section 1505. Note, **a limited liability company cannot act as its own agent** and no domestic or foreign corporation may file pursuant to Section 1505 unless the corporation is currently authorized to engage in business in California and is in good standing on the records of the Secretary of State.

If an individual is designated as agent, complete Items 3 and 4. If a corporation is designated as agent, complete Item 3 and proceed to Item 5 (do not complete Item 4).

Item 5. Check the appropriate provision indicating whether the limited liability company is to be managed by one manager, more than one manager or all limited liability company members. Only one box may be checked.

Item 6. Attach any other information to be included in Form LLC-1, provided that the information is not inconsistent with law.

Item 7. Form LLC-1 must be signed by the organizer. The person signing Form LLC-1 need not be a member or manager of the limited liability company.

- If Form LLC-1 is signed by an attorney-in-fact, the signature should be followed by the words "Attorney-in-fact for (name of person)."
- If Form LLC-1 is signed by an entity, the person who signs on behalf of the entity should note their name and position/title and the entity name. Example: If a limited liability company ("Smith LLC") is the organizer, the signature of the person signing on behalf of the Smith LLC should be reflected as Joe Smith, Manager of Smith LLC, Organizer.
- If Form LLC-1 is signed by a trust, the trustee should sign as follows:_____, trustee for _____ trust (including the date of the trust, if applicable). Example: Mary Todd, trustee of the Lincoln Family Trust (U/T 5-1-94).

Any attachments to Form LLC-1 are incorporated by reference. All attachments should be 8 ½" x 11", one-sided and legible.

| LLC-1 | File # _____ |

State of California
Secretary of State

LIMITED LIABILITY COMPANY
ARTICLES OF ORGANIZATION

A $70.00 filing fee must accompany this form.

IMPORTANT – Read instructions before completing this form.

This Space For Filing Use Only

ENTITY NAME (End the name with the words "Limited Liability Company," or the abbreviations "LLC" or "L.L.C." The words "Limited" and "Company" may be abbreviated to "Ltd." and "Co.," respectively.)

1. NAME OF LIMITED LIABILITY COMPANY

PURPOSE (The following statement is required by statute and should not be altered.)

2. THE PURPOSE OF THE LIMITED LIABILITY COMPANY IS TO ENGAGE IN ANY LAWFUL ACT OR ACTIVITY FOR WHICH A LIMITED LIABILITY COMPANY MAY BE ORGANIZED UNDER THE BEVERLY-KILLEA LIMITED LIABILITY COMPANY ACT.

INITIAL AGENT FOR SERVICE OF PROCESS (If the agent is an individual, the agent must reside in California and both Items 3 and 4 must be completed. If the agent is a corporation, the agent must have on file with the California Secretary of State a certificate pursuant to Corporations Code section 1505 and Item 3 must be completed (leave Item 4 blank).

3. NAME OF INITIAL AGENT FOR SERVICE OF PROCESS

4. IF AN INDIVIDUAL, ADDRESS OF INITIAL AGENT FOR SERVICE OF PROCESS IN CALIFORNIA   CITY   STATE   ZIP CODE

CA

MANAGEMENT (Check only one)

5. THE LIMITED LIABILITY COMPANY WILL BE MANAGED BY:

☐ ONE MANAGER

☐ MORE THAN ONE MANAGER

☐ ALL LIMITED LIABILITY COMPANY MEMBER(S)

ADDITIONAL INFORMATION

6. ADDITIONAL INFORMATION SET FORTH ON THE ATTACHED PAGES, IF ANY, IS INCORPORATED HEREIN BY THIS REFERENCE AND MADE A PART OF THIS CERTIFICATE.

EXECUTION

7. I DECLARE I AM THE PERSON WHO EXECUTED THIS INSTRUMENT, WHICH EXECUTION IS MY ACT AND DEED.

_____   _____
DATE   SIGNATURE OF ORGANIZER

_____
TYPE OR PRINT NAME OF ORGANIZER

LLC-1 (REV 04/2007)   APPROVED BY SECRETARY OF STATE

12. Sample Letter to Secretary of State
Accompanying Articles of Organization

Note: This letter is a version appropriate for use in Delaware, but can be modified for use in any state.

Michael Spadaccini
123 Elm Street
San Francisco, CA 94107
415-555-1212

(Date) _____

State of Delaware
Division of Corporations
401 Federal Street, Suite 4
Dover, DE 19901

To whom it may concern:

Enclosed you will find articles of organization for 17 Reasons, LLC. Please file the enclosed articles.

I have enclosed five copies of the filing and a check for $_____ to cover filing fees. Please return any necessary papers in the envelope that I have provided.

Yours truly,

Michael Spadaccini

13. Sample Letter to Registered Agent
Accompanying Articles of Organization

Michael Spadaccini
123 Elm Street
San Francisco, CA 94107
415-555-1212

(Date) _____

Harvard Business Services, Inc.
25 Greystone Manor
Lewes, DE 19958

To whom it may concern:

I have enclosed a copy of articles of incorporation I am filing today. As you can see, I have used you as our registered agents in the state of Delaware.

Please use the following contact information:

17 Reasons, LLC
c/o Michael Spadaccini
123 Elm Street
San Francisco, CA 94107

I have enclosed a check for $50.00 to cover the first year's services.

Yours truly,

Michael Spadaccini

14. Short-Form Operating Agreement for Member-Managed LLC

OPERATING AGREEMENT OF (nsert full name of LLC)

THIS OPERATING AGREEMENT (the "Agreement") is hereby entered into by the undersigned, who are owners and shall be referred to as Member or Members.

RECITALS

The Members desire to form (insert full name of LLC), a limited liability company (the "Company"), for the purposes set forth herein, and, accordingly, desire to enter into this Agreement in order to set forth the terms and conditions of the business and affairs of the Company and to determine the rights and obligations of its Members.

NOW, THEREFORE, the Members, intending to be legally bound by this Agreement, hereby agree that the limited liability company operating agreement of the Company shall be as follows:

ARTICLE I. DEFINITIONS

When used in this Agreement, the following terms shall have the meanings set forth below.

1.1 "Act" means the Limited Liability Company Law of the State in which the Company is organized or chartered, including any amendments or the corresponding provision(s) of any succeeding law.

1.2 "Capital Contribution(s)" means the amount of cash and the agreed value of property, services rendered, or a promissory note or other obligation to contribute cash or property or to perform services contributed by the Members for such Members' Interest in the Company, equal to the sum of the Members' initial Capital Contributions plus the Members' additional Capital Contributions, if any, made pursuant to Sections 4.1 and 4.2, respectively, less payments or distributions made pursuant to Section 5.1.

1.3 "Code" means the Internal Revenue Code of 1986 and the regulations promulgated thereunder, as amended from time to time (or any corresponding provision or provisions of succeeding law).

1.4 "Interest" or "Interests" means the ownership Interest, expressed as a number, percentage, or fraction, set forth in Table A, of a Member in the Company.

1.5 "Person" means any natural individual, partnership, firm, corporation, limited liability company, joint-stock company, trust, or other entity.

1.6 "Secretary of State" means the Office of the Secretary of State or the office charged with accepting articles of organization in the Company's state of organization.

ARTICLE II. FORMATION

2.1 Organization. The Members hereby organize the Company as a limited liability company pursuant to the provisions of the Act.

2.2 Effective Date. The Company shall come into being on, and this Agreement shall take effect from, the date the Articles of Organization of the Company are filed with the Secretary of State in the state of organization or charter.

2.3 Agreement: Invalid Provisions and Saving Clause. The Members, by executing this Agreement, hereby agree to the terms and conditions of this Agreement. To the extent any provision of this Agreement is prohibited or ineffective under the Act, this Agreement shall be deemed to be amended to the least extent necessary in order to make this Agreement effective under the Act. In the event the Act is subsequently amended or interpreted in such a way to validate any provision of this Agreement that was formerly invalid, such provision shall be considered to be valid from the effective date of such amendment or interpretation.

ARTICLE III. PURPOSE; NATURE OF BUSINESS

3.1 Purpose; Nature of Business. The purpose of the Company shall be to engage in any lawful business that may be engaged in by a limited liability company organized under the Act, as such business activities may be determined by the Member or Members from time to time.

3.2 Powers. The Company shall have all powers of a limited liability company under the Act and the power to do all things necessary or convenient to accomplish its purpose and operate its business as described in Section 3.1 here.

ARTICLE IV. MEMBERS AND CAPITAL CONTRIBUTIONS

4.1 Members and Initial Capital Contribution. The name, address, Interest, and value of the initial Capital Contribution of the Members shall be set forth on Table A attached hereto.

4.2 Additional Capital Contributions. The Members shall have no obligation to make any additional Capital Contributions to the Company. The Members may make additional Capital Contributions to the Company as the Members unanimously determine are necessary, appropriate, or desirable.

ARTICLE V. DISTRIBUTIONS AND ALLOCATIONS

5.1 Distributions and Allocations. All distributions of cash or other assets of the Company shall be made and paid to the Members at such time and in such amounts as the majority of the Members may determine. All items of income, gain, loss, deduction, and credit shall be allocated to the Members in proportion to their Interests.

ARTICLE VI. TAXATION

6.1 Income Tax Reporting. Each Member is aware of the income tax consequences of the allocations made by Article V here and agrees to be bound by the provisions of Article V here in reporting each Member's share of Company income and loss for federal and state income tax purposes.

6.2 Tax Treatment. Notwithstanding anything contained herein to the contrary and only for purposes of federal and, if applicable, state income tax purposes, the Company shall be classified as a partnership for such federal and state income tax purposes unless and until the Members unanimously determine to cause the Company to file an election under the Code to be classified as an association taxable as a corporation.

ARTICLE VII. MANAGEMENT BY MEMBERS

7.1 Management by Members. The Company shall be managed by its Members, who shall have full and exclusive right, power, and authority to manage the affairs of the Company and to bind the Company to contracts and obligations, to make all decisions with respect thereto, and to do or cause to be done any and all acts or things deemed by the Members to be necessary, appropriate, or desirable to carry out or further the business of the Company.

7.2 Voting Power in Proportion to Interest. The Members shall enjoy voting power and authority in proportion to their Interests. Unless expressly provided otherwise in this Agreement or the Articles of Organization, Company decisions shall be made by majority vote.

7.3 Duties of Members. The Members shall manage and administer the day-to-day operations and business of the Company and shall execute any and all reports, forms, instruments, documents, papers, writings, agreements, and contracts, including but not limited to deeds, bills of sale, assignments, leases, promissory notes, mortgages, and security agreements and any other type or form of document by which property or property rights of the Company are transferred or encumbered, or by which debts and obligations of the Company are created, incurred, or evidenced.

ARTICLE VIII. BOOKS AND RECORDS

8.1 Books and Records. The Members shall keep, or cause to be kept, at the principal place of business of the Company true and correct books of account, in which shall be entered fully and accurately each and every transaction of the Company. The Company's taxable and fiscal years shall end on December 31. All Members shall have the right to inspect the Company's books and records at any time, for any reason.

ARTICLE IX. LIMITATION OF LIABILITY; INDEMNIFICATION

9.1 Limited Liability. Except as otherwise required by law, the debts, obligations, and liabilities of the Company, whether arising in contract, tort, or otherwise, shall be solely the debts, obligations, and liabilities of the Company, and the Members shall not be obligated personally for any such debt, obligation, or liability of the Company solely by reason of being Members. The failure of the Company to observe any formalities or requirements relating to the exercise of its powers or the management of its business or affairs under this Agreement or by law shall not be grounds for imposing personal liability on the Members for any debts, liabilities, or obligations of the Company. Except as otherwise expressly required by law, the Members, in such Members' capacity as such, shall have no liability in excess of (a) the amount of such Members' Capital Contributions, (b) such Members' share of any assets and undistributed profits of the Company, and (c) the amount of any distributions required to be returned according to law.

9.2 Indemnification. The Company shall, to the fullest extent provided or allowed by law, indemnify, save harmless, and pay all judgments and claims against the Members, and each of the Company's or Members' agents, affiliates, heirs, legal representatives, successors, and assigns (each, an "Indemnified Party") from, against, and in respect of any and all liability, loss, damage, and expense incurred or sustained by the Indemnified Party in connection with the business of the Company or by reason of any act performed or omitted to be performed in connection with the activities of the Company or in dealing with third parties on behalf of the Company, including costs and attorneys' fees before and at trial and at all appellate levels, whether or not suit is instituted (which attorneys' fees may be paid as incurred), and any amounts expended in the settlement of any claims of liability, loss, or damage, to the fullest extent allowed by law.

9.3. Insurance. The Company shall not pay for any insurance covering liability of the Members or the

Company's or Members' agents, affiliates, heirs, legal representatives, successors, and assigns for actions or omissions for which indemnification is not permitted hereunder; provided, however, that nothing contained here shall preclude the Company from purchasing and paying for such types of insurance, including extended coverage liability and casualty and worker's compensation, as would be customary for any Person owning, managing, and/or operating comparable property and engaged in a similar business, or from naming the Members and any of the Company's or Members' agents, affiliates, heirs, legal representatives, successors, or assigns or any Indemnified Party as additional insured parties thereunder.

9.4 Non-Exclusive Right. The provisions of this Article IX shall be in addition to and not in limitation of any other rights of indemnification and reimbursement or limitations of liability to which an Indemnified Party may be entitled under the Act, common law, or otherwise.

ARTICLE X. AMENDMENT

10.1 Amendment. This Agreement may not be altered or modified except by the unanimous written consent or agreement of the Members as evidenced by an amendment hereto whereby this Agreement is amended or amended and restated.

ARTICLE XI. WITHDRAWAL

11.1 Withdrawal of a Member. No Member may withdraw from the Company except by written request of the Member given to each of the other Members and with the unanimous written consent of the other Members (the effective date of withdrawal being the date on which the unanimous written consent of all of the other Members is given) or upon the effective date of any of the following events:

(a) the Member makes an assignment of his or her property for the benefit of creditors;

(b) the Member files a voluntary petition of bankruptcy;

(c) the Member is adjudged bankrupt or insolvent or there is entered against the Member an order for relief in any bankruptcy or insolvency proceeding;

(d) the Member seeks, consents to, or acquiesces in the appointment of a trustee or receiver for, or liquidation of the Member or of all or any substantial part of the Member's property;

(e) the Member files an answer or other pleading admitting or failing to contest the material allegations of a petition filed against the Member in any proceeding described in Subsections 11.1 (a) through (d);

(f) if the Member is a corporation, the dissolution of the corporation or the revocation of its articles of incorporation or charter;

(g) if the Member is an estate, the distribution by the fiduciary of the estate's Interest in the Company;

(h) if the Member is an employee of the Company and he or she resigns, retires, or for any reason ceases to be employed by the Company in any capacity; or

(i) if the other Members owning more than fifty percent (50%) of the Interests vote or request in writing that a Member withdraw and such request is given to the Member (the effective date of withdrawal being the date on which the vote or written request of the other Members is given to the Member).

11.2 Valuation of Interest. The value of the withdrawing Member's Interest in all events shall be equal to the greater of the following: (a) the amount of the Member's Capital Contribution or (b) the amount of the Member's share of the Members' equity in the Company, plus the amount of any unpaid and outstanding loans or advances made by the Member to the Company (plus any due and unpaid interest thereon, if interest on the loan or advance has been agreed to between the Company and the Member), calculated as of the end of the fiscal quarter immediately preceding the effective date of the Member's withdrawal.

11.3 Payment of Value. The value shall be payable as follows: (a) If the value is equal to or less than $500, at closing, and (b) If the value is greater than $500, at the option of the Company, $500 at closing with the balance of the purchase price paid by delivering a promissory note of the Company dated as of the closing date and bearing interest at the prime rate published in *The Wall Street Journal* as of the effective date of withdrawal, with the principal amount being payable in five (5) equal annual installments beginning one (1) year from closing and with the interest on the accrued and unpaid balance being payable at the time of payment of each principal installment.

11.4 Closing. Payment of the value of the departing Member's Interest shall be made at a mutually agreeable time and date on or before thirty (30) days from the effective date of withdrawal. Upon payment of the value of the Interest as calculated in Section 11.3 above: (a) the Member's right to receive any and all further payments or distributions on account of the Member's ownership of the Interest in the Company shall cease; (b) the Member's loans or advances to the Company shall be paid and satisfied in full; and (c) the Member shall no longer be a Member or creditor of the Company on account of the Capital Contribution or the loans or advances.

11.5 Limitation on Payment of Value. If payment of the value of the Interest would be prohibited by any statute or law prohibiting distributions that would

(a) render the Company insolvent; or

(b) be made at a time that the total Company liabilities (other than liabilities to Members on account of their Interests) exceed the value of the Company's total assets;

then the value of the withdrawing Member's Interest in all events shall be $1.00.

ARTICLE XII. MISCELLANEOUS PROVISIONS

12.1 Assignment of Interest and New Members. No Member may assign such person's Interest in the Company in whole or in part except by the vote or written consent of the other Members owning more than fifty percent (50%) of the Interests. No additional Person may be admitted as a Member except by the vote or written consent of the Members owning more than fifty percent (50%) of the Interests.

12.2 Determinations by Members: Except as required by the express provisions of this Agreement or of the Act:

(a) Any transaction, action, or decision which requires or permits the Members to consent to, approve, elect, appoint, adopt, or authorize or to make a determination or decision with respect thereto under this Agreement, the Act, the Code, or otherwise shall be made by the Members owning more than fifty percent (50%) of the Interests.

(b) The Members shall act at a meeting of Members or by consent in writing of the Members. Members may vote or give their consent in person or by proxy.

(c) Meetings of the Members may be held at any time, upon call of any Member or Members owning, in the aggregate, at least ten percent (10%) of the Interests.

(d) Unless waived in writing by the Members owning more than fifty percent (50%) of the Interests (before or after a meeting), at least two (2) business days, prior notice of any meeting shall be given to each Member. Such notice shall state the purpose for which such meeting has been called. No business may be conducted or action taken at such meeting that is not provided for in such notice.

(e) Members may participate in a meeting of Members by means of conference telephone or similar communications equipment by means of which all Persons participating in the meeting can hear each other, and such participation shall constitute presence in person at such meeting.

(f) The Members shall cause to be kept a book of minutes of all meetings of the Members in which there shall be recorded the time and place of such meeting, by whom such meeting was called, the notice thereof given, the names of those present, and the proceedings thereof. Copies of any consents in writing shall also be filed in such minute book.

12.3 Binding Effect. This Agreement shall be binding upon and inure to the benefit of the undersigned Members, their legal representatives, heirs, successors, and assigns. This Agreement and the rights and duties of the Members hereunder shall be governed by, and interpreted and construed in accordance with, the laws of the Company's state of organization or charter, without regard to principles of choice of law.

12.5 Headings. The article and section headings in this Agreement are inserted as a matter of convenience and are for reference only and shall not be construed to define, limit, extend, or describe the scope of this Agreement or the intent of any provision.

12.6 Number and Gender. Whenever required by the context here, the singular shall include the plural, and vice versa, and the masculine gender shall include the feminine and neuter genders, and vice versa.

12.7 Entire Agreement and Binding Effect. This Agreement constitutes the sole operating agreement among the Members and supersedes and cancels any prior agreements, representations, warranties, or communications, whether oral or written, between the Members relating to the affairs of the Company and the conduct of the Company's business. No amendment or modification of this Agreement shall be effective unless approved in writing as provided in Section 10.1. The Articles of Organization and this Agreement are binding upon and shall inure to the benefit of the Members and Agent(s) and shall be binding upon their successors, assigns, affiliates, subsidiaries, heirs, beneficiaries, personal representatives, executors, administrators, and guardians, as applicable and appropriate.

IN WITNESS WHEREOF, this Agreement has been made and executed by the Members effective as of the date first written above.

_____ (Member)

_____ (Member)

_____ (Member)

Table A: Name, Address and Initial Capital Contribution of the Members

Name and Address of Member	Value of Initial Capital Contribution	Nature of Member's Initial Capital Contribution (i.e., cash, services, property)	Percentage Interest of Member

15. Short-Form Operating Agreement for Manager-Managed LLC

OPERATING AGREEMENT OF (insert full name of LLC)

THIS OPERATING AGREEMENT (the "Agreement") is hereby entered into by the undersigned, who are owners and shall be referred to as Member or Members.

RECITALS

The Members desire to form (insert full name of LLC), a limited liability company (the "Company"), for the purposes set forth herein, and, accordingly, desire to enter into this Agreement in order to set forth the terms and conditions of the business and affairs of the Company and to determine the rights and obligations of its Members.

NOW, THEREFORE, the Members, intending to be legally bound by this Agreement, hereby agree that the limited liability company operating agreement of the Company shall be as follows:

ARTICLE I. DEFINITIONS

When used in this Agreement, the following terms shall have the meanings set forth below.

1.1 "Act" means the Limited Liability Company Law of the State in which the Company is organized or chartered, including any amendments or the corresponding provision(s) of any succeeding law.

1.2 "Capital Contribution(s)" means the amount of cash and the agreed value of property, services rendered, or a promissory note or other obligation to contribute cash or property or to perform services contributed by the Members for such Members' Interest in the Company, equal to the sum of the Members' initial Capital Contributions plus the Members' additional Capital Contributions, if any, made pursuant to Sections 4.1 and 4.2, respectively, less payments or distributions made pursuant to Section 5.1.

1.3 "Code" means the Internal Revenue Code of 1986 and the regulations promulgated thereunder, as amended from time to time (or any corresponding provision or provisions of succeeding law).

1.4 "Interest" or "Interests" means the ownership Interest, expressed as a number, percentage, or fraction, set forth in Table A, of a Member in the Company.

1.5 "Manager" or "Managers" means the natural person or persons who have authority to govern the Company according to the terms of this Agreement.

1.6 "Person" means any natural individual, partnership, firm, corporation, limited liability company, joint-stock company, trust, or other entity.

1.7 "Secretary of State" means the Office of the Secretary of State or the office charged with accepting articles of organization in the Company's state of organization.

ARTICLE II. FORMATION

2.1 Organization. The Members hereby organize the Company as a limited liability company pursuant to the provisions of the Act.

2.2 Effective Date. The Company shall come into being on, and this Agreement shall take effect from, the date the Articles of Organization of the Company are filed with the Secretary of State in the state of organization or charter.

2.3 Agreement: Invalid Provisions and Saving Clause. The Members, by executing this Agreement, hereby agree to the terms and conditions of this Agreement. To the extent any provision of this Agreement is prohibited or ineffective under the Act, this Agreement shall be deemed to be amended to the least extent necessary in order to make this Agreement effective under the Act. In the event the Act is subsequently amended or interpreted in such a way to validate any provision of this Agreement that was formerly invalid, such provision shall be considered to be valid from the effective date of such amendment or interpretation.

ARTICLE III. PURPOSE; NATURE OF BUSINESS

3.1 Purpose; Nature of Business. The purpose of the Company shall be to engage in any lawful business that may be engaged in by a limited liability company organized under the Act, as such business activities may be determined by the Manager or Managers from time to time.

3.2 Powers. The Company shall have all powers of a limited liability company under the Act and the power to do all things necessary or convenient to accomplish its purpose and operate its business as described in Section 3.1 here.

ARTICLE IV. MEMBERS AND CAPITAL CONTRIBUTIONS

4.1 Members and Initial Capital Contribution. The name, address, Interest, type of property, and value of the initial Capital Contribution of the Members shall be set forth on Table A attached hereto.

4.2 Additional Capital Contributions. The Members shall have no obligation to make any additional Capital Contributions to the Company. The Members may make additional Capital Contributions to the Company as the Members unanimously determine are necessary, appropriate, or desirable.

ARTICLE V. DISTRIBUTIONS AND ALLOCATIONS

5.1 Distributions and Allocations. All distributions of cash or other assets of the Company shall be made and paid to the Members at such time and in such amounts as a majority of the Managers may determine. All items of income, gain, loss, deduction, and credit shall be allocated to the Members in proportion to their Interests.

ARTICLE VI. TAXATION

6.1 Income Tax Reporting. Each Member is aware of the income tax consequences of the allocations made by Article V here and agrees to be bound by the provisions of Article V here in reporting each Member's share of Company income and loss for federal and state income tax purposes.

6.2 Tax Treatment. Notwithstanding anything contained herein to the contrary and only for purposes of federal and, if applicable, state income tax purposes, the Company shall be classified as a partnership for such federal and state income tax purposes unless and until the Members determine to cause the Company to file an election under the Code to be classified as an association taxable as a corporation.

ARTICLE VII. MANAGERS AND AGENTS

7.1 Management by Manager(s). The Members shall elect and appoint the Manager(s), who shall have the full and exclusive right, power, and authority to manage the affairs of the Company and to bind the Company to contracts and obligations, to make all decisions with respect thereto, and to do or cause to be done any and all acts or things deemed by the Members to be necessary, appropriate, or desirable to carry out or further the business of the Company. All decisions and actions of the Manager(s) shall be made by majority vote of the Manager(s) as provided in Section 12.3. No annual meeting shall be required to reappoint Manager(s). Such Person(s) shall serve in such office(s) at the pleasure of the Members and until his, her, or their successors are duly elected and appointed by the Members. Until further action of the Members as provided herein, the Manager(s) whose names appear on Table B below are the Manager(s) of the Company.

7.2 Agents. Without limiting the rights of the Members, the Manager(s), or the Company, the Manager(s) shall appoint the Person(s) who is (are) to act as the agent(s) of the Company to carry out and further the decisions and actions of the Members or the Manager(s), to manage and the administer the day-to-day operations and business of the Company, and to execute any and all reports, forms, instruments, documents, papers, writings, agreements, and contracts, including but not limited to deeds, bills of sale, assignments, leases, promissory notes, mortgages, and security agreements and any other type or form of document by which property or property rights of the Company are transferred or encumbered, or by which debts and obligations of the Company are created, incurred, or evidenced, which are necessary, appropriate, or beneficial to carry out or further such decisions or actions and to manage and administer the day-to-day operations and business.

ARTICLE VIII. BOOKS AND RECORDS

8.1 Books and Records. The Managers shall keep, or cause to be kept, at the principal place of business of the Company true and correct books of account, in which shall be entered fully and accurately each and every transaction of the Company. The Company's taxable and fiscal years shall end on December 31. All Members shall have the right to inspect the Company's books and records at any time, for any reason.

ARTICLE IX. LIMITATION OF LIABILITY; INDEMNIFICATION

9.1 Limited Liability. Except as otherwise required by law, the debts, obligations, and liabilities of the Company, whether arising in contract, tort, or otherwise, shall be solely the debts, obligations, and liabilities of the Company, and the Members shall not be obligated personally for any such debt, obligation, or liability of the Company solely by reason of being Members. The failure of the Company to observe any formalities or requirements relating to the exercise of its powers or the management of its business or affairs under this Agreement or by law shall not be grounds for imposing personal liability on the Members for any debts, liabilities, or obligations of the Company. Except as otherwise expressly required by law, the Members, in such Members' capacity as such, shall have no liability in excess of (a) the amount of such Members' Capital Contributions, (b) such Members' share of any assets and undistributed profits of the Company, and (c) the amount of any distributions required to be returned according to law.

9.2 Indemnification. The Company shall, to the fullest extent provided or allowed by law, indemnify, save harmless, and pay all judgments and claims against the Members or Manager(s), and each of the Company's, Members', or Manager(s)' agents, affiliates, heirs, legal representatives, successors, and assigns (each, an "Indemnified Party") from, against, and in respect of any and all liability, loss, damage, and expense incurred or sustained by the Indemnified Party in connection with the business of the Company or by reason of any act performed or omitted to be performed in connection with the activities of the Company or in dealing with third parties on behalf of the Company, including costs and attorneys' fees before and at trial and at all appellate levels, whether or not suit is instituted (which attorneys' fees may be paid as incurred), and any amounts expended in the settlement of any claims of liability, loss, or damage, to the fullest extent allowed by law.

9.3. Insurance. The Company shall not pay for any insurance covering liability of the Members or the Manager(s) or the Company's, Members', or Manager(s)' agents, affiliates, heirs, legal representatives, successors, and assigns for actions or omissions for which indemnification is not permitted hereunder; provided, however, that nothing contained here shall preclude the Company from purchasing and paying for such types of insurance, including extended coverage liability and casualty and worker's compensation, as would be customary for any Person owning, managing, and/or operating comparable property and engaged in a similar business, or from naming the Members or the Manager(s) and any of the Company's, Members', or Manager(s)' agents, affiliates, heirs, legal representatives, successors, or assigns or any Indemnified Party as additional insured parties thereunder.

9.4 Non-Exclusive Right. The provisions of this Article IX shall be in addition to and not in limitation of any other rights of indemnification and reimbursement or limitations of liability to which an Indemnified Party may be entitled under the Act, common law, or otherwise.

ARTICLE X. AMENDMENT

10.1 Amendment. This Agreement may not be altered or modified except by the unanimous written consent or agreement of the Members as evidenced by an amendment hereto whereby this Agreement is amended or amended and restated.

ARTICLE XI. WITHDRAWAL

11.1 Withdrawal of a Member. No Member may withdraw from the Company except by written request of the Member given to each of the other Members and with the unanimous written consent of the other Members (the effective date of withdrawal being the date on which the unanimous written consent of all of the other Members is given) or upon the effective date of any of the following events:

(a) the Member makes an assignment of his or her property for the benefit of creditors;

(b) the Member files a voluntary petition of bankruptcy;

(c) the Member is adjudged bankrupt or insolvent or there is entered against the Member an order for relief in any bankruptcy or insolvency proceeding;

(d) the Member seeks, consents to, or acquiesces in the appointment of a trustee or receiver for, or liquidation of the Member or of all or any substantial part of the Member's property;

(e) the Member files an answer or other pleading admitting or failing to contest the material allegations of a petition filed against the Member in any proceeding described in Subsections 11.1 (a) through (d);

(f) if the Member is a corporation, the dissolution of the corporation or the revocation of its articles of incorporation or charter;

(g) if the Member is an estate, the distribution by the fiduciary of the estate's Interest in the Company;

(h) if the Member is an employee of the Company and he or she resigns, retires, or for any reason ceases to be employed by the Company in any capacity; or

(i) if the other Members owning more than fifty percent (50%) of the Interests vote or request in writing that a Member withdraw and such request is given to the Member (the effective date of withdrawal being the date on which the vote or written request of the other Members is given to the Member).

11.2 Valuation of Interest. The value of the withdrawing Member's Interest in all events shall be equal to the greater of the following: (a) the amount of the Member's Capital Contribution or (b) the amount of the Member's share of the Members' equity in the Company, plus the amount of any unpaid and outstanding loans or advances made by the Member to the Company (plus any due and unpaid interest thereon, if interest on the loan or advance has been agreed to between the Company and the Member), calculated as of the end of the fiscal quarter immediately preceding the effective date of the Member's withdrawal.

11.3 Payment of Value. The value shall be payable as follows: (a) If the value is equal to or less than $500, at closing, and (b) If the value is greater than $500, at the option of the Company, $500 at closing with the balance of the purchase price paid by delivering a promissory note of the Company dated as of the closing date and bearing interest at the prime rate published in *The Wall Street Journal* as of the effective date of withdrawal, with the principal amount being payable in five (5) equal annual installments beginning one (1) year from closing and with the interest on the accrued and unpaid balance being payable at the time of payment of each principal installment.

11.4 Closing. Payment of the value of the departing Member's Interest shall be made at a mutually agreeable time and date on or before thirty (30) days from the effective date of withdrawal. Upon payment of the value of the Interest as calculated in Section 11.3 above: (a) the Member's right to receive any and all further payments or distributions on account of the Member's ownership of the Interest in the Company shall cease; (b) the Member's loans or advances to the Company shall be paid and satisfied in full; and (c) the Member shall no longer be a Member or creditor of the Company on account of the Capital Contribution or the loans or advances.

11.5 Limitation on Payment of Value. If payment of the value of the Interest would be prohibited by any statute or law prohibiting distributions that would

(a) render the Company insolvent; or

(b) be made at a time that the total Company liabilities (other than liabilities to Members on account of their Interests) exceed the value of the Company's total assets;

then the value of the withdrawing Member's Interest in all events shall be $1.00.

ARTICLE XII. MISCELLANEOUS PROVISIONS

12.1 Assignment of Interest and New Members. No Member may assign such person's Interest in the Company in whole or in part except by the vote or written consent of the other Members owning more than fifty percent (50%) of the Interests. No additional Person may be admitted as a Member except by the vote or written consent of the Members owning more than fifty percent (50%) of the Interests.

12.2 Determinations by Members: Except as required by the express provisions of this Agreement or of the Act:

(a) Any transaction, action, or decision which requires or permits the Members to consent to, approve, elect, appoint, adopt, or authorize or to make a determination or decision with respect thereto under this Agreement, the Act, the Code, or otherwise shall be made by the Members owning more than fifty percent (50%) of the Interests.

(b) The Members shall act at a meeting of Members or by consent in writing of the Members. Members may vote or give their consent in person or by proxy.

(c) Meetings of the Members may be held at any time, upon call of any Manager or a Member or Members owning, in the aggregate, at least ten percent (10%) of the Interests.

(d) Unless waived in writing by the Members owning more than fifty percent (50%) of the Interests (before or after a meeting), at least two (2) business days' prior notice of any meeting shall be given to each Member. Such notice shall state the purpose for which such meeting has been called. No business may be conducted or action taken at such meeting that is not provided for in such notice.

(e) Members may participate in a meeting of Members by means of conference telephone or similar communications equipment by means of which all Persons participating in the meeting can hear each other, and such participation shall constitute presence in person at such meeting.

(f) The Managers shall cause to be kept a book of minutes of all meetings of the Members in which there shall be recorded the time and place of such meeting, by whom such meeting was called, the notice thereof given, the names of those present, and the proceedings thereof. Copies of any consents in writing shall also be filed in such minutes book.

12.3 Determinations by Managers. Except as required by the express provisions of this Agreement or of the Act and if there shall be more than one Manager:

(a) Any transaction, action, or decision which requires or permits the Managers to consent to, approve, elect, appoint, adopt, or authorize or to make a determination or decision with respect thereto under this Agreement, the Act, the Code, or otherwise shall be made by a majority of the Managers.

(b) The Managers shall act only at a meeting of the Managers or by consent in writing of the Managers. Managers may vote or give their consent in person only and not by proxy.

(c) Meetings of the Managers may be held at any time, upon call of any agent of the Company appointed pursuant to Section 7.2 of this Agreement or any Manager.

(d) Notice of any meeting shall be given to a majority of the Managers at any time prior to the meeting, in writing or by verbal communication. Such notice need not state the purpose for which such meeting has been called.

(e) The Managers may participate in a meeting of the Managers by means of conference telephone or similar communications equipment by means of which all Persons participating in the meeting can hear each other, and such participation shall constitute presence in person at such meeting.

(f) The Managers may cause to be kept a book of minutes of all meetings of the Managers in which there shall be recorded the time and place of such meeting, by whom such meeting was called, the notice thereof given, the names of those present, and the proceedings thereof. Copies of any consents in writing shall also be filed in such minute book.

12.4 Binding Effect. This Agreement shall be binding upon and inure to the benefit of the undersigned, their legal representatives, heirs, successors, and assigns. This Agreement and the rights and duties of the Members hereunder shall be governed by, and interpreted and construed in accordance with, the laws of the State of Florida, without regard to principles of choice of law.

12.5 Headings. The article and section headings in this Agreement are inserted as a matter of convenience and are for reference only and shall not be construed to define, limit, extend, or describe the scope of this Agreement or the intent of any provision.

12.6 Number and Gender. Whenever required by the context here, the singular shall include the plural, and vice versa, and the masculine gender shall include the feminine and neuter genders, and vice versa.

12.7 Entire Agreement and Binding Effect. This Agreement constitutes the sole operating agreement among the Members and supersedes and cancels any prior agreements, representations, warranties, or communications, whether oral or written, between the Members relating to the affairs of the Company and the conduct of the Company's business. No amendment or modification of this Agreement shall be effective unless approved in writing as provided in Section 10.1. The Articles of Organization and this Agreement are binding upon and shall inure to the benefit of the Members and Agent(s) and shall be binding upon their successors, assigns, affiliates, subsidiaries, heirs, beneficiaries, personal representatives, executors, administrators, and guardians, as applicable and appropriate.

IN WITNESS WHEREOF, this Agreement has been made and executed by the Members effective as of the date first written above.

_____ (Member)

_____ (Member)

_____ (Member)

Table A: Name, Address, and Initial Capital Contribution of the Members

Name and Address of Member	Value of Initial Capital Contribution	Nature of Member's Initial Capital Contribution (i.e., cash, services, property)	Percentage Interest of Member

Table B: Managers

Name of Manager	Address of Manager

16. Membership Ledger

Date of Original Issue	Member Name	Percentage Interest	Disposition of Shares (transferred or surrendered stock certificate)

17. Investment Representation Letter

Note: The following Investment Representation Letter should be executed by each LLC member and delivered to the company. The Representation Letter seeks to ensure company compliance with securities laws, by asking owners to certify that they are joining the LLC as an investment, and not to trade shares in the LLC.

(insert date)

To whom it may concern,

I am delivering this letter to Olde Craft, LLC in connection with my purchase of a 25% interest in Olde Craft, Inc. for a total sum of $75,000.00. I represent the following:

I am purchasing the shares in my own name and for my own account, for investment and not with an intent to sell or for sale in connection with any distribution of such stock; and no other person has any interest in or right with respect to the shares; nor have I agreed to give any person any such interest or right in the future.

I recognize that the shares have not been registered under the Federal Securities Act of 1933, as amended, or qualified under any state securities law, and that any sale or transfer of the shares is subject to restrictions imposed by federal and state law.

I also recognize that I cannot dispose of the shares absent registration and qualification or an available exemption from registration and qualification. I understand that no federal or state securities commission or other government body has approved of the fairness of the shares offered by the corporation and that the Commissioner has not and will not recommend or endorse the shares.

I have not seen or received any advertisement or general solicitation with respect to the sale of the shares.

I have a preexisting personal or business relationship with the Company or one or more of its officers, directors, or controlling persons and I am aware of its character and general financial and business circumstances.

I acknowledge that during the course of this transaction and before purchasing the shares I have been provided with financial and other written information about the Company. I have been given the opportunity by the Company to obtain any information and ask questions concerning the Company, the shares, and my investment that I felt necessary; and to the extent I availed myself of that opportunity, I have received satisfactory information and answers.

In reaching the decision to invest in the shares, I have carefully evaluated my financial resources and investment position and the risks associated with this investment, and I acknowledge that I am able to bear the economic risks of this investment.

_____

John Miller

18. Appointment of Proxy for Members' Meeting

Note: Use the following form when a Member wants to give his or her vote to another person at a meeting of an LLC's membership.

APPOINTMENT OF PROXY FOR (Annual/Special) MEETING

MadHatter, LLC

SHAREHOLDER: John Miller

PERCENTAGE INTEREST HELD BY SHAREHOLDER: 32%

I, the undersigned, as record holder of a 32% interest in MadHatter, LLC, revoke any previous proxies and appoint the person whose name appears just below this paragraph as my proxy to attend the member's meeting on _____ and any adjournment of that meeting.

The person I want to appoint as my proxy is _____

The proxy holder is entitled to cast a total number of votes equal to, but not exceeding the number of shares which I would be entitled to cast if I were personally present.

I authorize my proxy holder to vote and otherwise represent me with regard to any business that may come before this meeting in the same manner and with the same effect as if I were personally present.

I may revoke this proxy at any time. This proxy will lapse three months after the date of its execution.

If you are signing for a business entity, state your title:

Date (*important*):_____

_____
Name

_____
Title

Note: All proxies must be signed. Sign exactly as your name appears on your stock certificate. Joint shareholders must each sign this proxy. If signed by an attorney in fact, the Power of Attorney must be attached.

19. Call for Meeting of Members

Note: This "call" is an instruction by LLC members to the managers that the members want to call a meeting of members. This serves as official notice. This call is required only in manager-managed LLCs; if a member in a member-managed LLC wants to call a meeting of members, he or she would skip the call and simply send a notice of meeting of members to all other members. The next form is a notice of meeting of members.

CALL FOR MEETING OF LLC MEMBERS

TO: The Managers of MadHatter, LLC

(insert date)

The party or parties whose name appears below are members of MadHatter, LLC, and own percentage interests entitled to cast not less than 10 percent of MadHatter's votes. We hereby call a meeting of the members of MadHatter to be held _____ (date), at _____ (time), for the purpose of considering and acting upon the following matters:

(Insert matters to be considered, such as "A proposal that John Jones be removed as a manager of MadHatter.")

You are directed to give notice of this meeting of the members, in the manner prescribed by MadHatter's operating agreement and by law, to all members entitled to receive notice of the meeting.

Date _____

_____

_____

_____

20. Notice of Meeting of LLC Members

Note: This form is an LLC's announcement to its members that a meeting of members has been called.

NOTICE OF MEETING OF MEMBERS OF OLDECRAFT, LLC

Certain members of OldeCraft, LLC, have called a meeting of the members of OldeCraft pursuant to OldeCraft's operating agreement.

Therefore, this is your official notice as an OldeCraft member that a meeting of members of OldeCraft, LLC, will be held on _____ (date), at _____ (time), at _____ (address), to consider and act on the following matters:

(insert matters to be considered, such as "A proposal that John Jones be removed from the board of directors.")

If you do not expect to be present at the meeting and wish your shares to be voted, you may complete the attached form of proxy and mail it in the enclosed addressed envelope.

Date _____

_____
John Wilson, Manager

21. Minutes of Meeting of LLC Members

Note: While LLC members and managers enjoy far fewer corporate formalities than corporation owners, an LLC must still maintain records of its meetings. When an LLC's members meet to formally vote on any matter, the results of that vote should be committed to written minutes.

MINUTES OF MEETING OF MEMBERS OF OLDECRAFT, LLC

The members of OLDECRAFT, LLC, held a meeting on _____ (date), at _____(time), at _____(place). The meeting was called by John Miller and the company managers mailed notice to all members that the meeting would take place.

The following members were present at the meeting, in person or by proxy, representing membership interests as indicated:

> John Jones, 50%
> John Smith, 30%
> John Miller, 20%

Also present were Michael Spadaccini, attorney to the company, and Lisa Jones, wife of John Jones, and the company's president and sole manager.

The company's president called the meeting to order and announced that she would chair the meeting, that a quorum was present, and that the meeting was held pursuant to a written notice of meeting given to all members of the company. A copy of the notice was ordered inserted in the minute book immediately preceding the minutes of this meeting.

The minutes of the previous meeting of shareholders were then read and approved.

The chairperson then announced that the election of a manager was in order. Lisa Jones stated that she could no longer serve as manager of the company. John Smith was then elected to serve until the next meeting of members, and until the manager's successor was duly elected and qualified, as follows:

(Include agreement for selecting new manager here.)

There being no further business to come before the meeting, on motion duly made, seconded, and adopted, the meeting was adjourned.

_____
John Smith, Manager

22. Action by Written Consent of LLC Members

Note: Most company votes are taken by written consent rather than by notice and meeting and an in-person vote. Use the following form when you wish to take a company action in writing, rather than by a noticed meeting. Keep in mind, however, that your operating agreement and articles may require more than a simple majority to pass certain actions. Written consents are important company records and should be maintained in the record books.

ACTION BY WRITTEN CONSENT OF SHAREHOLDERS OF OLDECRAFT, LLC

The undersigned members of OldeCraft, LLC, owning of record the number of shares entitled to vote as set forth, hereby consent to the following company actions. The vote was unanimous. (For actions where a unanimous vote is not required: "A vote of 66% was required to take the actions listed below, and 80% of the membership interest in the company have given their consent."):

1. Pete Wilson is hereby removed as manager of the company.

2. The number of managers of the company is increased from one to two.

John Smith and John Miller, both also members, are hereby elected to serve as company managers until the next meeting of members.

DATED: _____

_____
John Smith

Percentage Owned: _____

DATED: _____

_____
John Miller

Percentage Owned:_____

23. Written Consent of Members Approving a Certificate of Amendment of Articles of Organization Changing an LLC's Name

ACTION OF MEMBERS BY WRITTEN CONSENT TO APPROVE AN AMENDMENT TO ARTICLES OF ORGANIZATION CHANGING LLC NAME

The undersigned, who comprise all the members of PLASTICWORLD, LLC, agree unanimously to the following:

RESOLVED, that the Certificate of Amendment of Articles of Organization presented to the undersigned members, specifically changing the name of the company to PLASTICUNIVERSE, LLC is approved.

Date _____

_____

Scott Bess

_____

Brian Bess

CHAPTER 4

Forms for Corporations

THE *SAMPLE CALIFORNIA ARTICLES OF Incorporation* are suitable articles of incorporation for a basic California corporation. Similarly, the *Sample Delaware Certificate of Incorporation* is a suitable certificate of incorporation for a basic Delaware corporation. The *Sample Nevada Articles of Incorporation (Long Form, with Full Indemnity Provisions)* are suitable articles of incorporation for a Nevada corporation; this sample is a long form, with provisions that indemnify officers and directors from lawsuits and claims made against them as a result of their duties to the corporation.

The *Optional Provisions for Inclusion in Articles of Incorporation* are a set of optional provisions that one can include in articles of incorporation that authorize two separate classes of stock. The *Sample Letter to Secretary of State Accompanying Articles of Incorporation* is a sample letter that one can include when presenting corporation paperwork for filing with a Secretary of State.

A *registered agent* is a person or entity authorized and obligated to receive legal papers on behalf of a corporation. The *Sample Letter to Registered Agent* (which is intended to accompany articles of incorporation) is a simple cover letter that you should deliver to your registered agent upon the organization of your corporation. Keep in mind that your state of organization may use a different term than "registered agent." Typical equivalents include "agent for service of process" and "local agent."

An *incorporator* is the person or entity that organizes a corporation and files its articles of incorporation. The incorporator enjoys certain powers: he or she can take corporate actions before directors and officers are appointed. For example, an incorporator can amend the articles of incorporation, approve bylaws, and appoint directors. Typically, an incorporator's power is quite broad. The *Sample Action by Incorporator Appointing Directors and Approving Bylaws* is a written resolution undertaken by the incorporator that appoints directors and approves bylaws for governance of the corporation.

Bylaws cover such matters as holding meetings, voting, quorums, elections, and the powers of directors and officers. The *Sample Corporate Bylaws* are simple, universal bylaws usable in any state. Consider, however, that these simple bylaws may not take advantage of favorable laws in your particular state of incorporation.

If and when you want to issue stock as a corporation, refer to the *Blank Stock Certificate* on the Web site supporting this book. This would ultimately be given to a shareholder with his or her name and the number of shares printed on the form. To finalize your incorporation, you must have an organizational meeting of the board of directors. You must also prepare minutes of this meeting. Because the format of the meeting is relatively standard, the minutes are nearly always drafted beforehand, and followed like a script. The *Sample Minutes of Organizational Meeting of the Board of Directors* (included on the Web) is such a document.

The *Shareholder's Agreement* (on the Web) is an agreement among the shareholders of a corporation that covers various matters such as a commitment to vote particular persons as directors and allow other shareholders to have a right of first refusal to purchase the shares of departing shareholders. Shareholders' agreements are complex documents best handled by an attorney, but this sample should give you some insight into the devices available in such a document.

The *Share Transfer Ledger* is a ledger indicating the owners of a corporation and their proportion of ownership, as well as transfers of such ownership. All corporations should begin the ledger upon the formation of the corporation and should diligently update the ledger when shares are transferred, gifted, sold, repurchased by the corporation, or when new shares are issued. Each member admitted to the corporation should execute the *Investment Representation Letter*. The investment representa-

tion letter offers some measure of protection to the entity because the member being admitted to the corporation makes certain representations regarding his or her qualifications and fitness to serve as a member of the corporation. Also, in the investment representation letter, the member makes certain representations regarding his or her investment objectives, which are necessary to comply with state and federal securities laws.

A *proxy* is an authorization by one member giving another person the right to vote the member's shares. Proxy also refers to the document granting such authority. We have included several proxy forms here: The *Appointment of Proxy for Annual or Special Shareholders' Meeting* a simple proxy form in which shareholder's grant their proxy for a shareholder's meeting and the *Long-Form Appointment of Proxy for Annual or Special Shareholders' Meeting*, which serves the same purpose but is a more thorough and complex document.

A *call* is an instruction by a corporation's shareholders to the corporation's officers and managers that the shareholders want to call a meeting of shareholders. This *Call for Special Meeting of Shareholders* (on the Web) serves as official notice to the managers that the members wish to call a meeting. The *Notice of Special Meeting of Shareholders* is a notice to shareholders that a meeting has been called.

Annual and special meetings of shareholders and of directors must be recorded. The written record of the actions taken at such meetings are called *minutes*. Minutes are simple to prepare and are often short. We have included several sample minutes here. The *Minutes of Annual or Special Meeting of Shareholders* is appropriate for documenting a shareholder meeting. As an alternative to a formally called meeting, subject to certain restrictions, shareholders or directors may take an action without a meeting if their action is memorialized in a written consent. A *written consent* is a formal written document that sets forth a corporate action or resolution to be taken or made, and is signed by the shareholders or directors consenting to the action. The *Action by Written Consent of Shareholder(s)* is such a document.

The *Call for Special Meeting of Directors* serves as official notice to the directors that either an officer or director wishes to call a meeting of a corporation's board of directors. The *Minutes of Annual Meeting of Directors* is a sample document memorializing the actions taken at an annual meeting of directors. The *Minutes of Special Meeting of Directors* (on the Web) memorializes the actions taken at a special meeting of directors.

A corporation's directors, like shareholders, can vote by written consent in lieu of a formally noticed and held meeting. The *Action of Directors by Written Consent to Approve Stock* allows directors to take such action. Note, however, that most bylaws require the unanimous vote of directors to utilize a written consent. A more specific use of the written consent form is the *Written Consent of Directors Approving a Certificate of Amendment of Articles of Incorporation Changing Corporation's Name* in which the directors unanimously vote to amend the corporation's charter to change the corporation's name.

The *Certificate of Amendment of Articles of Incorporation Changing Corporation's Name* is the formal and official document that a corporation would file with a Secretary of State in its state of incorporation that formally amends its articles of incorporation to change its name, while the *Certificate of Amendment of Articles of Incorporation Electing Close Corporation Status* formally effects a change to the corporation's status from regular corporation to close corporation. A *close corporation*, generally speaking, is a smaller corporation that elects close corporation status and is therefore entitled to operate without the strict formalities normally required in the operation of standard corporations. Many small business owners find this benefit invaluable. In essence, a close corporation is a corporation whose shareholders and directors are entitled to operate much like a partnership.

IRS Tax Form SS-4 is the form by which a business entity obtains its Federal Tax ID Number (included in Chapter 1). The *IRS Tax Form 2553* is the tax form under which a corporation elects "S" corporation status. Subchapter S of the IRS Code permits eligible smaller corporations to avoid double taxation and be taxed as partnerships. Corporations that make such an election are known as "S" corporations. An S corporation differs from a standard C corporation solely with respect to its taxation.

A corporation must meet certain conditions to be eligible for a subchapter S election. First, the corporation must have no more than 75 shareholders. In calculating the 75-shareholder limit, a husband and wife count as one shareholder. Also, only the following entities may be shareholders: individuals, estates, certain trusts, certain partnerships, tax-exempt charitable organizations, and other S corporations (but only if the other S corporation is the sole shareholder). S corporations may only have one class of stock. A corporation must make the subchapter S election no later than two months and 15 days after the first day of the taxable year—it cannot wait until the end of the taxable year to elect. Subchapter S election requires the consent of all shareholders.

The states treat S corporations differently. Some states disregard subchapter S status entirely, offering no tax break. Other states honor the federal election automatically. Finally, some states require the filing of a state-specific form to complete subchapter S election.

24. Sample California Articles of Incorporation

ARTICLES OF INCORPORATION
OF
(CORPORATION NAME)

1. The name of this corporation is (Corporation Name).

2. The purpose of the corporation is to engage in any lawful act or activity for which a corporation may be organized under the General Corporation Law of California other than the banking business, the trust company business, or the practice of a profession permitted to be incorporated by the California Corporations Code.

3. The name and address in the State of California of this corporation's initial agent for service of process is (insert name and address of initial agent for service of process).

4. This corporation is authorized to issue only one class of shares of stock; and the total number of shares which this corporation is authorized to issue is one million (1,000,000) shares.

5. The liability of the directors of the corporation for monetary damages shall be eliminated to the fullest extent permissible under California law.

Dated:

_____

Donald Leland, Incorporator

25. Nevada Articles of Incorporation, Long Form with Full Indemnity Provisions

DEAN HELLER
Secretary of State
206 North Carson Street
Carson City, Nevada 89701-4299
(775) 684 5708
Website: secretaryofstate.biz

Articles of Incorporation
(PURSUANT TO NRS 78)

Important. Read attached instructions before completing form.

ABOVE SPACE IS FOR OFFICE USE ONLY

1. **Name of Corporation:**	
2. **Resident Agent Name and Street Address:** (must be a Nevada address where process may be served)	Name
	Street Address · City · **NEVADA** · Zip Code
	Optional Mailing Address · City · State · Zip Code
3. **Shares:** (number of shares corporation authorized to issue)	Number of shares with par value: · Par value: $ · Number of shares without par value:
4. **Names & Addresses, of Board of Directors/Trustees:** (attach additional page there is more than 3 directors/trustees)	1. Name
	Street Address · City · State · Zip Code
	2. Name
	Street Address · City · State · Zip Code
	3. Name
	Street Address · City · State · Zip Code
5. **Purpose:** (optional-see instructions)	The purpose of this Corporation shall be:
6. **Names, Address and Signature of Incorporator.** (attach additional page there is more than 1 incorporator)	Name · Signature
	Address · City · State · Zip Code
7. **Certificate of Acceptance of Appointment of Resident Agent:**	I hereby accept appointment as Resident Agent for the above named corporation.
	Authorized Signature of R. A. or On Behalf of R. A. Company · Date

This form must be accompanied by appropriate fees. See attached fee schedule.

26. Nevada Long Form with Optional Provisions and Continuation Sheet

The following sample is long-form articles suitable for use only in Nevada. In some states, the use of fill-in forms is optional. In Nevada, it is now mandatory. So, if you want long-form articles in Nevada, you have to build them in two parts. The first part is the standard Nevada form and the second part is your continuation page. Note that the Article numbers appear out of order. This is because the article numbers for "shares of stock" and "directors" must correspond to the Article numbers on the fill-in form. Thereafter, the Article numbers continue where the fill-in form leaves off.

CONTINUATION OF ARTICLES OF INCORPORATION OF TONOSILVER, INC., a Nevada Corporation

ARTICLE THREE. SHARES OF STOCK

Section 3.01. Number of Shares and Classes. The Corporation shall have two classes of stock. One class shall be Class A Common Stock, par value $0.001, of which 70,000,000 shares shall be authorized. The holders of the Class A Common Stock are entitled to one vote per share and are entitled to receive the net assets of the Corporation upon dissolution. The second class shall be Class B Common Stock, par value $0.001, of which 5,000,000 shares shall be authorized. The holders of the Class B Common Stock are entitled to ten votes per share and are not entitled to receive the net assets of the Corporation upon dissolution.

ARTICLE FOUR. DIRECTORS

Section 4.01. Board of Directors. The Board of Directors shall consist of not less than one (1) and not more than five (5) members.
Section 4.02. Change in Number of Directors. The number of Directors may be increased or decreased by a duly adopted amendment to the Bylaws of the Corporation.

ARTICLE EIGHT. DIRECTORS' AND OFFICERS' LIABILITY

A Director or Officer of the Corporation shall not be personally liable to this Corporation or its Stockholders for damages for breach of fiduciary duty as a Director or Officer, but this Article shall not eliminate or limit the liability of a Director or Officer for (i) acts or omissions which involve intentional misconduct, fraud, or a knowing violation of law or (ii) the unlawful payment of distributions. Any repeal or modification of this Article by the Stockholders of the Corporation shall be prospective only and shall not adversely affect any limitation on the personal liability of a Director or Officer of the Corporation for acts or omissions prior to such repeal or modification.

ARTICLE NINE. INDEMNITY

Every person who was or is a party to, or is threatened to be made a party to, or is involved in any action, suit, or proceeding, whether civil, criminal, administrative, or investigative, by reason of the fact that he, or a person of whom he is the legal representative, is or was a Director or Officer of the Corporation, or is or was serving at the request of the Corporation as a Director or Officer of another Corporation, or as its representative in a partnership, joint venture, trust, or other enterprise, shall be indemnified and held harmless to the fullest extent legally permissible under the laws of the State of Nevada from time to time against all expenses, liability, and loss (including attorneys' fees judgments, fines, and amounts paid or to be paid in settlement) reasonably incurred or suffered by him in connection therewith. Such right of indemnification shall be a contract right which may be enforced in any manner desired by such person. The expenses of Officers and Directors incurred in defending a civil or criminal action, suit, or proceeding must be paid by the Corporation as they are incurred and in advance of the final disposition of the action, suit, or proceeding, upon receipt of an undertaking by or on behalf of the Director or Officer to repay the amount if it is ultimately determined by a court of competent jurisdiction that he is not entitled to be indemnified by the Corporation. Such right of indemnification shall not be exclusive of any other right which such Directors, Officers, or representatives may have or hereafter acquire, and, without limiting the generality of such statement, they shall be entitled to their respective rights of indemnification under any bylaw, agreement, vote of Stockholders, provision of law, or otherwise, as well as their rights under this Article. Without limiting the application of the foregoing, the Stockholders or Board of Directors may adopt bylaws from time to time with respect to indemnification, to provide at all times the fullest indemnification permitted by the laws of the State of Nevada, and may cause the Corporation to purchase and maintain insurance on behalf of any person who is or was a Director or Officer of the Corporation, or is or was serving at the request of the Corporation as a Director or Officer of another Corporation, or as its representative in a partnership, joint venture, trust, or other enterprise against any liability asserted against such person and incurred in any such capacity or arising out of such status, whether or not the Corporation would have the power to indemnify such person. The indemnification provided in this Article shall continue as to a person who has ceased to be a Director, Officer, Employee, or Agent, and shall inure to the benefit of the heirs, executors and administrators of such person.

ARTICLE TEN. AMENDMENTS
This Corporation reserves the right to amend, alter, change, or repeal any provision contained in these Articles of Incorporation or its Bylaws, in the manner now or hereafter prescribed by statute or by these Articles of Incorporation or said Bylaws, and all rights conferred upon the Stockholders are granted subject to this reservation.

ARTICLE ELEVEN. POWERS OF DIRECTORS
In furtherance and not in limitation of the powers conferred by statute the Board of Directors is expressly authorized: (1) Subject to the Bylaws, if any, adopted by the Stockholders, to make, alter, or repeal the Bylaws of the Corporation; (2) To authorize and cause to be executed mortgages and liens, with or without limit as to amount, upon the real and personal property of the Corporation; (3) To authorize the guaranty by the Corporation of securities, evidences of indebtedness, and obligations of other persons, corporations, and business entities; (4) To set apart out of any of the funds of the Corporation available for distributions a reserve or reserves for any proper purpose and to abolish any such reserve; (5) By resolution, to designate one or more committees, each committee to consist of at least one Director of the Corporation, which to the extent provided in the resolution or in the Bylaws of the Corporation, shall have and may exercise the powers of the Board of Directors in the management of the business and affairs of the Corporation, and may authorize the seal of the Corporation to be affixed to all papers which may require it. Such committee or committees shall have such name or names as may be stated in the Bylaws of the Corporation or as may be determined from time to time by resolution adopted by the Board of Directors; and (6) To authorize the Corporation by its Officers or agents to exercise all such powers and to do all such acts and things as may be exercised or done by the Corporation, except and to the extent that any such statute shall require action by the Stockholders of the Corporation with regard to the exercising of any such power or the doing of any such act or thing.

In addition to the powers and authorities hereinbefore or by statute expressly conferred upon them, the Board of Directors may exercise all such powers and do all such acts and things as may be exercised or done by the Corporation, except as otherwise provided herein and by law.

27. Optional Provisions for Inclusion in Articles of Incorporation

a. Clause establishing a class of voting common stock and a class of non-voting common stock:

This corporation is authorized to issue two classes of shares: "Class A Common Stock" and "Class B Common Stock." This corporation may issue 1,000,000 shares of Class A Common Stock and 500,000 shares of Class B Common Stock. The Class B Common Stock has no voting rights. The Class A Common Stock has exclusive voting rights except as otherwise provided by law.

b. Clause establishing a class of voting common stock and a class of preferred stock:

This corporation is authorized to issue two classes of shares: "Common Stock" and "Preferred Stock." This corporation may issue 1,000,000 shares of Common Stock and 500,000 shares of Preferred Stock. The Common Stock has voting rights. The Preferred Stock has no voting rights except as otherwise provided by law.

The Preferred Stock has a liquidation preference. Upon the liquidation or dissolution of the corporation, holders of the Preferred Stock are entitled to receive out of the assets available for distribution to shareholders, before any payment to the holders of the Common Stock, the sum of $_____ per share. If the assets of the corporation are insufficient to pay this liquidation preference to the Preferred Stock, all of the entire remaining assets shall be paid to holders of the Preferred Stock and holders of the Common Stock shall receive nothing. After the liquidation preference has been paid or set apart for holders of the Preferred Stock, the remaining assets shall be paid to holders of the Common Stock.

The Preferred Stock has a dividend preference. Holders of the Preferred Stock are entitled to receive dividends on a noncumulative basis at the rate of $_____ per share, as and when declared by the board of directors from funds legally available for dividends and distributions. The holders of the Common Stock may not receive dividends or other distributions during any fiscal year of the corporation until dividends on the Preferred Stock in the total amount of $_____ per share during that fiscal year have been declared and paid or set apart for payment. The payment of such dividends is discretionary, and the holders of the Preferred Stock shall not enjoy a right to dividends if such dividends are not declared, even if the corporation has sufficient funds to lawfully pay such dividends.

28. Sample Letter to Secretary of State Accompanying Articles of Incorporation

Note: This letter is a version appropriate for use in Delaware, but can be modified for use in any state.

Michael Spadaccini
123 Elm Street
San Francisco, CA 94107
415-555-1212

September 28, 2004

State of Delaware
Division of Corporations
401 Federal Street, Suite 4
Dover, DE 19901

To whom it may concern:

Enclosed you will find articles of incorporation for Banquo Acquisition Corporation, a corporation that I wish to file in Delaware.

I have enclosed a filing fee of $74.00. Please return any necessary papers in the envelope that I have provided.

Yours truly,

Michael Spadaccini

29. Sample Letter to Registered Agent

Michael Spadaccini
123 Elm Street
San Francisco, CA 94107
415-555-1212

September 28, 2004

Harvard Business Services, Inc.
25 Greystone Manor
Lewes, DE 19958

To whom it may concern:

I have enclosed a copy of articles of incorporation I am filing today. As you can see, I have used you as our registered agents in the state of Delaware.

Please use the following contact information:

Banquo Acquisition Corporation
c/o Michael Spadaccini
801 Minnesota Street, Suite 7
San Francisco, CA 94107
Phone: (415) 282-7901

I have enclosed a check for $50.00 to cover the first year's services.

Yours truly,

Michael Spadaccini

30. Sample Action by Incorporator
Appointing Directors and Approving Bylaws

MINUTES OF ACTION OF INCORPORATOR TAKEN WITHOUT A MEETING BY WRITTEN CONSENT

The following action is taken by the incorporator of OLDE CRAFT, INC., by written consent, without a meeting on the date specified below.

The following resolution approving a form of bylaws for the governance of this corporation is adopted:

RESOLVED, that the bylaws presented to the incorporator be adopted as the bylaws of this corporation, and that a copy of those bylaws shall be inserted in the minute book of this corporation.

The following resolution electing the directors of the corporation is adopted:

RESOLVED, that pursuant to the foregoing bylaws, authorizing *three* directors, the following persons are hereby appointed as directors of this corporation for the ensuing year and until their successor(s) have been elected and qualified.

John Jones
John Smith
John Miller

The undersigned, the incorporator of this corporation, consents to the foregoing action.

Dated: _____

_____
Michael Spadaccini, Incorporator

31. Share Transfer Ledger

Stock Certificate Number	Date of Original Issue	Stockholder Name	Number of Shares	Disposition of Shares (transferred or surrendered stock certificate)

32. Investment Representation Letter

July 31, 2004

To whom it may concern,

I am delivering this letter to Olde Craft, Inc. in connection with my purchase of 100,000 shares of Olde Craft, Inc. for a total sum of $75,000.00. I represent the following:

I am purchasing the shares in my own name and for my own account, for investment and not with an intent to sell or for sale in connection with any distribution of such stock; and no other person has any interest in or right with respect to the shares; nor have I agreed to give any person any such interest or right in the future.

I recognize that the shares have not been registered under the Federal Securities Act of 1933, as amended, or qualified under any state securities law, and that any sale or transfer of the shares is subject to restrictions imposed by federal and state law.

I also recognize that I cannot dispose of the shares absent registration and qualification or an available exemption from registration and qualification. I understand that no federal or state securities commission or other government body has approved of the fairness of the shares offered by the corporation and that the Commissioner has not and will not recommend or endorse the shares.

I have not seen or received any advertisement or general solicitation with respect to the sale of the shares.

I have a preexisting personal or business relationship with the Company or one or more of its officers, directors, or controlling persons and I am aware of its character and general financial and business circumstances.

I acknowledge that during the course of this transaction and before purchasing the shares I have been provided with financial and other written information about the Company. I have been given the opportunity by the Company to obtain any information and ask questions concerning the Company, the shares, and my investment that I felt necessary; and to the extent I availed myself of that opportunity, I have received satisfactory information and answers.

In reaching the decision to invest in the shares, I have carefully evaluated my financial resources and investment position and the risks associated with this investment, and I acknowledge that I am able to bear the economic risks of this investment.

_____

John Miller

33. Appointment of Proxy for Annual or Special Shareholders' Meeting

APPOINTMENT OF PROXY FOR (ANNUAL/SPECIAL) MEETING

SuperCorp, Inc.

SHAREHOLDER: John Miller

NUMBER OF SHARES HELD: 100,000

I, the undersigned, as record holder of the shares of stock of SuperCorp, Inc. described above, revoke any previous proxies and appoint the person whose name appears just below this paragraph in the box to the right (**Note:** on a regular proxy form, this would appear) as my proxy to attend the (annual/special) shareholders' meeting on _____ and any adjournment of that meeting.

THE BOARD STRONGLY RECOMMENDS THAT YOU RETURN THIS PROXY IF YOU DO NOT INTEND TO APPEAR PERSONALLY AT THE (ANNUAL/SPECIAL) SHAREHOLDERS' MEETING.

The person I want to appoint as my proxy is _____

The proxy holder is entitled to cast a total number of votes equal to but not exceeding the number of shares which I would be entitled to cast if I were personally present.

I authorize my proxy holder to vote and otherwise represent me with regard to any business that may come before this meeting in the same manner and with the same effect as if I were personally present.

I may revoke this proxy at any time. This proxy will lapse three months after the date of its execution.

Please sign your name below and, if you are signing for a business entity, please state your title.

Date (*important*): _____

_____
Name

_____
Title

ALL PROXIES MUST BE SIGNED. PLEASE SIGN EXACTLY AS YOUR NAME APPEARS ON YOUR STOCK CER-TIFICATE. JOINT SHAREHOLDERS MUST EACH SIGN THIS PROXY. IF SIGNED BY AN ATTORNEY IN FACT, THE POWER OF ATTORNEY MUST BE ATTACHED.

IF YOU REQUIRE ASSISTANCE WITH THIS PROXY, PLEASE CONTACT THE CORPORATE SECRETARY, _____, AT 415-555-1212.

34. Action by Written Consent of Shareholder(s)

ACTION BY WRITTEN CONSENT OF SHAREHOLDER(S) OF SUPERCORP, INC.

The undersigned shareholder(s) of SuperCorp, Inc., owning of record the number of shares entitled to vote as set forth, hereby consent(s) to the following corporate actions:

1. John Smith is hereby elected to serve on the board of directors and to occupy the vacancy left by the resignation of John Jones. He shall serve until the next annual meeting of shareholders.

2. The corporation hereby elects to be a close corporation.

3. The Articles of Incorporation shall be amended to include language sufficient to make the close corporation election under state law.

Date _____

_____
John Smith

_____
Number of Shares Owned

Date _____

_____
John Miller

_____
Number of Shares Owned

35. Call for Special Meeting of Directors

CALL FOR SPECIAL MEETING OF DIRECTORS

TO: The Secretary of SuperCorp, Inc.

The party whose name appears below, the (director/CEO/president), by this notice hereby calls a special meeting of directors, which shall be held on _____ (date), at _____ (time), at _____ (place), to consider and act on the following proposals and such other business as may properly come before the board.

1. Acceptance of resignation of John Jones as corporate secretary.

2. Appointment of John Miller to position of corporate secretary.

3. Consideration of acquisition of Newcorp, Inc. by Supercorp, Inc.

You are directed to give notice of this special meeting, in the manner prescribed by the corporation's bylaws and by law, to all shareholders entitled to receive notice of the meeting.

Date: _____

_____
Name

_____
Position (i.e., director, CEO, president)

36. Action of Directors by Written Consent to Approve Stock

ACTION OF DIRECTOR(S) BY WRITTEN CONSENT TO APPROVE STOCK OPTION PLAN AND TO ISSUE SHARES OF STOCK

The undersigned, the director(s) of Evolution Water Company, Inc., agree unanimously to the following:

RESOLVED, that the undersigned directors waive notice of a special meeting of directors pursuant to the corporation's bylaws and hereby agree that the following actions and resolutions be taken by this written consent.

RESOLVED, that the "Evolution Water Company Stock Option Plan" presented to the undersigned directors and attached to this written consent as an exhibit is hereby adopted by the corporation.

RESOLVED FURTHER: That the officers of this corporation be, and they hereby are, authorized to sell and issue to the following persons the number of shares of capital stock of this corporation and for the consideration indicated opposite each name:

NAME	NUMBER OF SHARES	$ PER SHARE	TYPE AND AMOUNT OF CONSIDERATION
John Jones	100,000	$0.75	$75,000 in cash

Date _____

_____
Scott Bess, Director

_____
Brian Bess, Director

37. Action of Directors by Written Consent
Approving Purchase of Another Corporation

RESOLUTION OF THE BOARD OF DIRECTORS OF BALL PLAY INTERNATIONAL, INC.

The undersigned, who constitute the entire Board of Directors of Ball Play International, Inc., a Delaware corporation (the "Corporation"), acting pursuant to Article III of the Bylaws of the Corporation, and pursuant to Section 141(f) of the General Corporation Law of the State of Delaware, hereby adopt and approve the recitals and resolutions set forth below, which shall have the same force and effect as if adopted and approved at a duly held meeting.

The purpose of this resolution is to approve the purchase of a majority interest in the Telas Olefinas, a Mexico corporation.

WHEREAS, the Corporation and Telas Olefinas, a Mexico corporation affiliated with the Corporation, desire to engage in a private stock transaction whereby Telas Olefinas issues new and unissued securities of Telas Olefinas totaling 540 shares, which shall immediately following issuance represent 80% of the total outstanding securities of Telas Olefinas, to the Corporation for consideration; further, that the Purchase Price to be paid by the Corporation for the shares shall be the following: the Corporation shall forgive debt for which Telas Olefinas is obliged to the Corporation in the amount of $US 1,041,552.

RESOLVED, that the board of directors hereby approve the transaction on the preceding terms, and the Corporation, through and by the further action of any officer, is authorized to enter the transaction and to execute a Share Purchase and Subscription Agreement memorializing the transaction.

Witness our Signatures to be effective the 31st day of May, 2010.

_____   _____
Bob Emmett   Wolf D.H. Koch

_____
Larry Emmett

38. Action of Directors by Written Consent
Appointing Directors to Fill Vacant Board Seats

RESOLUTION OF THE BOARD OF DIRECTORS OF BALL PLAY INTERNATIONAL, INC.

The undersigned, who constitute the entire Board of Directors of Ball Play International, Inc., a Delaware corporation (the "Corporation"), acting pursuant to Article III of the Bylaws of the Corporation, and pursuant to Section 141 (f) of the General Corporation Law of the State of Delaware, hereby adopt and approve the recitals and resolutions set forth below, which shall have the same force and effect as if adopted and approved at a duly held meeting.

WHEREAS, available seats on the board of directors are five and only one seat is occupied, leaving four vacancies;

RESOLVED, that the sitting board of directors, consisting of one director, hereby avails himself of the power of appointment of vacant seats as outlined in the Bylaws and the General Corporation Law of the State of Delaware and appoints the following persons to serve as directors of the Corporation:

Dean Martin

Frank Sinatra

Harry Connick

Witness our Signatures to be effective the 18th day of December, 2010.

_____

Bill DeLander

39. Written Consent of Directors Approving a Certificate of Amendment of Articles of Incorporation Changing Corporation's Name

ACTION OF DIRECTOR(S) BY WRITTEN CONSENT TO APPROVE AN AMENDMENT TO ARTICLES OF INCORPORATION CHANGING CORPORATE NAME

The undersigned, the director(s) of Plasticworld.com, Inc., a California corporation, agree unanimously to the following:

RESOLVED, that the undersigned directors waive notice of a special meeting of directors pursuant to the corporation's bylaws and hereby agree that the following actions and resolutions be taken by this written consent.

RESOLVED, that the Certificate of Amendment of Articles of Incorporation presented to the undersigned directors, specifically changing the name of the corporation to PlasticUniverse, Inc., be approved by the directors.

Date _____

_____
Scott Bess, Director

_____
Brian Bess, Director

40. Certificate of Amendment of Articles of Incorporation Changing Corporation's Name

CERTIFICATE OF AMENDMENT OF
ARTICLES OF INCORPORATION

The undersigned certify that:

1. They are the president and secretary, respectively, of PlasticWorld.com, Inc., corporation number 10134944.

2. Article I of the Articles of Incorporation of this corporation is hereby amended to read as follows:

The name of this Corporation is hereby changed to PlasticUnverse, Inc.

3. The foregoing Amendment of Articles of Incorporation has been duly approved by the board of directors.

4. The foregoing Amendment of Articles of Incorporation has been duly approved by the required vote of shareholders in accordance with state law. The total number of outstanding shares of the corporation is 10,000,000. The number of shares voting in favor of the amendment equaled or exceeded the vote required. The percentage vote required was more than 50%.

We further declare, under penalty of perjury under the laws of the State of California, that the matters set forth in this certificate are true and correct of our own knowledge.

Dated _____

_____
Scott Bess, President

_____
Brian Bess, Secretary

41. Certificate of Amendment of Articles of Incorporation Electing Close Corporation Status

CERTIFICATE OF AMENDMENT OF
ARTICLES OF INCORPORATION

The undersigned certify that:

1. They are the president and secretary, respectively, of Evolution Water Company, Inc., corporation number 1059964.

2. Article V of the Articles of Incorporation of this corporation is hereby added, and the Articles of Incorporation are hereby amended to read as follows:

All of this Corporation's issued shares of all classes shall be held of record by not more than 35 persons, and this Corporation is a close corporation.

3. The foregoing Amendment of Articles of Incorporation has been duly approved by the board of directors.

4. The foregoing Amendment of Articles of Incorporation has been duly approved by the required vote of shareholders. The total number of outstanding shares of the corporation is 98,333. The vote with respect to this amendment was unanimous.

We further declare, under penalty of perjury under the laws of the State of California, that the matters set forth in this certificate are true and correct of our own knowledge.

Dated _____

_____
Donald Leland, President

_____
Alexandra Leland, Secretary

42. Sample Delaware Certificate of Dissolution

CERTIFICATE OF DISSOLUTION

The corporation organized and existing under the General Corporation Law of the State of Delaware DOES HEREBY CERTIFY AS FOLLOWS: The dissolution of said DEF Corporation has been duly authorized by all the stockholders of the Corporation entitled to vote on a dissolution in accordance with subsection (c) of Section 275 of the General Corporation Law of the State of Delaware. The date the dissolution was authorized is December 11, 2010. The following is a list of the names and addresses of the directors of the said corporation:

[Enter names and addresses of directors here]

The following is a list of the names and addresses of the officers of the said corporation:

[Enter names and addresses of officers here]

By: _____
    Signature of Authorized Officer

Name: _____
    Print or Type

Title: _____

43. Written Consent of Shareholders Approving a Conversion from a California Corporation to a Delaware Limited Liability Company

ACTION OF SHAREHOLDERS BY WRITTEN CONSENT TO APPROVE A CONVERSION OF CORPORATION TO LIMITED LIABILITY COMPANY

The undersigned, being all the shareholders of PLASTICWORLD, Inc., agree unanimously to the following:

RESOLVED, that the shareholders, following consultation, have agreed that it is in the best interests of PLASTICWORLD, Inc. to convert the legal status of the entity from a California Corporation to a Limited Liability Company chartered in Delaware, to be entitled PLASTICWORLD LLC.

To facilitate the tax reporting of the LLC, it is agreed that the conversion shall be filed so that it takes place on January 1, 2011. The officers of PLASTICWORLD, Inc. are authorized and directed to file the appropriate Certificate of Conversion with the Secretary of State of California and to file a Certificate of Conversion from a Delaware or Non-Delaware Corporation to a Delaware Limited Liability Company with the State of Delaware and to file a Certificate of Formation with the State of Delaware simultaneously with the Certificate of Conversion to accomplish the conversion.

Date: _____

_____
Scott Bess

_____
Brian Bess

44. Sample Certificate/Articles of Conversion from a California Corporation to a Delaware Limited Liability Company

Notes: The following document is a simple certificate of conversion document that converts a California corporation to a Delaware LLC. This document illustrates fairly clearly how conversion is accomplished. The states offer slightly different procedures for conversion, so we recommend that you use form specific to your state if attempting a conversion.

STATE OF DELAWARE CERTIFICATE OF CONVERSION FROM A CORPORATION TO A LIMITED LIABILITY COMPANY PURSUANT TO SECTION 18-214 OF THE LIMITED LIABILITY ACT

1. The jurisdiction where the Corporation first formed is California.
2. The jurisdiction immediately prior to filing this Certificate is California.
3. The date the corporation first formed is September 1, 2001.
4. The name of the Corporation immediately prior to filing this Certificate is Plasticworld, Inc.
5. The name of the Limited Liability Company as set forth in the Certificate of Formation is Plasticworld, LLC.
6. IN WITNESS WHEREOF, the undersigned being duly authorized to sign on behalf of the converting Limited

   Liability Company have executed this Certificate on the 12th day of November, 2010

By: _____ Scott Bess President

46. Notice to Remaining Members by a Member Desiring to Withdraw from a Corporation

Joan Donner
123 Elm Street
San Francisco, CA 94107
415-555-1212

September 28, 2010

Dear Brian, This is my formal notice that I will be withdrawing from my ownership in Tonosilver, Inc.

The shareholder's agreement states that:

Section 5.1. Voluntary Termination; Resignation. In the event any Shareholder voluntarily terminates his or her employment with the Corporation for any reason whatsoever, other than as provided in Section 4.2, the terminating Shareholder shall sell to the Corporation and the Corporation shall purchase from the Shareholder all of the terminating Shareholder's shares in the Corporation now owned or hereafter acquired and which are owned by the terminating Shareholder as of the date of termination for the purchase price determined in the manner provide in Article VI and upon the terms provided in Article VII.

We must next discuss the valuation of my interest. I suggest that we speak informally first. If we can't come to some resolution, we can then trigger the appraisal rights under the operating agreement. I'll await your response.

Yours,

Joan Donner

Form **2553**
(Rev. December 2007)

Department of the Treasury
Internal Revenue Service

Election by a Small Business Corporation
(Under section 1362 of the Internal Revenue Code)
► See Parts II and III on page 3 and the separate instructions.
► The corporation can fax this form to the IRS (see separate instructions).

OMB No. 1545-0146

Note.   This election to be an S corporation can be accepted only if all the tests are met under   Who May Elect   on page 1 of the instructions; all shareholders have signed the consent statement; an officer has signed below; and the exact name and address of the corporation and other required form information are provided.

Part I	Election Information

Type
or Print

	A Employer identification number
Name (see instructions)	
Number, street, and room or suite no. (If a P.O. box, see instructions.)	B Date incorporated
City or town, state, and ZIP code	C State of incorporation

D   Check the applicable box(es) if the corporation, after applying for the EIN shown in   A above, changed its   ☐ name or   ☐ address

E   Election is to be effective for tax year beginning (month, day, year) (see instructions) . . . . . ►___/___/___

Caution. A corporation (entity) making the election for its first tax year in existence will usually enter the beginning date of a short tax year that begins on a date other than January 1.

F   Selected tax year:

(1) ☐ Calendar year

(2) ☐ Fiscal year ending (month and day)   ► _____

(3) ☐ 52-53-week year ending with reference to the month of December

(4) ☐ 52-53-week year ending with reference to the month of   ► _____

If box (2) or (4) is checked, complete Part II

G   If more than 100 shareholders are listed for item J (see page 2), check this box if treating members of a family as one shareholder results in no more than 100 shareholders (see test 2 under   Who May Elect   in the instructions) ► ☐

H   Name and title of officer or legal representative who the IRS may call for more information

I   Telephone number of officer or legal representative
(   )

If this S corporation election is being filed with Form 1120S, I declare that I had reasonable cause for not filing Form 2553 timely, and if this election is made by an entity eligible to elect to be treated as a corporation, I declare that I also had reasonable cause for not filing an entity classification election timely. See below for my explanation of the reasons the election or elections were not made on time (see instructions).

Sign
Here
► Under penalties of perjury, I declare that I have examined this election, including accompanying schedules and statements, and to the best of my knowledge and belief, it is true, correct, and complete.

Signature of officer	Title	Date

For Paperwork Reduction Act Notice, see separate instructions.   Cat. No. 18629R   Form **2553** (Rev. 12-2007)

Form 2553 (Rev. 12-2007)   Page **2**

Part I	Election Information	(continued)				

J Name and address of each shareholder or former shareholder required to consent to the election. (See the instructions for column K.)	K Shareholders' Consent Statement. Under penalties of perjury, we declare that we consent to the election of the above-named corporation to be an S corporation under section 1362(a) and that we have examined this consent statement, including accompanying schedules and statements, and to the best of our knowledge and belief, it is true, correct, and complete. We understand our consent is binding and may not be withdrawn after the corporation has made a valid election. (Sign and date below.)		L Stock owned or percentage of ownership (see instructions)		M Social security number or employer identification number (see instructions)	N Shareholder's tax year ends (month and day)
	Signature	Date	Number of shares or percentage of ownership	Date(s) acquired		

Form **2553** (Rev. 12-2007)

Form 2553 (Rev. 12-2007)
Page **3**

Part II   Selection of Fiscal Tax Year   (see instructions)

Note. All corporations using this part must complete item O and item P, Q, or R.

O   Check the applicable box to indicate whether the corporation is:

    1. ☐ A new corporation adopting the tax year entered in item F, Part I.

    2. ☐ An existing corporation retaining the tax year entered in item F, Part I.

    3. ☐ An existing corporation changing to the tax year entered in item F, Part I.

P   Complete item P if the corporation is using the automatic approval provisions of Rev. Proc. 2006-46, 2006-45 I.R.B. 859, to request   (1) a natural business year (as defined in section 5.07 of Rev. Proc. 2006-46) or   (2) a year that satisfies the ownership tax year test (as defined in section 5.08 of Rev. Proc. 2006-46). Check the applicable box below to indicate the representation the corporation is making.

    1. Natural Business Year ▶ ☐ I represent that the corporation is adopting, retaining, or changing to a tax year that qualifies as its natural business year (as defined in section 5.07 of Rev. Proc. 2006-46) and has attached a statement showing separately for each month the gross receipts for the most recent 47 months (see instructions). I also represent that the corporation is not precluded by section 4.02 of Rev. Proc. 2006-46 from obtaining automatic approval of such adoption, retention, or change in tax year.

    2. Ownership Tax Year ▶ ☐ I represent that shareholders (as described in section 5.08 of Rev. Proc. 2006-46) holding more than half of the shares of the stock (as of the first day of the tax year to which the request relates) of the corporation have the same tax year or are concurrently changing to the tax year that the corporation adopts, retains, or changes to per item F, Part I, and that such tax year satisfies the requirement of section 4.01(3) of Rev. Proc. 2006-46. I also represent that the corporation is not precluded by section 4.02 of Rev. Proc. 2006-46 from obtaining automatic approval of such adoption, retention, or change in tax year.

Note. If you do not use item P and the corporation wants a fiscal tax year, complete either item Q or R below. Item Q is used to request a fiscal tax year based on a business purpose and to make a back-up section 444 election. Item R is used to make a regular section 444 election.

Q   Business Purpose—To request a fiscal tax year based on a business purpose, check box Q1. See instructions for details including payment of a user fee. You may also check box Q2 and/or box Q3.

    1. Check here ▶ ☐ if the fiscal year entered in item F, Part I, is requested under the prior approval provisions of Rev. Proc. 2002-39, 2002-22 I.R.B. 1046. Attach to Form 2553 a statement describing the relevant facts and circumstances and, if applicable, the gross receipts from sales and services necessary to establish a business purpose. See the instructions for details regarding the gross receipts from sales and services. If the IRS proposes to disapprove the requested fiscal year, do you want a conference with the IRS National Office?

    ☐ Yes   ☐ No

    2. Check here ▶ ☐ to show that the corporation intends to make a back-up section 444 election in the event the corporation's business purpose request is not approved by the IRS. (See instructions for more information.)

    3. Check here ▶ ☐ to show that the corporation agrees to adopt or change to a tax year ending December 31 if necessary for the IRS to accept this election for S corporation status in the event (1) the corporation's business purpose request is not approved and the corporation makes a back-up section 444 election, but is ultimately not qualified to make a section 444 election, or (2) the corporation's business purpose request is not approved and the corporation did not make a back-up section 444 election.

R   Section 444 Election—To make a section 444 election, check box R1. You may also check box R2.

    1. Check here ▶ ☐ to show that the corporation will make, if qualified, a section 444 election to have the fiscal tax year shown in item F, Part I. To make the election, you must complete Form 8716, Election To Have a Tax Year Other Than a Required Tax Year, and either attach it to Form 2553 or file it separately.

    2. Check here ▶ ☐ to show that the corporation agrees to adopt or change to a tax year ending December 31 if necessary for the IRS to accept this election for S corporation status in the event the corporation is ultimately not qualified to make a section 444 election.

Part III   Qualified Subchapter S Trust (QSST) Election Under Section 1361(d)(2)*

Income beneficiary's name and address	Social security number
Trust's name and address	Employer identification number

Date on which stock of the corporation was transferred to the trust (month, day, year) . . . . ▶   /   /

In order for the trust named above to be a QSST and thus a qualifying shareholder of the S corporation for which this Form 2553 is filed, I hereby make the election under section 1361(d)(2). Under penalties of perjury, I certify that the trust meets the definitional requirements of section 1361(d)(3) and that all other information provided in Part III is true, correct, and complete.

_____   _____

Signature of income beneficiary or signature and title of legal representative or other qualified person making the election   Date

*Use Part III to make the QSST election only if stock of the corporation has been transferred to the trust on or before the date on which the corporation makes its election to be an S corporation. The QSST election must be made and filed separately if stock of the corporation is transferred to the trust after the date on which the corporation makes the S election.

✪ Printed on recycled paper   Form **2553** (Rev. 12-2007)

CHAPTER 5

Partner Up!

FORMING A PARTNERSHIP REQUIRES COMmunication—not only with your state, but with your business partner, and family if applicable. The true definition of a *business partnership* is essentially two or more people in business for profit, including husbands and wives (if they are in business together and they have not formed any other type of entity). Included in this chapter are sample forms you'll need to file legally as business partners in addition to forms that will help you legally maintain your business relationship and determine what it will take to operate as successful pair.

To establish a partnership in the eyes of the IRS, it's required that the partners file *Form SS-4 Application for Employer Identification Number (EIN)*. The EIN is needed to apply for a business license and for tax reporting and banking functions.

The *Delaware Certificate of Limited Partnership* is the charter document used by a limited partnership organized in the State of Delaware; this form is included as a sample, but each state uses its own form. The *Sample General Partnership Agreement* is a simple, standard agreement between the owners of a partnership.

A *Partnership Ledger* is a written table listing the owners of a partnership and should be kept with the partnership agreement. The ledger must also indicate the percentage held by each partner. As new partners join the partnership through the sale of additional partnership interest (and a new partner's corresponding capital contribution), the new ownership is recorded on the ledger. The partnership ledger should also show transfers of partners' ownership interests, as when a partner passes away and transfers his or her interest through his or her will. Of course, your partnership ledger may never change—partners may simply not come and go from your partnership. Your ledger may reflect the initial partners and their initial contributions and percentage interests.

In the real world, most small company votes are taken by written consent rather than by notice and meeting and an in-person vote. Use the *Action by Written Consent of Partners* when you wish to take a partnership action in writing, rather than by a noticed meeting. Written consents are important company records and should be maintained in the records book. Compare this consent form to the minutes in the form previous to this one. You'll note that it is often far simpler to take votes by written consent.

48. Application for Employer Identification Number (EIN)

Form **SS-4** (Rev. July 2007) Department of the Treasury Internal Revenue Service	**Application for Employer Identification Number** (For use by employers, corporations, partnerships, trusts, estates, churches, government agencies, Indian tribal entities, certain individuals, and others.) ▶ See separate instructions for each line. ▶ Keep a copy for your records.	OMB No. 1545-0003 EIN	

Type or print clearly.	**1** Legal name of entity (or individual) for whom the EIN is being requested

2 Trade name of business (if different from name on line 1)	**3** Executor, administrator, trustee, "care of" name

4a Mailing address (room, apt., suite no. and street, or P.O. box)	**5a** Street address (if different) (Do not enter a P.O. box.)
4b City, state, and ZIP code (if foreign, see instructions)	**5b** City, state, and ZIP code (if foreign, see instructions)

6 County and state where principal business is located

7a Name of principal officer, general partner, grantor, owner, or trustor	**7b** SSN, ITIN, or EIN

8a Is this application for a limited liability company (LLC) (or a foreign equivalent)? . . . . ☐ Yes ☐ No	**8b** If 8a is "Yes," enter the number of LLC members . . . . ▶

8c If 8a is "Yes," was the LLC organized in the United States? . . . . ☐ Yes ☐ No

9a Type of entity (check only one box). Caution. If 8a is "Yes," see the instructions for the correct box to check.

☐ Sole proprietor (SSN) _____	☐ Estate (SSN of decedent) _____
☐ Partnership	☐ Plan administrator (TIN) _____
☐ Corporation (enter form number to be filed) ▶_____	☐ Trust (TIN of grantor) _____
☐ Personal service corporation	☐ National Guard ☐ State/local government
☐ Church or church-controlled organization	☐ Farmers' cooperative ☐ Federal government/military
☐ Other nonprofit organization (specify) ▶_____	☐ REMIC ☐ Indian tribal governments/enterprises
☐ Other (specify) ▶	Group Exemption Number (GEN) if any ▶

9b If a corporation, name the state or foreign country (if applicable) where incorporated	State	Foreign country

10 Reason for applying (check only one box)

☐ Started new business (specify type) ▶ _____	☐ Banking purpose (specify purpose) ▶_____
_____	☐ Changed type of organization (specify new type) ▶_____
	☐ Purchased going business
☐ Hired employees (Check the box and see line 13.)	☐ Created a trust (specify type) ▶_____
☐ Compliance with IRS withholding regulations	☐ Created a pension plan (specify type) ▶_____
☐ Other (specify) ▶	

11 Date business started or acquired (month, day, year). See instructions.	**12** Closing month of accounting year
	14 Do you expect your employment tax liability to be $1,000 or less in a full calendar year? ☐ Yes ☐ No (If you expect to pay $4,000 or less in total wages in a full calendar year, you can mark "Yes.")
13 Highest number of employees expected in the next 12 months (enter -0- if none). Agricultural · Household · Other	

15 First date wages or annuities were paid (month, day, year). Note. If applicant is a withholding agent, enter date income will first be paid to nonresident alien (month, day, year) . . . . ▶

16 Check one box that best describes the principal activity of your business.

☐ Construction ☐ Rental & leasing ☐ Transportation & warehousing	☐ Health care & social assistance ☐ Wholesale-agent/broker
☐ Real estate ☐ Manufacturing ☐ Finance & insurance	☐ Accommodation & food service ☐ Wholesale-other ☐ Retail
	☐ Other (specify)

17 Indicate principal line of merchandise sold, specific construction work done, products produced, or services provided.

18 Has the applicant entity shown on line 1 ever applied for and received an EIN? ☐ Yes ☐ No
If "Yes," write previous EIN here ▶

Third Party Designee	Complete this section **only** if you want to authorize the named individual to receive the entity's EIN and answer questions about the completion of this form.	
	Designee's name	Designee's telephone number (include area code) ( )
	Address and ZIP code	Designee's fax number (include area code) ( )

Under penalties of perjury, I declare that I have examined this application, and to the best of my knowledge and belief, it is true, correct, and complete.	Applicant's telephone number (include area code) ( )
Name and title (type or print clearly) ▶	Applicant's fax number (include area code) ( )
Signature ▶ Date ▶	

For Privacy Act and Paperwork Reduction Act Notice, see separate instructions. Cat. No. 16055N Form **SS-4** (Rev. 7-2007)

Form SS-4 (Rev. 7-2007)   Page 2

Do I Need an EIN?

File Form SS-4 if the applicant entity does not already have an EIN but is required to show an EIN on any return, statement, or other document. [1] See also the separate instructions for each line on Form SS-4.

IF the applicant...	AND...	THEN...
Started a new business	Does not currently have (nor expect to have) employees	Complete lines 1, 2, 4a–8a, 8b–c (if applicable), 9a, 9b (if applicable), and 10–14 and 16–18.
Hired (or will hire) employees, including household employees	Does not already have an EIN	Complete lines 1, 2, 4a–6, 7a–b (if applicable), 8a, 8b–c (if applicable), 9a, 9b (if applicable), 10–18.
Opened a bank account	Needs an EIN for banking purposes only	Complete lines 1–5b, 7a–b (if applicable), 8a, 8b–c (if applicable), 9a, 9b (if applicable), 10, and 18.
Changed type of organization	Either the legal character of the organization or its ownership changed (for example, you incorporate a sole proprietorship or form a partnership) [2]	Complete lines 1–18 (as applicable).
Purchased a going business [3]	Does not already have an EIN	Complete lines 1–18 (as applicable).
Created a trust	The trust is other than a grantor trust or an IRA trust[4]	Complete lines 1–18 (as applicable).
Created a pension plan as a plan administrator [5]	Needs an EIN for reporting purposes	Complete lines 1, 3, 4a–5b, 9a, 10, and 18.
Is a foreign person needing an EIN to comply with IRS withholding regulations	Needs an EIN to complete a Form W-8 (other than Form W-8ECI), avoid withholding on portfolio assets, or claim tax treaty benefits [6]	Complete lines 1–5b, 7a–b (SSN or ITIN optional), 8a, 8b–c (if applicable), 9a, 9b (if applicable), 10, and 18.
Is administering an estate	Needs an EIN to report estate income on Form 1041	Complete lines 1–6, 9a, 10–12, 13–17 (if applicable), and 18.
Is a withholding agent for taxes on non-wage income paid to an alien (i.e., individual, corporation, or partnership, etc.)	Is an agent, broker, fiduciary, manager, tenant, or spouse who is required to file Form 1042, Annual Withholding Tax Return for U.S. Source Income of Foreign Persons	Complete lines 1, 2, 3 (if applicable), 4a–5b, 7a–b (if applicable), 8a, 8b–c (if applicable), 9a, 9b (if applicable), 10 and 18.
Is a state or local agency	Serves as a tax reporting agent for public assistance recipients under Rev. Proc. 80-4, 1980-1 C.B. 581 [7]	Complete lines 1, 2, 4a–5b, 9a, 10 and 18.
Is a single-member LLC	Needs an EIN to file Form 8832, Classification Election, for filing employment tax returns, or for state reporting purposes [8]	Complete lines 1–18 (as applicable).
Is an S corporation	Needs an EIN to file Form 2553, Election by a Small Business Corporation [9]	Complete lines 1–18 (as applicable).

[1] For example, a sole proprietorship or self-employed farmer who establishes a qualified retirement plan, or is required to file excise, employment, alcohol, tobacco, or firearms returns, must have an EIN. A partnership, corporation, REMIC (real estate mortgage investment conduit), nonprofit organization (church, club, etc.), or farmers' cooperative must use an EIN for any tax-related purpose even if the entity does not have employees.

[2] However, do not apply for a new EIN if the existing entity only (a) changed its business name, (b) elected on Form 8832 to change the way it is taxed (or is covered by the default rules), or (c) terminated its partnership status because at least 50% of the total interests in partnership capital and profits were sold or exchanged within a 12-month period. The EIN of the terminated partnership should continue to be used. See Regulations section 301.6109-1(d)(2)(iii).

[3] Do not use the EIN of the prior business unless you became the "owner" of a corporation by acquiring its stock.

[4] However, grantor trusts that do not file using Optional Method 1 and IRA trusts that are required to file Form 990-T, Exempt Organization Business Income Tax Return, must have an EIN. For more information on grantor trusts, see the Instructions for Form 1041.

[5] A plan administrator is the person or group of persons specified as the administrator by the instrument under which the plan is operated.

[6] Entities applying to be a Qualified Intermediary (QI) need a QI-EIN even if they already have an EIN. See Rev. Proc. 2000-12.

[7] See also Household employer on page 4 of the instructions. Note. State or local agencies may need an EIN for other reasons, for example, hired employees.

[8] Most LLCs do not need to file Form 8832. See Limited liability company (LLC) on page 4 of the instructions for details on completing Form SS-4 for an LLC.

[9] An existing corporation that is electing or revoking S corporation status should use its previously-assigned EIN.

49. Delaware Certificate of Limited Partnership

STATE OF DELAWARE CERTIFICATE OF LIMITED PARTNERSHIP

•**The Undersigned,** desiring to form a limited partnership pursuant to the Delaware Revised Uniform Limited Partnership Act, 6 Delaware Code, Chapter 17, do hereby certify as follows:

•**First:** The name of the limited partnership is_____

_____

_____.

•**Second:** The address of its registered office in the State of Delaware is

_____ in the city of_____.

The name of the registered agent at such address is_____

_____

_____.

•**Third:** The name and mailing address of each general partner is as follows:

•**In Witness Whereof,** the undersigned has executed this Certificate of Limited Partnership of

____ _____as of_____.

By:

_____

General Partner

Name:_____

(Type or Print Name)

50. Sample General Partnership Agreement

GENERAL PARTNERSHIP AGREEMENT
Between
ANDREW LELAND and
DONALD LELAND

This general partnership agreement is made and entered into as of January 1, 2004, by and among Andrew Leland and Donald Leland (all of whom are hereinafter collectively sometimes referred to as "partners").

The parties hereto desire to form a general partnership (hereinafter referred to as the "Partnership"), under the laws of the State of _____ for the term and upon the conditions set forth in this agreement, and the Partners agree as follows:

1.1. FORMATION OF PARTNERSHIP. The parties hereby form a general partnership, and the name of the partnership shall be _____. This agreement shall supersede any previous partnership agreements between the parties to this agreement.

1.2. DEFINITIONS.

"Act" means the laws governing partnerships in the State of organization .

"Bankruptcy" shall be deemed to have occurred with respect to any Partner 60 days after the happening of any of the following: (1) the filing of an application by a Partner for, or a consent to, the appointment of a trustee of the Partner's assets; (2) the filing by a Partner of a voluntary petition in bankruptcy of the filing of a pleading in any court of record admitting in writing the Partner's inability to pay the Partner's debts as they become due; (3) the making by a Partner of a general assignment for the benefit of creditors; (4) the filing by a Partner of an answer admitting the material allegations of, or consenting to or defaulting in answering a bankruptcy petition filed against the Partner in any bankruptcy proceeding; or (5) the entry of an order, judgment, or decree by any court of competent jurisdiction adjudicating a Partner a bankrupt or appointing a trustee of the Partner's assets, and that order, judgment, or decree continuing unstayed and in effect for a period of 60 days.

"Capital Account" means with respect to each Partner, the account established on the books and records of the Partnership for each Partner under Section 2.1. Each Partner's Capital Account shall initially equal the cash and the agreed value of property (net of liabilities assumed or to which the property is subject) contributed by the Partner to the Partnership, and during the term of the Partnership shall be (1) increased by the amount of (a) Taxable Income allocated to the Partner, other than Taxable Income attributable to the difference between the agreed value and adjusted basis of the property at contribution, and (b) any money and the agreed value of property (net of any liabilities assumed or to which the property is subject) subsequently contributed to the Partnership, and (2) decreased by the amount of (a) Tax Losses allocated to the Partner, except (i) Tax Losses attributable to depreciation of contributed property, which shall decrease Capital Accounts only to the extent of depreciation computed as if the property were purchased by the Partnership at its agreed value, and (ii) Tax Losses attributable to the difference between the agreed value and adjusted basis of property of property at contribution (which shall not decrease the contributing Partner's Capital Account), and (b) all cash and the agreed value of property (net of liabilities assumed or to which the property is subject) distributed to such Partner, and shall otherwise be kept in accordance with applicable Treasury Regulations.

"Contract Price" shall be equal to the fair market value of the selling Partner's Interest as of the date of the event triggering the sale. The fair market value shall be determined within 60 days by a valuation of the selling Partner's Interest as if the net assets of the Partnership were sold for cash and the cash distributed in accordance with Section 9.1.

"Incapacity" or "Incapacitated" means the incompetence, insanity, interdiction, death, disability, or incapacity, as the case may be, of any Partner.

"Interest" means the entire ownership interest of a Partner in the Partnership.

"Managing Partner" means Donald Leland but in the event that he is at any time no longer a Partner, or is replaced by vote of the Partners, the term shall mean the party or parties then acting in that capacity.

"Net Income" with respect to any fiscal period means all cash revenues of the Partnership during that period (including interest or other earning on the funds of the Partnership), less the sum of the following to the extent made from those cash revenues:

(a) All principal and interest payments on any indebtedness of the Partnership.

(b) All cash expenses incurred incident to the operations of the Partnership's business.

(c) Funds set aside as reserves for contingencies, working capital, debt service, taxes, insurance, or other costs or expenses incident to the conduct of the Partnership's business, which the Partners deem reasonably necessary or appropriate.

"Partnership Percentage" means the following percentages:

Name	Percentage
Donald Leland	50%
Andrew Leland	50%

Distributions or allocations made in proportion to or in accordance with the Partnership Percentages of the Partners shall be based upon relative Partnership Percentages as of the record date for distributions and in accordance with Section 706(c) and (d) of the Internal Revenue Code (IRC) for allocations.

"Operating Partner" means Andrew Leland but in the event that he is at any time no longer a Partner, or is replaced by vote of the Partners, the term shall mean the party or parties then acting in that capacity.

"Taxable Income" and "Tax Losses" respectively, shall mean the net income or net losses of the Partnership as determined for federal income tax purposes, and all items required to be separately stated by Section 702 of the IRC and the Regulations thereunder.

1.3. BUSINESS OF THE PARTNERSHIP. The business purpose for which this Partnership is organized is _____. Any modification of the business purpose outlined in this section shall not void this agreement.

1.4. NAMES AND ADDRESSES OF PARTNERS. The names and addresses of the Partners are:

Donald Leland, _____; and

Andrew Leland, _____.

1.5. TERM. The term of the Partnership shall begin on _____ and shall continue until the earlier of December 31, 2050, or until dissolved by an act or event specified in the Agreement or by the law as one effecting dissolution.

1.6. BUSINESS OFFICES. The principal place of business of the Partnership shall be _____. The Partners may, from time to time, change the principal place of business of the Partnership. The Partners may in their discretion establish additional places of business of the Partnership.

2.1 INITIAL CAPITAL CONTRIBUTIONS. The Partner's initial Capital Contributions are deemed made as of this Agreement. The Partners shall initially make Capital Contributions as follows:

(a) Donald Leland shall contribute the following property: _____; and

(b) Andrew Leland shall contribute the following property: _____.

2.2. PARTNER'S ASSESSMENTS. In addition to the Capital Contributions required by Section 2.1, each Partner shall be obligated to make additional Capital Contributions, as needed to maintain the profitability of the Partnership. All additional Capital Contributions shall be made in accordance with the Partnership Percentages and within 30 days after the Partners have received notice thereof from the Managing Partner. The Managing Partner shall call these assessments based upon his estimate of all costs, expenses, or charges with respect to operation of the Partnership, less the expected revenues from such operations. Any increases in the Capital Contributions of the Partners pursuant to this Section shall be noted on Annex A attached hereto and incorporated by reference.

2.3. INTEREST ON CAPITAL CONTRIBUTIONS. No Partner shall be paid interest on any Capital Contribution.

2.4. WITHDRAWAL AND RETURN OF CAPITAL CONTRIBUTIONS. No Partner shall be entitled to withdraw any part of his Capital Contribution, or to receive any distributions from the Partnership except as provided by this Agreement.

2.5. LOANS BY PARTNER. The Partners may (but shall not be obligated to) loan or advance to the Partnership such funds as are necessary for the Partnership's operations, provided, however, that interest on those loans or advances shall not be in excess of five percent.

3.1. DISTRIBUTIONS. Net Income shall be distributed among the Partners in proportion to their Partnership Percentages.

3.2. ALLOCATION OF PROFITS AND LOSSES FOR TAX PURPOSES. The Taxable Income to be allocated among the Partners shall be allocated among them in accordance with the previous section concerning distributions. Tax Losses to allocated among the Partners shall be allocated among them in accordance with their respective Partnership Percentages.

4.1. BOOKS OF ACCOUNT, RECORDS, AND REPORTS. Proper and complete records and books of account shall be kept by the Operating Partner in which shall be entered fully and accurately all transactions and other matters relative to the Partnership's business as are usually entered into records and books of account maintained by persons engaged in businesses of a like character, including a Capital Account for each Partner. The Partnership books and records shall be prepared in accordance with generally accepted accounting practices, consistently applied, and shall be kept on a cash basis except in circumstances in which the Managing Partner determines that another bases of accounting will be in the best interests of the Partnership. The books and records shall at all times be maintained at the principal place of business of the Partnership and shall be open to the inspection and examination of the Partners or their duly authorized representatives during reasonable business hours.

4.2. REPORTS TO PARTNERS. As soon as practicable in the particular case, the Operating Partner shall deliver to every other Partner:

(a) Such information concerning the Partnership after the end of each fiscal year as shall be necessary for the preparation by such a Partner of his income or other tax returns.

(b) An unaudited statement prepared by the Operating Partner setting forth, as of the end of and for each fiscal year, a profit and loss statement and a balance sheet of the Partnership and a statement showing the amounts allocated to or against each Interest during that year.

4.3. FISCAL YEAR. The fiscal year of the Partnership shall end on the thirty-first day of December in each year.

4.4. PARTNERSHIP FUNDS. The funds of the Partnership shall be deposited in such bank account or accounts, or invested in such interest-bearing or non interest-bearing investments, as shall be designated by the Managing Partner. All withdrawals from any such bank accounts shall be made by the duly authorized agent or agents of any Partner. Partnership funds shall be held in the name of the Partnership and shall not be commingled with those of any other person.

5.1. INCAPACITATION. Within 90 days after a Partner becomes Incapacitated, his executor, administrator, committee, or analogous fiduciary (the "Representative") shall sell that Interest to the remaining Partners. The Representative shall notify the other Partners in writing within the 90 day period and the other Partners must purchase the Incapacitated Partner's Interest. The purchase price of an Interest sold pursuant to this Section shall be the Contract Price, and payment for the Interest shall be made in the manner set forth in Section 5.5.

5.2. BANKRUPTCY. At the Bankruptcy of any Partner, that Partner (an "Inactive Partner") or his representative shall cease to have any voice in the conduct of the affairs of the partnership and all acts, consents, and decisions with respect to the Partnership shall thereafter be made by the other Partners. The Inactive Partner shall, nonetheless, remain liable for his share of any losses of the Partnership or contributions to the Partnership as provided herein, and shall be entitled to receive his share of Taxable Income, Tax Losses, and Net Income. For six months from and after the date of the Bankruptcy of any Partner, the other Partners shall have the irrevocable option to purchase the Inactive Partner's Interest in the Partnership. That purchase shall be made in proportion to the respective Partnership Percentages of the other Partners at the time or in such other proportion as they may mutually agree. Should the other Partners exercise their option to purchase the Inactive Partner's Interest, they shall notify the Inactive Partner or his representative of their intention to do so within this six-month period. The purchase price of any Interest purchased pursuant to this Section shall be the Contract Price, and shall be payable at the time and in the manner specified in Section 5.5. Should the other Partners not exercise the option to purchase the Inactive Partner's Interest, the Inactive Partner shall remain such in accordance with the provisions set forth above.

5.3. SALE OF PARTNERSHIP INTEREST. If a Partner desires to offer for sale his Interest in the Partnership, such Partner (the "Selling Partner") shall give written notice to the other Partners (the "Buying Partner[s]"). Within 30 days after receipt of the notice, the Buying Partner(s) shall notify the Selling Partner of their intent to purchase the Interest of the Selling Partner. The purchase price of an Interest sold pursuant to this Section shall be the Contract Price, and payment for the Interest shall be made in the manner set forth in Section 5.5. If the Buying Partners fail to notify the Selling Partner that they intend to purchase his or her interest within the 30-day period, the Selling Partner shall have the right to withdraw from the Partnership. If a Partner withdraws, the Partner shall be entitled to a payment from the Partnership equal to the Contract Price and payable at the time and in the manner set forth in Section 5.5. Any amounts received pursuant to this Section shall constitute complete and full discharge of all amounts owing to the withdrawing Partner on account of his Interest as a Partner in the Partnership.

5.4. ASSIGNMENT. A Partner may not assign any part of his Interest in the Partnership.

5.5. PAYMENT; TIME AND MANNER.

(a) Any Interest transferred to other Partners or the Partnership pursuant to this Agreement shall be paid for, at the purchaser's option, either (1) all in cash at the time of transfer of the Interest, or (2) by a down payment computed in accordance with paragraph (b) below and delivery of a promissory note signed by the purchaser(s).

(b) If the purchaser(s) elects the second option in paragraph (a) above, (s)he shall pay as a down payment 33 percent. The remaining portion shall be represented by a promissory note of the purchasers, and providing for four equal annual installments of the remaining unpaid portion of the Contract Price, each installment due on the anniversary of the transfer of the interest. The promissory note shall provide that interest at an annual rate of 5 percent (compounded semi-annually) shall be paid with each payment of principal (or such higher interest rate as shall be necessary to avoid the imputation of interest pursuant to Section 483 of the IRC), from the date of acquisition of the Interest on the portion of the note remaining unpaid from time to time.

6.1. ADJUSTMENT OF PARTNERSHIP PERCENTAGES. If a Partner withdraws pursuant to Section 5.3, the Partnership Percentages of the remaining Partners shall immediately be recalculated so that each Partner's Partnership Percentage is equal to (1) his Capital Contribution, divided by (2) the aggregate Capital Contributions of all remaining Partners. If the Partners purchase an Interest pursuant to Sections 5.1, 5.2, or 5.3, the Partnership Percentage of the selling Partner shall be added to that of the purchasing Partners, pro rata.

6.2. VOTING. All decisions or actions required by the Partners pursuant to this Agreement (including amendment hereof) shall be made or taken by the affirmative vote (at a meeting or, in lieu thereof, by written consent of the required percentage in Interest) of Partners having 100 percent of the aggregate Partnership Percentages.

7.1. MANAGEMENT AND ADMINISTRATION OF BUSINESS. Except as otherwise provided in this agreement, all Partners shall have the authority to manage the day-to-day operations and affairs of the Partnership and to make decisions regarding the business of the Partnership. Any action taken by any Partner shall constitute the act of and serve to bind the Partnership.

7.2. ACTS REQUIRING UNANIMOUS CONSENT. The following acts may be done only with the unanimous consent of the partners: (a) Borrowing money in the Partnership's name, other than in the ordinary course of the Partnership's business; (b) Capital expenditures in excess of $500.00; and (c) Amendment of this agreement.

8.1. LIABILITY AND INDEMNIFICATION. No Partner shall be liable, responsible, or accountable in damages or otherwise to the Partnership or any Partner for any action taken or failure to act on behalf of the Partnership within the scope of the authority conferred on any Partner by this Agreement or by law unless the act or omission was performed or omitted fraudulently or in bad faith or constituted negligence. The Partnership shall indemnify and hold harmless the Partners from and against any loss, expense, damage, or injury suffered or sustained by them by reason of any acts, omissions arising out of their activities on behalf of the Partnership or in furtherance of the interests of the Partnership, including but not limited to any judgment, award, settlement, reasonable attorneys' fees, and other costs or expenses incurred in connection with the defense of any actual or threatened action, proceeding, or claim, if the acts, omissions, or alleged acts or omissions upon which the actual or threatened action, proceeding, or claims are based were for a purpose reasonably believed to be in the best interests of the Partnership and were not performed or omitted fraudulently or in bad faith or as a result of negligence by a Partner and were not in violation of the Partner's fiduciary obligation to the Partnership. Any such indemnification shall be first from the assets of the Partnership, and then from all Partners and borne among them in accordance with their Partnership Percentages.

8.2. LIMITS ON PARTNERS' POWERS. Anything in this Agreement to the contrary notwithstanding, no Partner shall cause the Partnership to (a) Commingle the Partnership's funds with those of any other person, or employ or permit another to employ those funds or assets in any manner except for the exclusive benefit of the Partnership (except to the extent that funds are temporarily retained by agents of the Partnership), or (b) Reimburse any Partner for expenses incurred by any Partner except for the actual cost to the Partner of goods, materials, or services (including reasonable travel and entertainment expenses) used for or by the Partnership.

9.1. DISSOLUTION OF THE PARTNERSHIP. The happening of any one of the following events shall work an immediate dissolution of the Partnership:

(a) The sale or other disposition of all or substantially all of the assets of the Partnership.

(b) The affirmative vote for dissolution of the Partnership by Partners having at least 34 percent of the aggregate Partnership Percentages.

(c) The Bankruptcy or Incapacity of any Partner; provided that the remaining Partners shall continue the business of the Partnership unless the Partnership is dissolved under subparagraph (b) above.

(d) The expiration of the term of the Partnership.

9.2. WINDING UP. If the Partnership is dissolved and its business is not continued under Section 9.1, the Managing Partner or his/her successor shall commence to wind up the affairs of the Partnership and to liquidate the Partnership's assets. The Partners shall continue to share profits and losses during the period of liquidation in accordance with Sections 3.1 and 3.2. Following the occurrence of any of the events set forth in Section 9.1, the Partners shall determine whether the assets of the Partnership are to be sold or whether the assets are to be distributed to the Partners. If assets are distributed to the Partners, all such assets shall be valued at their then fair market value as determined by the Partners and the difference, if any, of the fair market value over (or under) the adjusted basis of such property to the Partnership shall be credited (or charged) to the Capital Accounts of the Partners in accordance with the provisions of Section 1.2. Such fair market value shall be used for purposes of determining the amount of any distribution to a Partner pursuant to Section 9.3. If the Partners are unable to agree on the fair market value of any asset of the Partnership, the fair market value shall be the average of two appraisals, one prepared by a qualified appraiser selected by Partners having 50 percent or more of the aggregate Partnership Percentages, and the other selected by the remaining Partners.

9.3. DISTRIBUTIONS UPON DISSOLUTION. Subject to the right of the Partners to set up such cash reserves as may be deemed reasonably necessary for any contingent or unforeseen liabilities or obligations of the Partnership, the proceeds of the liquidation and any other funds of the Partnership shall be distributed.

(a) To creditors, in the order of priority as provided by law except those liabilities to Partners in their capacities as Partners.

(b) To the Partners for loans, if any, made by them to the Partnership, or reimbursement for Partnership expenses paid by them.

(c) To the Partners in proportion to their respective Capital Accounts until they have received an amount equal to their Capital Accounts immediately prior to such distribution, but after adjustment for gain or loss with respect to the disposition of the Partnership's assets incident to the dissolution of the Partnership and the winding up of its affairs, whether or not the disposition occurs prior to the dissolution of the Partnership.

(d) To the Partners in accordance with their Partnership Percentages.

9.4. DEFICIT CAPITAL ACCOUNT RESTORATION. If, upon the dissolution and liquidation of the Partnership, after crediting all income upon sale of the Partnership's assets that have been sold and after making the allocations provided for in Section 9.3, any Partner has a negative Capital Account, then the Partner shall be obligated to contribute to the Partnership an amount equal to the negative Capital Account for distribution to creditors, or to Partners with positive Capital Account balances, in accordance with this Section.

10.1. FINAL REPORTS. Within a reasonable time following the completion of the liquidation of the Partnership's properties, the Managing Partner shall supply to each of the other Partners a statement that shall set forth the assets and liabilities of the Partnership as of the date of complete liquidation, and each Partner's portion of distributions pursuant to Section 9.3.

10.2. RIGHTS OF PARTNERS. Each Partner shall look solely to the assets of the Partnership for all distributions with respect to the Partnership and his Capital Contribution (including the return thereof), and share of profits, and shall have no recourse therefor (upon dissolution or otherwise) against any other Partner except as otherwise provided in this agreement.

10.3. TERMINATION. Upon the completion of the liquidation of the Partnership and the distribution of all Partnership funds, the Partnership shall terminate.

10.4. NOTICES. All notices and demands required or permitted under this Agreement shall be in writing and may be sent by certified or registered mail or similar delivery service, postage prepaid, to the Partners at their addresses as shown from time to time on the records of the Partnership, and shall be deemed given when mailed or delivered to the service. Any Partner may specify a different address by notifying the Managing Partner in writing of the different address.

10.5. SEVERABILITY. If any portion of this agreement be deemed by a competent court to be void or unenforceable, the remaining portions shall remain in full force and effect.

10.6. ENTIRE AGREEMENT. This is the entire agreement of the parties. Any oral representations or modifications concerning this instrument shall be of no force or effect unless contained in a subsequent written modification signed by the party to be charged.

IN WITNESS WHEREOF, the undersigned have executed this Agreement as of this date:

_____.

_____

Andrew Leland

_____

Donald Leland

Table A: Name, address and initial capital contribution of the Partners

Name and Address of Partner	Value of Initial Capital Contribution	Nature of Partner's Initial Capital Contribution, i.e., cash, services, property	Percentage Interest of Partner

51. Partnership Ledger

Date of Original Issue	Partner Name	Percentage Interest	Disposition of Shares (transferred or surrendered stock certificate)

52. Action by Written Consent of Partners

Note: In the real world, most small company votes are taken by written consent rather than by notice and meeting and an in-person vote. Use the following form when you wish to take a company action in writing, rather than by a noticed meeting. Keep in mind, however, that your operating agreement and articles may require more than a simple majority to pass certain actions. Written consents are important company records and should be maintained in the record books. Compare this consent form to the minutes in the form just previous to this one. You'll note that it is often far simpler to take votes by written consent.

ACTION BY WRITTEN CONSENT OF PARTNERS OF PALOS VERDES PARTNERS

The undersigned members of Palos Verdes Partners, owning the following number of shares:

> John Jones, 50%
> Judy Smith, 30%
> John Miller, 20%

hereby consent(s) to the following company actions.

1. Lisa Johnson is hereby admitted as a partner to the partnership, and her capital contribution of $10,000 in cash is accepted.

2. The partnership percentages are hereby adjusted to accommodate the new partner; the new partnership percentages would be as follows, effective immediately after this resolution is adopted:

> John Jones, 45%
> Judy Smith, 27%
> John Miller, 18%
> Lisa Johnson, 10%

The three current partners all voted in favor of admitting Lisa Johnson.

John Smith and John Miller, both also members, are hereby elected to serve as company managers until the next meeting of members.

Dated _____

_____
John Smith
Percentage Owned _____

Dated _____

_____
John Miller
Percentage Owned _____

Dated _____

_____
Judy Smith
Percentage Owned _____

CHAPTER 6

Opening: Your Place of Business

N O MATTER WHERE YOU DECIDED TO establish your business (physically speaking) there are forms involved. Whether your budget accommodates a Class-A floor within a 20-story building or your type of business requires 3,000 square feet of warehouse space, it helps to have a prior understanding of the paperwork involved.

The *Sample Commercial Lease* is an example of one of the generic forms needed to rent space for your business. It's imperative to know in advance that there may be variations depending on the specific space being leased. As with any agreement, it's important to read it thoroughly as several thousand dollars could be at stake when it's all said and done. Once you've established where your business will operate, your next step may include the lease of specific equipment. Equipment leas-

ing agreements differ in each state, however, the *Sample California Agreement to Lease Equipment* is a general template of what to expect. The *Sample Janitorial Service Agreement* is included for business owners whose current commercial contracts don't include janitorial or similar services.

If you own the business, you should have a premium parking space, right? As logical as it may seem, not all business owners are provided with designated parking spaces as part of a commercial lease agreement. The *Sample Parking Agreement* can be a resource for business owners whose current lease agreements don't include a place to park.

As a tenant, you're able to request commercial improvements. Use the sample *Tenant Improvement Form for Property Improvements*, which can help you alter your current working environment.

53. Sample Commercial Lease

This Commercial Lease is hereby made between _____, the "Lessor," and _____, the "Lessee," concerning the following property: _____, the "Premises." Lessee hereby leases from Lessor the Premises.

1. **Term and Rent.** Lessor will lease the above Premises for an initial term of _____ years and _____ months, beginning on _____, 20_____ and ending on _____, 20_____, as provided herein at the monthly rent of $ _____, payable in equal installments in advance on the first day of each month for that month's rental, during the term of the lease. All rental payments shall be made to Lessor, at the following address: _____.

2. **Use.** Lessee shall use and occupy the Premises for _____. The Premises shall be used for no other purpose. Lessor represents that the Premises may lawfully be used for such purpose.

3. **Care and Maintenance of Premises.** Lessee acknowledges that the Premises are in good order and repair, unless otherwise indicated herein. Lessee shall, at his own expense and at all times, maintain the Premises in good and safe condition, including electrical wiring, plumbing and heating installations, and any other system or equipment upon the Premises and shall surrender the same, at termination hereof, in as good a condition as received, normal wear and tear excepted. Lessee shall be responsible for all repairs required, excepting the roof, exterior walls, structural foundations, and the following: _____, which shall be maintained by Lessor. Lessee shall also maintain in good condition such portions adjacent to the Premises, such as sidewalks, driveways, lawns, and shrubbery, which would otherwise be required to be maintained by Lessor.

4. **Alterations.** Lessee shall not, without first obtaining the written consent of Lessor, make any alterations, additions, or improvements, in, to, or about the Premises.

5. **Ordinances and Statues.** Lessee shall comply with all statutes, ordinances, and requirements of all municipal, state, and federal authorities now in force, or which may hereafter be in force, pertaining to the Premises, occasioned by or affecting the use thereof by Lessee.

6. **Assignment and Subletting.** Lessee shall not assign this lease or sublet any portion of the Premises without prior written consent of the Lessor, which shall not be unreasonably withheld. Any such assignment or subletting without consent shall be void and, at the option of the Lessor, may terminate this lease.

7. **Utilities.** All applications and connections for necessary utility services on the demised Premises shall be made in the name of Lessee only, and Lessee shall be solely liable for utility charges as they become due, including those for sewer, water, gas, electricity, and telephone services.

8. **Entry and Inspection.** Lessee shall permit Lessor or Lessor's agents to enter upon the Premises at reasonable times and upon reasonable notice, for the purpose of inspecting the same, and will permit Lessor, at any time within sixty (60) days prior to the expiration of this lease, to place upon the Premis-

es any usual "To Let" or "For Lease" signs and permit persons desiring to lease the same to inspect the Premises thereafter.

9. **Possession.** If Lessor is unable to deliver possession of the Premises at the commencement hereof, Lessor shall not be liable for any damage caused thereby, nor shall this lease be void or voidable, but Lessee shall not be liable for any rent until possession is delivered. Lessee may terminate this lease if possession is not delivered within ten (10) days of the commencement of the term hereof.

10. **Indemnification of Lessor.** Lessor shall not be liable for any damage or injury to Lessee, or any other person, or to any property, occurring on the demised Premises or any part thereof, and Lessee agrees to hold Lessor harmless from any claims for damages, no matter how caused.

11. **Insurance.** Lessee, at his expense, shall maintain public liability insurance including bodily injury and property damage insuring Lessee and Lessor with minimum coverage as follows:

_____

_____

Lessee shall provide Lessor with a Certificate of Insurance showing Lessor as additional insured. The Certificate shall provide for a ten-day written notice to Lessor in the event of cancellation or material change of coverage. To the maximum extent permitted by insurance policies that may be owned by Lessor or Lessee, Lessee and Lessor, for the benefit of each other, waive any and all rights of subrogation that might otherwise exist.

12. **Eminent Domain.** If the Premises or any part thereof or any estate therein, or any other part of the building materially affecting Lessee's use of the Premises, shall be taken by eminent domain, this lease shall terminate on the date when title vests pursuant to such taking. The rent, and any additional rent, shall be apportioned as of the termination date, and any rent paid for any period beyond that date shall be repaid to Lessee. Lessee shall not be entitled to any part of the award for such taking or any payment in lieu thereof, but Lessee may file a claim for any taking of fixtures and improvements owned by Lessee and for moving expenses.

13. **Destruction of Premises.** In the event of a partial destruction of the Premises during the term hereof, from any cause, Lessor shall forthwith repair the same, provided that such repairs can be made within sixty (60) days under existing governmental laws and regulations, but such partial destruction shall not terminate this lease, except that Lessee shall be entitled to a proportionate reduction of rent while such repairs are being made, based upon the extent to which the making of such repairs shall interfere with the business of Lessee on the Premises. If such repairs cannot be made within said sixty (60) days, Lessor, at his option, may make the same within a reasonable time, this lease continuing in effect with the rent proportionately abated as aforesaid, and in the event that Lessor shall not elect to make such repairs that cannot be made within sixty (60) days, this lease may be terminated at the option of either party. In the event that the building in which the demised Premises may be situated is destroyed to an extent of not less than one-third of the replacement costs thereof, Lessor may elect to terminate this lease whether the demised Premises be injured or not. A total destruction of the building in which the Premises may be situated shall terminate this lease.

14. **Lessor's Remedies on Default.** If Lessee defaults in the payment of rent, or any additional rent, or

defaults in the performance of any of the other covenants or conditions hereof, Lessor may give Lessee notice of such default and if Lessee does not cure any such default within sixty (60) days, after the giving of such notice (or if such other default is of such nature that it cannot be completely cured within such period, if Lessee does not commence such curing within such sixty (60) days and thereafter proceed with reasonable diligence and in good faith to cure such default), then Lessor may terminate this lease on not less than thirty (30) days' notice to Lessee. On the date specified in such notice, the term of this lease shall terminate and Lessee shall then quit and surrender the Premises to Lessor, but Lessee shall remain liable as hereinafter provided. If this lease shall have been so terminated by Lessor, Lessor may at any time thereafter resume possession of the Premises by any lawful means and remove Lessee or other occupants and their effects. No failure to enforce any term shall be deemed a waiver.

15. **Common Area Expenses.** In the event the Premises are situated in a shopping center or in a commercial building in which there are common areas, Lessee agrees to pay his pro-rata share of maintenance, taxes, and insurance for the common areas.

16. **Attorney's Fees.** In case suit should be brought for recovery of the Premises, or for any sum due hereunder, or because of any act which may arise out of the possession of the Premises, by either party, the prevailing party shall be entitled to all costs incurred in connection with such action, including a reasonable attorney's fee.

17. **Notices.** Any notice that either party may or is required to give shall be given by mailing the same, postage prepaid, to Lessee at the Premises, or Lessor at the address shown below [give address], or at such other places as may be designated by the parties from time to time.

18. **Heirs, Assigns, Successors.** This lease is binding upon and inures to the benefit of the heirs, assigns, and successors in interest to the parties.

19. **Subordination.** This lease is and shall be subordinated to all existing and future liens and encumbrances against the property.

20. **Entire Agreement.** The foregoing constitutes the entire agreement between the parties and may be modified only by a writing signed by both parties. The following Exhibits, if any, have been made a part of this lease before the parties' execution hereof:

[Insert any exhibits here]

Signed this _____ day of _____, 20____.

_____
Signature of Lessor

_____
Signature of Lessee

54. Sample California Agreement to Lease Equipment

This agreement to lease equipment ("Lease") is made effective _____ [Date], between

_____ , ("Lessor") and

_____ ,("Lessee").

Lessor desires to lease ("Equipment") to Lessee, and Lessee desires to lease from Lessor.

In consideration of the mutual covenants and promises hereinafter set forth, the parties hereto agree as follows:

1. **Lease.**

   Lessor hereby leases to Lessee, and Lessee hereby leases from Lessor, the following described equipment (the "Equipment"):

2. **Term.**

   The term of this Lease is effective _____ [Effective Date] and ends _____ [End Date] thereafter.

3. **Shipping.**

   Lessee shall be responsible for shipping the Equipment to Lessee's premises.

4. **Rent and Deposit (Installments).**

A. The monthly rent for the Equipment shall be paid in advance in installments of _____ [Installment Amount] each month, beginning on _____ [Date of First Payment] and on the first day of each month thereafter through the effective dates of the contract. Payments will be given to Lessee or mailed to address designated by Lessee at [Address for Payments]. Any installment payment not made by the____(day) of the month shall be considered overdue and in addition to Lessor's other remedies, Lessor may levy a late payment charge equal to ___(%) per month on any overdue amount. Rent for any partial month shall be prorated.

B. Lessee shall pay a deposit in the following amount prior to taking possession of the Equipment: _____ [Deposit Amount]. The deposit will be refunded to Lessee following Lessee's performance of all obligations in this Lease.

5. **Use.**

   Lessee shall use the Equipment in a careful and proper manner and shall comply with and conform to all national, state, municipal, police and other laws, ordinances and regulations in any way relating to the possession, use or maintenance of the Equipment.

   _____

   _____

   _____

55. Sample Janitorial Service Agreement

Company (Janitorial)_____

Address: _____

Effective Date: _____

("Janitor") and _____ located at _____ ("Company") hereby agree to enter into this contract on the terms and conditions set forth on _____ and continuing till _____ (duration of contract). In consideration of the premises and the obligations hereinafter set forth and for other good and valuable consideration, the receipt and sufficiency of which are hereby acknowledged, the parties agree as follows:

1. **Services.** Company accepts Janitor's proposal dated _____ ("Proposal") to provide cleaning services at Company's facilities as described in the proposal, and Janitor agrees to perform the services described in the Proposal as modified by the terms and conditions contained in this agreement.

2. **Access Requirements.** Janitor shall assign to Company only Janitor employees that have completed, to Company's satisfaction, Company's standard safety training program. Company has the right to refuse access to its facilities to Janitor employees who have not completed such training and shall not be obligated in any manner to Janitor by such refusal.

3. **Cost.** Company shall pay Janitor for actual time which Janitor employees work at Company at the rate of ($_____) per hour, pro-rated for any partial hour worked, not to exceed _____ (_____) hours per week.

4. **Payment Schedule.** Janitor shall bill Company every four (4) weeks from the Effective Date for actual time worked at Company during the previous four (4) week period. Company shall not be obligated to pay any payment due at a time when Janitor is in breach of this Agreement until the breach is remedied to the satisfaction of Company.

5. **Renewal.** This Agreement shall automatically renew under the terms specified herein for a one (1) year period on the expiration of the current term unless either party notifies the other in writing at least thirty (30) days prior to the expiration of the current term that this Agreement shall not be renewed.

6. **Cancellation for Convenience.** Either party may terminate this Agreement by sending written notice to the other party thirty (30) days prior to the date on which the Agreement shall terminate.

7. **Presence of Hazardous Materials.** Janitor acknowledges that Company stores and uses hazardous materials throughout Company's facilities. Janitor assumes the risk of harm to its employees, their property or the property of Janitor resulting from contact with hazardous materials while Janitor's employees or property are on Company's.

8. **Compliance with Laws.** All services rendered by Janitor and its employees pursuant to this Agreement shall conform with and be in full compliance with all applicable laws, rules, ordinances and regulations adopted or required by any federal, state, or local government. Janitor shall be entirely and solely responsible for the payment of employee and employer payroll taxes, contributions, and/or assessments, whether pertaining to federal, state, or local requirements, workers' compensation insurance, or other insurance for Janitor and all of its employees providing the services specified in this Agreement.

9. **Insurance.** Janitor agrees to maintain insurance in commercially reasonable amounts calculated to protect Company and Janitor from any and all claims of any kind or nature for worker's compensation, as required by the state where this contract is performed, and for damage to property or personal injury, including death, arising from acts or omissions of Janitor in performing its duties under this agreement, whether the acts or omissions are those of Janitor, its employees, or agents, or anyone directly or indirectly engaged or employed by Janitor or its agents.

10. **Independent Contractor Status.** The parties intend this Agreement to create an independent contractor relationship. Neither Janitor nor its employees or agents are to be considered agents or employees of Company for any purpose, including that of federal and state taxation, federal, state, and local employment laws, or employee benefits. Janitor, not Company, shall furnish all labor, tools, equipment, vehicles, licenses, and registrations necessary to perform the services.

11. **Assignment/Sub-Contracting.** Janitor shall not assign its rights, delegate its duties, or subcontract any part of its obligations under this Agreement without prior written consent of Company.

12. **Conflicts between Agreements.** The terms of this Agreement shall control over any conflicting terms in the Proposal or any referenced agreement or document.

13. **Indemnification.** Janitor shall indemnify, defend and hold Company, its parent company, subsidiaries, officers and employees harmless from and against any and all claims, actions, suits, demands, assessments or judgments asserted and any and all losses, liabilities, damages, costs and expenses (including, without limitation, reasonable attorneys' fees to the extent permitted by law, accounting fees and investigation costs) alleged or incurred by third Parties arising out of or relating to any operations, acts or omissions of Janitor or any of its employees or agents in the exercise of Janitor's rights or the performance or observance of Janitor's obligations under this Agreement.

14. **Survival.** All provisions that logically ought to survive termination of this Agreement shall survive.

15. **Severability.** If any provision of this Agreement, or the application thereof to any person or circumstance, shall be held invalid or unenforceable by any court of competent jurisdiction, the remainder of this Agreement or the application of such provisions to persons or circumstances, other than those as to which it is held invalid or unenforceable, shall not be affected thereby.

16. **Entire Agreement.** This Agreement, consisting of the Proposal and this document, constitutes the entire agreement with respect to the subject matter herein and supersedes all prior or contemporaneous oral or written agreements concerning such services.

IN WITNESS WHEREOF, the Parties have executed this Agreement as of the date first written above.

Janitor Company _____

a _____ corporation   a _____ corporation

By: _____   By: _____

Name: _____   Name: _____

Its: _____   Its: _____

56. Sample Parking Space Agreement

Name: _____

Company: _____

Address: _____

Date of Agreement:

On (date) _____, between "Tenant" _____, of _____(company) and hereinafter referred to as "Landlord"_____, of _____("Landlord Company")_____.

Landlord desires to lease to Tenant and Tenant desires to lease from Landlord the premises generally described as _____(description of leased space).

It is agreed as follows:

Landlord hereby leases to "Tenant" parking space located at the following designated space:

(space number) _____

(effective dates) _____

Payment Terms:

Tenant agrees to pay $_____in advance on (date)_____of each month to Landlord by mail or in person at the following address:_____.

Upon Receipt of Payment:

Once Landlord receives payment, Landlord agrees to issue:

■ Receipt stating the name of Tenant

■ Designated parking space

■ Total rent paid

■ Effective dates

Landlord shall not be liable for any damage or theft of property from said parking space.

The vehicle(s) to be parked in "parking space" shall have current registration and insurance, as verified by Landlord.

Verified: Date:_____

IN WITNESS WHEREOF, the parties hereto have executed this Agreement on the date first above written.

_____

_____

57. Tenant Improvement Form for Property Improvements

Tenant:_____

Building Address:_____

Description of Work:

_____

_____

_____

_____

_____

_____

In consideration of approval, the Tenant agrees:

1.

2.

3.

CHAPTER 7

Money Money Money and the Forms to Get It

HOW THE BUSINESS IS GOING TO BE financed or capitalized is highly dependent on how your business is funded. If your business is not self-funded, you'll need to know how to apply for the type of financing that fits your business entity, model, and short and long-term plans. As far as the forms you'll need, it all depends on the type of loan you apply for.

A credit analysis is one of the first things a bank will assess when a person or business requests a loan. If you don't know yours or your business' credit score, it's imperative to obtain it via your personal credit report. The three credit bureaus are TransUnion, Equifax, and Experian. You can obtain your report by calling each bureau or applying for it on the bureau's website. Once you receive your report, review it for errors and other potentially disputable information. Use the *Sample Credit Dispute Letter* in this chapter to challenge information that's possibly hurting your credit score.

If you're seeking grant money, use the *Sample Grant Proposal* (included on the Web) as an example of how you can take your grand vision and portray it in writing with clear measurable objectives.

Qualifying for financing doesn't have to be a chore so long as you're prepared with the proper arsenal of paperwork—and proof. Use the *Sample Loan Request* form to request small business loans from banks or federal programs.

Refer to the *Sample Cover Letter* for the loan application to ensure your request is formally prepared, making it easier for the lender to review your application and assess its key points.

If your business model is devised for high growth, you may be seeking venture capital (VC). To be considered for venture capital, your potential investors will ask for an executive summary. Even if you have an executive summary prepared, review the *Sample Executive Summary* in this chapter to show you what information VCs expect to see in a finalized document.

The SBA is another resource business owners can use to fund their operations. A variety of loans are available through the SBA, which recommends having the following forms prepared to qualify for its Basic 7(a) loan: Review *SBA Loan Application*, where you'll see where to provide a description of how the loan funds will be used, the purpose for the funding, and the amount and type of loan.

Also from the SBA is the *SBA Schedule of Collateral*. On this form, list real property and other assets to be held as collateral. Also required by the SBA when submitting a loan application is the completion of the *SBA Personal Financial History* and *Personal Financial Statement*. The SBA requires financial statements for all owners, partners, officers, and stockholders owning 20% or more of the business.

Qualifying for financing doesn't have to be a chore so long as you're prepared with the proper arsenal of paperwork—and proof.

58. Sample Cover Letter for Loan Application

Business Name_____

Address_____

Date_____

Lender's name, bank name, and address

_____

_____

Re: Loan Request for $_____ (loan amount)

Dear (Lender)_____:

I am requesting a small business loan of $_____. I have experience in this industry including

_____ (mention experience and qualifications).

The market for this business is _____

_____

_____ (include a short description of your business'

industry and expected growth).

My customer base and overall market includes _____

_____

(provide short description of target market and its demographics).

The competition includes _____

_____

(include a brief paragraph about your competition and what differentiates your business from the pack).

I am investing $_____ of my own money. My collateral consists of business assets having a fair

market value of $_____ and personal assets valued at $_____ .

Please review the attached business plan which details the reasons for the loan request. If you have any questions,

please contact me at _____ (include a phone number).

Sincerely,

_____ (Your signature)

_____ (print name)

59. Sample Credit Dispute Letter

Your Name
123 Your Street Address
Your City, ST 01234

The Credit Bureau
Bureau Address
Anytown, State 56789

Date

Dear Credit Bureau,

This letter serves as a formal complaint that you are reporting inaccurate credit information.

I am very distressed that you have included the below information in my credit profile due to its damaging effects on my good credit standing. As you are no doubt aware, credit reporting laws ensure that bureaus report only accurate credit information. No doubt the inclusion of this inaccurate information is a mistake on either your or the reporting creditor's part.

The following information therefore needs to be verified and deleted from the report as soon as possible:

I am disputing the negative information on my credit report for the following reason:

_____

_____

_____

_____

_____

CREDITOR AGENCY, acct. 123-34567-ABC
Please delete the above information as quickly as possible.

Sincerely,

[Signature]

Your Name
SSN# 123-45-6789
Attachment included.

60. Sample Executive Summary

Executive Summary
Company Name

Contact Name and Title
Street Address
City, State, Zip
Phone:
Email:
Website

Business and Industry Description

Company Background: _____

Problem and Solution: _____

Products and Services: _____

Specialties (Technology, Proprietary Products and Services): _____

Markets: _____

Competitors: _____

Business Model: _____

Management Team

Owner(s):
Title_____

Relevant
Experience:_____

Board Members and
Advisors:_____

Finances
Bank:

Legal Representation/Retainer:_____ Amount of Financing Sought: _____

Current Investor(s) (if applicable): _____

Intended use of invested funds: _____

_____

Financial Projections (Five Year Plan)

Revenue: _____

61. SBA Loan Application

OMB Approval No. 3245-0016
Expiration Date: 11/30/2012

U. S. Small Business Administration
APPLICATION FOR BUSINESS LOAN

Individual	Full Address

Name of Applicant Business	Tax I.D. No. or SSN

Full Street Address of Business	Tel. No. (inc. Area Code)

City	County	State	Zip	Number of Employees (including subsidiaries and affiliates)

Type of Business	Date Business Established	At Time of Application _____
		If Loan is Approved _____

Bank of Business Account and Address	Subsidiaries or Affiliates (Separate for above) _____

Use of Proceeds: (Enter Gross Dollar Amounts Rounded to the Nearest Hundreds)	Loan Requested		Loan Request
Land Acquisition		Pay off SBA Loan	
New Construction/ Expansion Repair		Pay off Bank Loan (Non SBA Associated)*	
Acquisition and/or Repair of Machinery and Equipment		Other Debt Payment (Non SBA Associated)	
Inventory Purchase		All Other	
Working Capital (including Accounts Payable)		Total Loan Requested	
Acquisition of Existing Business		Term of Loan - (Requested Maturity)	___ Yrs.

CURRENT AND PREVIOUS SBA AND OTHER GOVERNMENT DEBT: Complete the chart below if you, your business, any principal of your business, any affiliate of your business, any other business currently owned by a principal, or any business previously owned by you or a principal of your business has received or applied for any direct or guaranteed financial assistance from the Federal Government, including student loans and disaster loans. All current, previous, and pending Government debt must be listed, including loans that have been paid in full or those that resulted in a loss to the Government. (Note: Loans that resulted in a loss to the Government include loans that were charged off, compromised, or discharged as a result of bankruptcy. The amount of the loss is the outstanding principal balance of the loan that the Government had to write off after all collection activities (including compromise) were finalized.)

Name of Agency Agency Loan #	Borrower's Name	Original Amount of Loan	Date of Application	Loan Status	Outstanding Balance	$ Amount of Loss to the Government.
1. #		$			$	$
2. #		$			$	$
3. #		$			$	$
4. #		$			$	$

ASSISTANCE: Did you commit to pay -- or have you paid -- anyone (including the lender) to assist you in either obtaining this loan (such as a broker, consultant or referral agent) or in preparing the application or application materials for this loan (such as a loan packager)? Yes ☐   No ☐

If "yes," complete SBA Form 159 **(7a) - (Fee Disclosure Form and Compensation Agreement) for each party that was paid or will be paid.)**

Note: The estimated burden completing this form is 12.0 hours per response. You will not be required to respond to collection of information unless it displays a currently valid OMB approval number. Comments on the burden should be sent to the U.S. Small Business Administration, Chief, AIB, 409 3rd St., S.W., Washington, DC. 20416 and Desk Office for Small Business Administration, Office of Management and Budget, New Executive Building, room 10202 Washington, D.C. 20503. OMB Approval (3245-0016). **PLEASE DO NOT SEND FORMS TO OMB. SUBMIT COMPLETED APPLICATION TO LENDER OF CHOICE.**

SBA Form 4 (9-09) Previous Edition Obsolete

Page 1

ALL EXHIBITS MUST BE SIGNED AND DATED BY PERSON SIGNING THIS FORM

BUSINESS INDEBTEDNESS: Furnish the following information on all outstanding installment debts, contracts, notes, and mortgages payable. Indicate by an asterisk (*) items to be paid by loan proceeds and reasons for paying them. (Present balance should agree with the latest balance sheet submitted).

To Whom Payable	Original Amount	Original Date	Present Balance	Rate of Interest	Maturity Date	Monthly Payment	Security	Current or Past Due
Acct. #	$		$			$		
Acct. #	$		$			$		
Acct. #	$		$			$		
Acct. #	$		$			$		
Acct. #	$		$			$		

MANAGEMENT (Proprietor, partners, officers, directors, all holders of outstanding stock –100% of ownership must be shown.) Use separate sheet if necessary.

Name and Social Security Number Position/Title	Complete Address	% Owned		*Gender
			*Veteran Status Veteran Yes☐ No☐ If yes, service-disabled? Yes☐ No☐	
Race * :Amer. Indian or Alaska Native☐ Asian☐ Black or African-Amer.☐ Native Haw. or Pacific Islander☐ White☐			*Ethnicity:Hispanic or Latino☐ Not Hisp or Lantino☐	
			*Veteran Status Veteran Yes☐ No☐ If yes, service-disabled? Yes☐ No☐	
Race * :Amer. Indian or Alaska Native☐ Asian☐ Black or African-Amer.☐ Native Haw. or Pacific Islander☐ White☐			*Ethnicity:Hispanic or Latino☐ Not Hisp or Lantino☐	
			*Veteran Status Veteran Yes☐ No☐ If yes, service-disabled? Yes☐ No☐	
Race * :Amer. Indian or Alaska Native☐ Asian☐ Black or African-Amer.☐ Native Haw. or Pacific Islander☐ White☐			*Ethnicity:Hispanic or Latino☐ Not Hisp or Lantino☐	
			*Veteran Status Veteran Yes☐ No☐ If yes, service-disabled? Yes☐ No☐	
Race * :Amer. Indian or Alaska Native☐ Asian☐ Black or African-Amer.☐ Native Haw. or Pacific Islander☐ White☐			*Ethnicity:Hispanic or Latino☐ Not Hisp or Lantino☐	

*This data is collected for statistical purposes only. It has no bearing on the credit decision. Disclosure is voluntary. One or more boxes for race may be selected

For Guaranty Loans please provide an original and one copy (Photocopy is Acceptable) of the Application Form and all Exhibits to the participating Lender. For Direct Loans submit one original copy of the application and Exhibits to SBA.

1. Submit SBA Form 912 (Statement of Personal History) for each proprietor (if sole proprietorship), partner (if a partnership), and by each officer, director, and owner of 20% or more of the company's stock (if a corporation, limited liability company or development company).

2. If your collateral consists of (A) Land and Building, (B) Machinery and Equipment, (C) Furniture and Fixtures, (D) Accounts Receivable, (E) Inventory, (F) Other, please provide an itemized list that contains serial and identification numbers for all articles that had an original value of greater than $5,000. Include a legal description of Real Estate offered as collateral. Label it Exhibit A.

3. Furnish a signed current personal balance sheet (SBA Form 413 may be used for this purpose) for (1) each proprietor; or (2) each limited partner who owns 20% or more interest and each general partner; or (3) each stockholder owning 20% or more of voting stock. Include the assets and liabilities of the spouse and any minor children.

Also, include the tax i.d. number [EIN or Social Security Number (SSN)] Label it Exhibit B.

4. Include the financial statements listed below: a, b, c for the last three years; also a, b, c, and d as of the same date, - current within 90 days of filing the application; and statement *e*, if applicable. **All** information must be signed and dated. (a) Balance Sheet; (b) Profit and Loss Statement (if not available, explain why and substitute Federal income tax forms); (c) Reconciliation of Net Worth; (d) Aging of Accounts Receivable and and Payable (summary); (e) Projection of earnings for at least one year where financial statements for the last three years are unavailable or when SBA requests them, Label it Exhibit C. (Contact SBA for a referral if assistance with preparation is wanted.)

5. Provide a brief history of your company and a paragraph describing the expected benefits it will receive from the loan. Label it Exhibit D.

6. Provide a brief description similar to a resume of the education, technical and business background for all the people listed under Management. Label it Exhibit E.

SBA Form 4 (9-09) Previous Edition Obsolete   Page 2

7. Submit the name, addresses, tax I.D. number (EIN or SSN), and current personal financial statement of any co-signers who are not otherwise affiliated with the business and any guarantors for the loan not covered by 3. above. Exhibit F.

8. Include a list of any machinery or equipment or other non-real estate assets to be purchased with loan proceeds and the cost of each item as quoted by the seller. Include the seller's name and address. Exhibit G.

9. Have you or any officer of your company ever been involved in bankruptcy or insolvency proceedings? [ ]Yes [ ]No. If yes, please provide the details as Exhibit H.

10. Are you or your business involved in any pending lawsuits? [ ]Yes [ ]No. If yes, provide the details as Exhibit I.

11. Do you or your spouse or any member of your household, or anyone who owns, manages, or directs your business or their spouses or members of their households work for the Small Business Administration, Small Business Advisory Council, SCORE or ACE, any Federal Agency, or the participating lender? [ ]Yes [ ]No. If yes, please provide the name and address of the person and the office where employed. Label this Exhibit J.

12. Does your business, its owners or majority stockholders own or have a controlling interest in other businesses? [ ]Yes [ ]No. If yes, please provide their names and the relationship with your company along with financial data requested in question 4. Label this Exhibit K.

13. Do you buy from, sell to, or use the services of any concern in which someone in your company has a significant financial interest? [ ]Yes [ ]No. If yes, provide details on a separate sheet of paper. Exhibit L.

14. Is your business is a franchise, [ ]Yes [ ]No. If yes, include a copy of the franchise agreement and a copy of the FTC disclosure statement supplied to you by the Franchisor. Label this Exhibit M.

CONSTRUCTION LOANS ONLY

15. Include as a separate exhibit the estimated cost of the project and a statement of the source of any additional funds. Label this Exhibit N.

16. Provide copies of preliminary construction plans and specifications. Label this as Exhibit O. Final plans will be required prior to disbursement.

EXPORT LOANS

17. Does your business currently export, or will it start exporting, pursuant to this loan (if approved) ?
Check here: [ ]Yes [ ]No

18. If you answered yes to item 17, what is your estimate of the total export sales this loan would support? $ _____

19. Would you like information on Exporting?
Check here: [ ]Yes [ ]No

COUNSELING/TRAINING

20. Have you received counseling or training from SBA (e.g., SCORE, ACE, SBDC, WBC, etc.) ?
Check here: [ ]Yes [ ]No

SUBMIT COMPLETED APPLICATION TO LENDER OF CHOICE.

AGREEMENTS AND CERTIFICATIONS

AGREEMENTS:

By signing below you agree to the following:

(a) Agreements of non-employment of SBA Personnel. I agree that if SBA approves this application I will not, for at least two years, hire as an employee or consultant anyone that was employed by the SBA during the one year period prior to the loan disbursement.

(b) Waiver of Claims. As consideration for any Management, Technical, and/or Business Development Assistance that may be provided, I waive all claims against SBA and its consultants.

(c) Criminal Background. I authorize the SBA's Office of Inspector General to request criminal record information about me from criminal justice agencies for the purpose of determining my eligibility for assistance under the Small Business Act.

(d) Reimbursement of Expenses. I agree to pay for or reimburse SBA for the cost of any surveys, title or mortgage examinations, appraisals, credit reports, etc., performed by non-SBA personnel provided I have given my consent.

(e) Reporting. I agree to report to the SBA Office of the Inspector General, Washington, DC 20416 any federal government employee who offers, in return for any type of compensation, to help get this loan approved.

READ THE FOLLOWING CAREFULLY -- FALSE STATE-MENTS ARE SUBJECT TO CRIMINAL PROSECUTION:

If you knowingly make a false statement, you can be fined up to $250,000 and/or imprisoned for not more than five years under 18 USC 1001; if submitted to a Federally insured institution, under 18 USC 1014 by Imprisonment of not more than twenty years and/or a fine of not more than $1,000,000

CERTIFICATIONS:
By signing below you certify as to the following:

(a) **All information in this Application and the Exhibits is true and complete to the best of your knowledge.** You understand that this information is being submitted to a lender and SBA so they can decide to make a loan or give a loan guaranty, and that the lender and SBA are relying on this information.

(b) You have not paid anyone employed by the Federal Government for help in getting this loan. You understand that you do not need to pay any other third-party for assistance in locating a lender or preparing this Application or Exhibits, and **you certify that you will disclose all parties that were paid for such assistance** to the Lender and will complete the SBA Form 159 for all such persons.

(c) I have read a copy of the "Statements Required By Law And Executive Order," which is attached to this application and agree to comply with the requirements in this Notice.

If Applicant is a proprietor or general partner, sign below.

By: _____

If Applicant is a Corporation, sign below:

_____
Corporate Name and Seal   Date

By: _____
         Signature of President

Attested by: _____
       Signature of Corporate Secretary

Other than the person that signed on page 3, each Partner, each Stockholder owning 20% or more, and each Guarantor must sign below. In addition, if a husband and wife collectively own 20% or more of a company, each spouse must also sign. No one should sign more than once.

Business Name:_____

APPLICANT'S CERTIFICATION

READ THE FOLLOWING CAREFULLY -- FALSE STATEMENTS ARE SUBJECT TO CRIMINAL PROSECUTION:
If you knowingly make a false statement, you can be fined up to $250,000 and/or imprisoned for not more than five years under 18 USC 1001; if submitted to a Federally insured institution, under 18 USC 1014 by Imprisonment of not more than twenty years and/or a fine of not more than $1,000,000

By signing below you certify as to the following:

(a) You have reviewed (1) the responses to the question about debt on page 1 of the application; (2) the responses to questions 11, 12, and 13 (application-page 3), and (3) any financial statement that <u>you</u> were required to complete as Exhibit B or F to the application and **certify that <u>as to you personally</u> all information in this Application and Financial Statement is true and complete to the best of your knowledge**. You acknowledge that this information is being submitted to a lender and SBA so they can decide to make a loan or give a loan guaranty, and that the lender and SBA are relying on this information.

(b) You have read a copy of the "Statements Required By Law And Executive Order," which is attached to this application and agree to comply with the requirements in this Notice.

_____   _____
Signature   Date
Check all that apply: [ ] guarantor [ ] owner-indicate percentage owned: [   ] [ ] partner-indicate whether [ ] general or [ ] limited

_____   _____
Signature   Date
Check all that apply: [ ] guarantor [ ] owner-indicate percentage owned: [   ] [ ] partner-indicate whether [ ] general or [ ] limited

_____   _____
Signature   Date
Check all that apply: [ ] guarantor [ ] owner-indicate percentage owned: [   ] [ ] partner-indicate whether [ ] general or [ ] limited

_____   _____
Signature   Date
Check all that apply: [ ] guarantor [ ] owner-indicate percentage owned: [   ] [ ] partner-indicate whether [ ] general or [ ] limited

_____   _____
Signature   Date
Check all that apply: [ ] guarantor [ ] owner-indicate percentage owned: [   ] [ ] partner-indicate whether [ ] general or [ ] limited

_____   _____
Signature   Date
Check all that apply: [ ] guarantor [ ] owner-indicate percentage owned: [   ] [ ] partner-indicate whether [ ] general or [ ] limited

_____   _____
Signature   Date
Check all that apply: [ ] guarantor [ ] owner-indicate percentage owned: [   ] [ ] partner-indicate whether [ ] general or [ ] limited

SBA Form 4 (9-09) Previous Edition Obsolete   Page 4

PLEASE READ, DETACH, AND RETAIN FOR YOUR RECORDS
STATEMENTS REQUIRED BY LAW AND EXECUTIVE ORDER

Federal executive agencies, including the Small Business Administration (SBA), are required to withhold or limit financial assistance, to impose special conditions on approved loans, to provide special notices to applicants or borrowers and to require special reports and data from borrowers in order to comply with legislation passed by the Congress and Executive Orders issued by the President and by the provisions of various inter-agency agreements. SBA has issued regulations and procedures that implement these laws and executive orders, and they are contained in Parts 112, 113, 116, and 117, Title 13, Code of Federal Regulations Chapter 1, or Standard Operating Procedures.

Freedom of Information Act (5 U.S.C. 552)
This law provides, with some exceptions, that SBA must supply information reflected in agency files and records to a person requesting it. Information about approved loans that will be automatically released includes, among other things, statistics on our loan programs (individual borrowers are not identified in the statistics) and other information such as the names of the borrowers (and their officers, directors, stockholders or partners), the collateral pledged to secure the loan, the amount of the loan, its purpose in general terms and the maturity. Proprietary data on a borrower would not routinely be made available to third parties. All requests under this Act are to be addressed to the nearest SBA office and be identified as a Freedom of Information request.

Privacy Act (5 U.S.C. 552a)

A person can request to see or get copies of any personal information that SBA has in his or her file when that file is retrievable by individual identifiers such as name or social security numbers. Requests for information about another party may be denied unless SBA has the written permission of the individual to release the information to the requestor or unless the information is subject to disclosure under the Freedom of Information Act.

Under the provisions of the Privacy Act, you are not required to provide your social security number. Failure to provide your social security number may not affect any right, benefit or privilege to which you are entitled. Disclosures of name and other personal identifiers are, however, required for a benefit, as SBA requires an individual seeking assistance from SBA to provide it with sufficient information for it to make a character determination. In determining whether an individual is of good character, SBA considers the person's integrity, candor, and disposition toward criminal actions. In making loans pursuant to section 7(a)(6) of the Small Business Act (the Act), 15 USC Section 636(a)(6), SBA is required to have reasonable assurance that the loan is of sound value and will be repaid or that it is in the best interest of the Government to grant the assistance requested. Additionally, SBA is specifically authorized to verify your criminal history, or lack thereof, pursuant to section 7(a)(1)(B), 15 USC Section 636(a)(1)(B). Further, for all forms of assistance, SBA is authorized to make all investigations necessary to ensure that a person has not engaged in acts that violate or will violate the Act or the Small Business Investment Act, 15 USC Sections 634(b)(11) and 687(b)(a). For these purposes, you are asked to voluntarily provide your social security number to assist SBA in making a character determination and to distinguish you from other individuals with the same or similar name or other personal identifier.

The Privacy Act authorizes SBA to make certain "routine uses" of information protected by that Act. One such routine use for SBA's loan system of records is that when this information indicates a violation or potential violation of law, whether civil, criminal, or administrative in nature, SBA may refer it to the appropriate agency, whether Federal, State, local or foreign, charged with responsibility for or otherwise involved in investigation, prosecution, enforcement or prevention of such violations. Another routine use of personal information is to assist in obtaining credit bureau reports, including business credit reports on the small business borrower and consumer credit reports and scores on the principals of the small business and guarantors on the loan for purposes of originating, servicing, and liquidating small business loans and for purposes of routine periodic loan portfolio management and lender monitoring. See, 69 F.R. 58598, 58617 (and as amended from time to time) for additional background and other routine uses.

SBA Form 4 (9-09) Previous Edition Obsolete

Page 5

Right to Financial Privacy Act of 1978 (12 U.S.C. 3401)
This is notice to you as required by the Right of Financial Privacy Act of 1978, of SBA's access rights to financial records held by financial institutions that are or have been doing business with you or your business, including any financial institutions participating in a loan or loan guarantee. The law provides that SBA shall have a right of access to your financial records in connection with its consideration or administration of assistance to you in the form of a Government loan or loan guaranty agreement. SBA is required to provide a certificate of its compliance with the Act to a financial institution in connection with its first request for access to your financial records, after which no further certification is required for subsequent accesses. The law also provides that SBA's access rights continue for the term of any approved loan or loan guaranty agreement. No further notice to you of SBA's access rights is required during the term of any such agreement.

The law also authorizes SBA to transfer to another Government authority any financial records included in an application for a loan, or concerning an approved loan or loan guarantee, as necessary to process, service or foreclose on a loan or loan guarantee or to collect on a defaulted loan or loan guarantee. No other transfer of your financial records to another Government authority will be permitted by SBA except as required or permitted by law.

Flood Disaster Protection Act (42 U.S.C. 4011)
Regulations have been issued by the Federal Insurance Administration (FIA) and by SBA implementing this Act and its amendments. These regulations prohibit SBA from making certain loans in an FIA designated floodplain unless Federal flood insurance is purchased as a condition of the loan. Failure to maintain the required level of flood insurance makes the applicant ineligible for any future financial assistance from SBA under any program, including disaster assistance.

Executive Orders -- Floodplain Management and Wetland Protection (42 F.R. 26951 and 42 F.R. 26961)
The SBA discourages any settlement in or development of a floodplain or a wetland. This statement is to notify all SBA loan applicants that such actions are hazardous to both life and property and should be avoided. The additional cost of flood preventive construction must be considered in addition to the possible loss of all assets and investments in future floods.

Occupational Safety and Health Act (15 U.S.C. 651 et seq.)
This legislation authorizes the Occupational Safety and Health Administration in the Department of Labor to require businesses to modify facilities and procedures to protect employees or pay penalty fees. In some instances the business can be forced to cease operations or be prevented from starting operations in a new facility. Therefore, in some instances SBA may require additional information from an applicant to determine whether the business will be in compliance with OSHA regulations and allowed to operate its facility after the loan is approved and disbursed. Signing this form as borrower is a certification that the OSA requirements that apply to the borrower's business have been determined and the borrower to the best of its knowledge is in compliance.

Civil Rights Legislation
All businesses receiving SBA financial assistance must agree not to discriminate in any business practice, including employment practices and services to the public, on the basis of categories cited in 13 C.F.R., Parts 112, 113, and 117 of SBA Regulations. This includes making their goods and services available to handicapped clients or customers. All business borrowers will be required to display the "Equal Employment Opportunity Poster" prescribed by SBA.

Equal Credit Opportunity Act (15 U.S.C. 1691)
The Federal Equal Credit Opportunity Act prohibits creditors from discriminating against credit applicants on the basis of race, color, religion, national origin, sex, marital status or age (provided that the applicant has the capacity to enter into a binding contract); because all or part of the applicant's income derives from any public assistance program, or because the applicant has in good faith exercised any right under the Consumer Credit Protection Act. The Federal agency that administers compliance with this law concerning this creditor is the Federal Trade Commission, Equal Credit Opportunity, Washington, D.C. 20580.

SBA Form 4 (5-09) Previous Edition Obsolete   Page 6

Executive Order 11738 -- Environmental Protection (38 C.F.R. 25161)

The Executive Order charges SBA with administering its loan programs in a manner that will result in effective enforcement of the Clean Air Act, the Federal Water Pollution Act and other environmental protection legislation. SBA must, therefore, impose conditions on some loans. By acknowledging receipt of this form and presenting the application, the principals of all small businesses borrowing $100,000 or more in direct funds stipulate to the following:

1. That any facility used, or to be used, by the subject firm is not cited on the EPA list of Violating Facilities.

2. That subject firm will comply with all the requirements of Section 114 of the Clean Air Act (42 U.S.C. 7414) and Section 308 of the Water Act (33 U.S.C 1318) relating to inspection, monitoring, entry, reports and information, as well as all other requirements specified in Section 114 and Section 308 of the respective Acts, and all regulations and guidelines issued thereunder.

3. That subject firm will notify SBA of the receipt of any communication from the Director of the Environmental Protection Agency indicating that a facility utilized, or to be utilized, by subject firm is under consideration to be listed on the EPA List of Violating Facilities.

Debt Collection Act of 1982 Deficit Reduction Act of 1984 (31 U.S.C. 3701 et seq. and other titles)

These laws require SBA to aggressively collect any loan payments which become delinquent. SBA must obtain your taxpayer identification number when you apply for a loan. If you receive a loan, and do not make payments as they come due, SBA may take one or more of the following actions:

- Report the status of your loan(s) to credit bureaus
- Hire a collection agency to collect your loan
- Offset your income tax refund or other amounts due to you from the Federal Government
- Suspend or debar you or your company from doing business with the Federal Government
- Refer your loan to the Department of Justice or other attorneys for litigation
- Foreclose on collateral or take other action permitted in the loan instruments.

Immigration Reform and Control Act of 1986 (Pub. L. 99-603)

If you are an alien who was in this country illegally since before January 1, 1982, you may have been granted lawful temporary resident status by the United States Immigration and Naturalization Service pursuant to the Immigration Reform and Control Act of 1986 (Pub. L. 99-603). For five years from the date you are granted such status, you are not eligible for financial assistance from the SBA in the form of a loan or guaranty under section 7(a) of the Small Business Act unless you are disabled or a Cuban or Haitian entrant. When you sign this document, you are making the certification that the Immigration Reform and Control Act of 1986 does not apply to you, or if it does apply, more than five years have elapsed since you have been granted lawful temporary resident status pursuant to such 1986 legislation.

Lead-Based Paint Poisoning Prevention Act (42 U.S.C. 4821 et seq.)

Borrowers using SBA funds for the construction or rehabilitation of a residential structure are prohibited from using lead-based paint (as defined in SBA regulations) on all interior surfaces, whether accessible or not, and exterior surfaces, such as stairs, decks, porches, railings, windows and doors, which are readily accessible to children under 7 years of age. A "residential structure" is any home, apartment, hotel, motel, orphanage, boarding school, dormitory, day care center, extended care facility, college or other school housing, hospital, group practice or community facility and all other residential or institutional structures where persons reside.

Executive Order 12549, Debarment and Suspension (13 C.F.R. 145)

1. The prospective lower tier participant certifies, by submission of this loan application, that neither it nor its principals are presently debarred, suspended, proposed for debarment, declared ineligible, or voluntarily excluded from participation in this transaction by any Federal department or agency.

2. Where the prospective lower tier participant is unable to certify to any of the statements in this certification, such prospective participants shall attach an explanation to the loan application.

SBA Form 4 (4-09) Previous Edition Obsolete   Page 7

62. SBA Schedule of Collateral

OMB Approval No.: 3245-0016
Expiration Date: 11/30/2012

U.S. SMALL BUSINESS ADMINISTRATION
SCHEDULE OF COLLATERAL
Exhibit A

Applicant		
Street Address		
City	State	Zip Code

LIST ALL COLLATERAL TO BE USED AS SECURITY FOR THIS LOAN

Section I – REAL ESTATE

Attach a copy of the deed(s) containing a full legal description of the land and show the location (street address) and city where the deed(s) is recorded. Following the address below, give a brief description of the improvements, such as size, type of construction, use, number of stories, and present condition (use additional sheet if more space is required).

LIST OF PARCELS OF REAL ESTATE					
Address	Year Acquired	Original Cost	Market Value	Amount of Lien	Name of Lienholder

Description(s)

SBA Form 4, Schedule A (09-09) Previous Editions Obsolete
SUBMIT COMPLETED APPLICATION TO LENDER OF CHOICE

Section II- PERSONAL PROPERTY

All items with an original value greater than $5,000 listed herein must show manufacturer or make, model, year, and serial number. Items with no serial number must be clearly identified (use additional sheet if more space is required).

Description-Show Manufacturer, Model, Serial No.	Year acquired	Original Cost	Market Value	Current Lien Balance	Name of Lienholder

All information contained herein it TRUE and CORRECT to the best of knowledge. **If you knowingly make a false statement or overvalue a security to obtain a guaranteed loan from SBA, you can be fined up to $250,000 and/or imprisoned for not more than five years under 18 USC 1001; if submitted to a Federally insured institution, under 18 USC 1014 by Imprisonment of not more than twenty years and/or a fine of not more than $1,000,000.** I authorize the SBA's Office of Inspector General to request criminal record information about me from criminal justice agencies for the purpose of determining my eligibility for programs authorized by the Small Business Act, as amended.

Name _____   Date _____

Name _____   Date _____

NOTE: The estimated burden for completing this form is 0.5 hours per response. You will not be required to respond to collection of information unless it displays a currently valid OMB approval number. Comments on the burden should be sent to the U.S. Small Business Administration, Chief, AIB, 409 3rd. St., S.W. Washington, D.C., 20416 and Desk Office for Small Business Administration, Office of Management and Budget, New Executive Office Building, Room 10202, Washington, D.C. 20503. **OMB Approval (3245-0016).**

SBA Form 4, Schedule A (09-09) Previous Editions Obsolete

63. SBA Statement of Personal History

Return Executed Copies 1, 2, and 3 to SBA

OMB APPROVAL NO.3245-0178
Expiration Dat e: 12/31/2009

United States of America
SMALL BUSINESS ADMINISTRATION
STATEMENT OF PERSONAL HISTORY

Please Read Carefull y - Print or T ype

Each member of the small business or the development company requesting assistance must submit this form in TR IPLICATE for filing with the SBA application. This form must be filled out and submitted by:

1. By the proprietor, if a sole proprietorship.

2. By each partner, if a partnership.

3. By each officer, director, and additionally by each holder of 20% or more of the ownership stock, if a corporation, limited liability company, or a development company.

Name and Address of Applicant (Firm Name)(Street, City, State, and ZIP Code)

SBA District/Disaster Area Office

Amount Applied for (when applicable) | File No. (if known)

1. Personal Statement of: (State name in full, if no middle name, state (NMN), or if initial only, indicate initial.) List all former names used, and dates each name was used. Use separate sheet if necessary.

First | Middle | Last

2. Give the percentage of ownership or stocked owned or to be owned in the small business or the development company | Social Security No.

3. Date of Birth (Month, day, and year)

4. Place of Birth: (City & State or Foreign Country)

Name and Address of participating lender or surety co. (when applicable and kno wn)

5. U.S. Citizen? ☐ YES ☐ NO
If No, are you a Lawful Permanent resident alien: ☐ YES ☐ NO
If non- U.S. citizen provide alien registration number:

6. Present residence address:
From:
To:
Address:

Home Telephone No. (Include A/C):
Business Telephone No. (Include A/C):

Most recent prior address (omit if over 10 years ago):
From:
To:
Address:

PLEASE SEE REVERSE SIDE FOR EXPLANATION REGARDING DISCLOSURE OF INFORMATION AND THE USES OF SUCH INFORMATION.

IT IS IMPORTANT THAT THE NEXT THREE QUESTIONS BE ANSWERED COMPLETELY. AN ARREST OR CONVICTION RECORD WILL NOT NECESSARILY DISQUALIFY YOU; HOWEVER, AN UNTRUTHFUL ANSWER WILL CAUSE YOUR APPLICATION TO BE DENIED.

IF YOU ANSWER "YES" TO 7, 8, OR 9, FURNISH DETAILS ON A SEPARATE SHEET. INCLUDE DATES, LOCATION, FINES, SENTENCES, WHETHER MISDEMEANOR OR FELONY, DATES OF PAROLE/PROBATION, UNPAID FINES OR PENALTIES, NAME(S) UNDER WHICH CHARGED, AND ANY OTHER PERTINENT INFORMATION.

7. Are you presently under indictment, on parole or probation?
☐ Yes ☐ No (If yes, indicate date parole or probation is to expire.)

8. Have you ever been charged with and or arrested for any criminal offense other than a minor motor vehicle violation? Include offenses which have been dismissed, discharged, or not prosecu ted (All arres ts and cha rges must be disclosed and explained on an attached sheet.)
☐ Yes ☐ No

9. Have you ever been convicted, placed on pretrial diversion, or placed on any form of probati on, including adjudication withheld pending probation, for any criminal offense other than a minor vehicle violation?
☐ Yes ☐ No

10. I authorize the Small Business Administration Office of Inspector General to request criminal record information about me from criminal justice agencies for the purpose of determining my eligibility for programs authorized by the Small Business Act, and the Small Business Investment Act.

CAUTION: Knowingly making a false statement on this form is a violation of Federal law and could result in criminal prosecution, significant civil penalties, and a denial of your loan, surety bond, or other program participation. A false statement is punishable under 18 USC 1001 by imprisonment of not more than five years and/or a fine of not more than $10,000; under 15 USC 645 by imprisonment of not more than two years and/or a fine of not more than $5,000; and, if submitted to a Federally insured institution, under 18 USC 1014 by imprisonment of not more than thirty years and/or a fine of not more than $1,000,000.

Signature | Title | Date

Agency Use Only

11. ☐ Fingerprints Waived
Date | Approving Authority

☐ Fingerprints Required
Date | Approving Authority

Date Sent to OIG

12. ☐ Cleared for Processing
Date | Approving Authority

13. ☐ Request a Character Evaluation
Date | Approving Authority

(Required whenever 7, 8 or 9 are answered "yes" even if cleared for processing.)

PLEASE NOTE: The estimated burden for completing this form is 15 minutes per re sponse. You are not required to respond to any collection of information unl ess it displays a currently valid OMB approval number. Comments on the burden should be sent to U.S. Small Business Administration, Chief, AIB, 409 3rd St., S.W., Washington D.C. 20416 and Desk Officer for the Small Business Administration, Office of Management and Budget, New Executive Office Building, Room 10202, Washington, D.C. 20503. OMB Approval 3245-0178. PLEASE DO NOT SEND FORMS TO OMB.

SBA 912 (12-06) SOP 5010.4 Previous Edition Obsolete

This form was electronically produced by Elite Federal Forms, Inc.

NOTICES REQUIRED BY LAW

The following is a brief summary of the laws applicable to this solicitation of information.

Paperwork Reduction Act (44 U.S.C. Chapter 35)

SBA is collecting the information on this form to make a character and credit eligibility decision to fund or deny you a loan or other form of assistance. The information is required in order for SBA to have sufficient information to determine whether to provide you with the requested assistance. The information collected may be checked against criminal history indices of the Federal Bureau of Investigation.

Privacy Act (5 U.S.C. § 552a)

Any person can request to see or get copies of any personal information that SBA has in his or her file, when that file is retrievable by individual identifiers, such as name or social security numbers. Requests for information about another party may be denied unless SBA has the written permission of the individual to release the information to the requestor or unless the information is subject to disclosure under the Freedom of Information Act.

Under the provisions of the Privacy Act, you are not required to provide your social security number. Failure to provide your social security number may not affect any right, benefit or privilege to which you are entitled. Disclosures of name and other personal identifiers are, however, required for a benefit, as SBA requires an individual seeking assistance from SBA to provide it with sufficient information for it to make a character determination. In determining whether an individual is of good character, SBA considers the person's integrity, candor, and disposition toward criminal actions. In making loans pursuant to section 7(a)(6) the Small Business Act (the Act), 15 USC § 636 (a)(6), SBA is required to have reasonable assurance that the loan is of sound value and will be repaid or that it is in the best interest of the Government to grant the assistance requested. Additionally, SBA is specifically authorized to verify your criminal history, or lack thereof, pursuant to section 7(a)(1)(B), 15 USC § 636(a)(1)(B). Further, for all forms of assistance, SBA is authorized to make all investigations necessary to ensure that a person has not engaged in acts that violate or will violate the Act or the Small Business Investment Act,15 USC §§ 634(b)(11) and 687b(a). For these purposes, you are asked to voluntarily provide your social security number to assist SBA in making a character determination and to distinguish you from other individuals with the same or similar name or other personal identifier.

When this information indicates a violation or potential violation of law, whether civil, criminal, or administrative in nature, SBA may refer it to the appropriate agency, whether Federal, State, local, or foreign, charged with responsibility for or otherwise involved in investigation, prosecution, enforcement or prevention of such violations. See 56 Fed. Reg. 8020 (1991) for other published routine uses.

64. SBA Personal Financial Statement

OMB APPROVAL NO. 3245-0188
EXPIRATION DATE: 8/31/2011

PERSONAL FINANCIAL STATEMENT

U.S. SMALL BUSINESS ADMINISTRATION

As of _____ , _____

Complete this form for: (1) each proprietor, or (2) each limited partner who owns 20% or more interest and each general partner, or (3) each stockholder owning 20% or more of voting stock, or (4) any person or entity providing a guaranty on the loan.

Name	Business Phone
Residence Address	Residence Phone
City, State, & Zip Code	
Business Name of Applicant/Borrower	

ASSETS	(Omit Cents)	LIABILITIES	(Omit Cents)
Cash on hand & in Banks	$	Accounts Payable	$
Savings Accounts	$	Notes Payable to Banks and Others	$
IRA or Other Retirement Account	$	(Describe in Section 2)	
Accounts & Notes Receivable	$	Installment Account (Auto)	$
Life Insurance-Cash Surrender Value Only	$	Mo. Payments $ _____	
(Complete Section 8)		Installment Account (Other)	$
Stocks and Bonds	$	Mo. Payments $ _____	
(Describe in Section 3)		Loan on Life Insurance	$
Real Estate	$	Mortgages on Real Estate	$
(Describe in Section 4)		(Describe in Section 4)	
Automobile-Present Value	$	Unpaid Taxes	$
Other Personal Property	$	(Describe in Section 6)	
(Describe in Section 5)		Other Liabilities	$
Other Assets	$	(Describe in Section 7)	
(Describe in Section 5)		Total Liabilities	$
		Net Worth	$
Total	$	**Total**	$

Section 1. Source of Income		Contingent Liabilities	
Salary	$	As Endorser or Co-Maker	$
Net Investment Income	$	Legal Claims & Judgments	$
Real Estate Income	$	Provision for Federal Income Tax	$
Other Income (Describe below)*	$	Other Special Debt	$

Description of Other Income in Section 1.

*Alimony or child support payments need not be disclosed in "Other Income" unless it is desired to have such payments counted toward total income.

Section 2. Notes Payable to Banks and Others.   (Use attachments if necessary. Each attachment must be identified as a part of this statement and signed.)

Name and Address of Noteholder(s)	Original Balance	Current Balance	Payment Amount	Frequency (monthly,etc.)	How Secured or Endorsed Type of Collateral

SBA Form 413 (10-08) **Previous Editions Obsolete**

This form was electronically produced by Elite Federal Forms, Inc.

Personal Recycling Program   Printed on Recycled Paper

(tumble)

Section 3. Stocks and Bonds. (Use attachments if necessary. Each attachment must be identified as a part of this statement and signed).

Number of Shares	Name of Securities	Cost	Market Value Quotation/Exchange	Date of Quotation/Exchange	Total Value

Section 4. Real Estate Owned. (List each parcel separately. Use attachment if necessary. Each attachment must be identified as a part of this statement and signed.)

	Property A	Property B	Property C
Type of Property			
Address			
Date Purchased			
Original Cost			
Present Market Value			
Name & Address of Mortgage Holder			
Mortgage Account Number			
Mortgage Balance			
Amount of Payment per Month/Year			
Status of Mortgage			

Section 5. Other Personal Property and Other Assets. (Describe, and if any is pledged as security, state name and address of lien holder, amount of lien, terms of payment and if delinquent, describe delinquency)

Section 6.   Unpaid Taxes.   (Describe in detail, as to type, to whom payable, when due, amount, and to what property, if any, a tax lien attaches.)

Section 7.   Other Liabilities.   (Describe in detail.)

Section 8.   Life Insurance Held.   (Give face amount and cash surrender value of policies - name of insurance company and beneficiaries)

I authorize SBA/Lender to make inquiries as necessary to verify the accuracy of the statements made and to determine my creditworthiness. I certify the above and the statements contained in the attachments are true and accurate as of the stated date(s). These statements are made for the purpose of either obtaining a loan or guaranteeing a loan. I understand FALSE statements may result in forfeiture of benefits and possible prosecution by the U.S. Attorney General (Reference 18 U.S.C. 1001).

Signature: Date: Social Security Number:

Signature: Date: Social Security Number:

PLEASE NOTE: The estimated average burden hours for the completion of this form is 1.5 hours per response. If you have questions or comments concerning this estimate or any other aspect of this information, please contact Chief, Administrative Branch, U.S. Small Business Administration, Washington, D.C. 20416, and Clearance Officer, Paper Reduction Project (3245-0188), Office of Management and Budget, Washington, D.C. 20503. **PLEASE DO NOT SEND FORMS TO OMB.**

CHAPTER 8

HR Essentials

TTRACTING AND HIRING THE RIGHT employee for your firm is essential to your business's success. In this chapter, you will find forms and worksheets to help you attract and evaluate suitable candidates. These forms are applicable to nearly any industry. A *New Employee Welcome Letter* is included—but before it can be used—there's a lot of pre-work to be done to find the right person for the job.

You will find two employment applications, the *Application for Employment—Short Form* and the *Application for Employment—Long Form*. The short form will likely be sufficient for most hires, while the long form is more appropriate for longer-term and executive positions.

As part of the employment application process, insist that your applicants execute the *Authorization to Release Employment Applicant Information*. This important form authorizes the applicant's former employer to release information about the applicant's work history and personal characteristics.

Most former employers will insist on receiving such an authorization before divulging any information.

You will also find two versions of a *Pre-Employment Reference Check via Phone*. These two forms are scripts that you should use when making telephone contact with an applicant's former employer. If you wish to contact your applicant's former employer by letter, use the *Pre-Employment Reference Check via Letter* form.

Once you have narrowed your employee search to a handful of candidates, summarize their critical strengths and weaknesses with the *Applicant Comparison Summary Form*. Rate each candidate's qualifications for critical job requirements, such as computer skills, foreign languages, and the like. You can rate each applicant's individual skills with *Applicant Rating Form, Part One* and *Applicant Rating Form, Part Two*.

Once you have found your ideal candidate, you can use the *Offer of Employment and Employment Contract*. This form formally announces the offer of employment and documents the terms of the employment agreement. Save a copy in the employee's file. Finally, once you've secured your new employee, use the *New Employee Announcement* to announce the new employee to your other employees

Now that you've got the best candidate in the door, it's important to keep him or her there and to maintain adequate records. You should maintain a master database of your employees with the *Employee Master Database*. With this form you can maintain an accurate and convenient master list of the name, Social Security number, date of birth, address, and hire date of each current or former employee. (Always maintain records for five years after an employee leaves.) You can also maintain records of whether the employee is current or former and full- or part-time. The Employee Master Database also contains columns for whether your employees have executed an employment agreement, stock option agreement, employee handbook acknowledgment, non-disclosure agreement, and W-4 form. Once you have these documents on file, indicate this by writing "OF" in the appropriate cell.

65. New Employee Welcome Letter

Date

Dear (New Employee Name):

We're writing to welcome you to [Name of Company] and to tell you how much we are looking forward to you joining our team. Our organization will benefit from your experience, acumen, and skill set. [Name of Company] has succeeded for the past [number of years in business] as a result of our hard-working staff and overall team spirit.

Please join our employee orientation scheduled for [Date] at [Time]. [Attendees] will be present to discuss your position as well as the necessary human resource policies.

Today, your agenda is scheduled as follows:

8 am_____

9 am_____

10 am_____

11am_____

12 pm_____

1pm_____

2pm_____

3pm_____

4pm_____

5pm_____

We'd like to once again welcome you to [Name of Company]! I am available at any time to answer questions.

Best Regards,

(Name of Manager)

66. Application for Employment–Short Form

Our policy is to provide equal employment opportunity to all qualified persons without regard to race, creed, color, religious belief, sex, age, national origin, ancestry, physical or mental disability, or veteran status.

Name

Last _____ First _____ Middle_____

Date _____

Street Address _____

City _____ State _____ ZIP _____

Telephone _____

Social Security # _____

Position applied for _____

How did you hear of this opening? _____

When can you start? _____ Desired Wage $_____

Are you a U.S. citizen or otherwise authorized to work in the U.S. on an unrestricted basis? (You may be required to provide documentation.) ❏ Yes ❏ No

Are you looking for full-time employment? ❏ Yes   ❏ No

If no, what hours are you available? _____

Are you willing to work swing shift? ❏ Yes   ❏ No

Are you willing to work graveyard? ❏ Yes   ❏ No

Have you ever been convicted of a felony? (This will not necessarily affect your application.) ❏ Yes   ❏ No

If yes, please describe conditions. _____
_____
_____
_____
_____

Education	School Name and Location	Year	Major	Degree
High School	_____	_____	_____	_____
College	_____	_____	_____	_____
College	_____	_____	_____	_____
Post-College	_____	_____	_____	_____
Other Training	_____	_____	_____	_____

In addition to your work history, are there other skills, qualifications, or experience that we should consider?
_____
_____
_____
_____
_____
_____

Employment History (Start with most recent employer)

Company Name _____

Address _____ Telephone _____

Date Started _____ Starting Wage _____ Starting Position _____

Date Ended _____ Ending Wage _____ Ending Position _____

Name of Supervisor _____

May we contact? ❏ Yes ❏ No

Responsibilities _____

Reason for leaving _____

Company Name _____

Address _____ Telephone _____

Date Started _____ Starting Wage _____ Starting Position _____

Date Ended _____ Ending Wage _____ Ending Position _____

Name of Supervisor _____

May we contact? ❏ Yes ❏ No

Responsibilities _____

Reason for leaving _____

Company Name _____

Address _____ Telephone _____

Date Started _____ Starting Wage _____ Starting Position _____

Date Ended _____ Ending Wage _____ Ending Position _____

Name of Supervisor _____

May we contact? ❏ Yes ❏ No

Responsibilities _____

Reason for leaving _____

Attach additional information if necessary.

I certify that the facts set forth in this application for employment are true and complete to the best of my knowledge. I understand that if I am employed, false statements on this application shall be considered sufficient cause for dismissal. This company is hereby authorized to make any investigations of my prior educational and employment history.

I understand that employment at this company is "at will," which means that either I or this company can terminate the employment relationship at any time, with or without prior notice, and for any reason not prohibited by statute. All employment is continued on that basis. I understand that no supervisor, manager, or executive of this company, other than the president, has any authority to alter the foregoing.

Signature_____ Date _____

67. Application for Employment–Long Form

Our policy is to provide equal employment opportunity to all qualified persons without regard to race, creed, color, religious belief, sex, age, national origin, ancestry, physical or mental disability, or veteran status.

Name
Last _____ First _____ Middle_____
Date _____
Street Address _____
City _____ State _____ ZIP _____
Telephone _____
Social Security # _____

Position applied for _____
How did you hear of this opening? _____
When can you start? _____ Desired Wage $_____

Are you a U.S. citizen or otherwise authorized to work in the U.S. on an unrestricted basis? (You may be required to provide documentation.) ❑ Yes ❑ No
Are you looking for full-time employment? ❑ Yes ❑ No
If no, what hours are you available? _____
Are you willing to work swing shift? ❑ Yes ❑ No
Are you willing to work graveyard? ❑ Yes ❑ No

Have you ever been convicted of a felony? (This will not necessarily affect your application.) ❑ Yes ❑ No
If yes, please describe conditions. _____
_____
_____
_____
_____

Employment Desired
Have you ever applied for employment here? ❑ Yes ❑ No
When? _____
Where?_____
Have you ever been employed by this company? ❑ Yes ❑ No
When? _____
Where?_____
Are you presently employed? ❑ Yes ❑ No
May we contact your present employer? ❑ Yes ❑ No
Are you available for full-time work? ❑ Yes ❑ No
Are you available for part-time work? ❑ Yes ❑ No
Will you relocate? ❑ Yes ❑ No
Are you willing to travel? ❑ Yes ❑ No If yes, what percent? _____
Date you can start _____
Desired position _____

Desired starting salary _____

Please list applicable skills _____

_____

_____

Education: School Name and Location   Year   Major Degree

High School _____   _____ _____ _____

College _____   _____ _____ _____

College _____   _____ _____ _____

Post-College _____   _____ _____ _____

Other Training _____   _____ _____ _____

In addition to your work history, are there other skills, qualifications, or experience that we should consider?

_____

_____

_____

_____

_____

Please list any scholastic honors received and offices held in school.

_____

_____

Are you planning to continue your studies? ❏ Yes ❏ No

If yes, where and what courses of study?

_____

_____

Company Name _____

Address _____ Telephone _____

Date Started _____ Starting Wage _____ Starting Position _____

Date Ended _____ Ending Wage _____ Ending Position _____

Name of Supervisor _____

May we contact? ❏ Yes ❏ No

Responsibilities _____

_____

Reason for leaving _____

Company Name _____

Address _____ Telephone _____

Date Started _____ Starting Wage _____ Starting Position _____

Date Ended _____ Ending Wage _____ Ending Position _____

Name of Supervisor _____

May we contact? ❏ Yes ❏ No

Responsibilities _____

_____

Reason for leaving _____

Company Name _____

Address _____ Telephone _____

Date Started _____ Starting Wage _____ Starting Position _____

Date Ended _____ Ending Wage _____ Ending Position _____

Name of Supervisor _____

May we contact? ❏ Yes   ❏ No

Responsibilities _____

_____

Reason for leaving _____

Company Name _____

Address _____ Telephone _____

Date Started _____ Starting Wage _____ Starting Position _____

Date Ended _____ Ending Wage _____ Ending Position _____

Name of Supervisor _____

May we contact? ❏ Yes   ❏ No

Responsibilities _____

_____

Reason for leaving _____

Company Name _____

Address _____ Telephone _____

Date Started _____ Starting Wage _____ Starting Position _____

Date Ended _____ Ending Wage _____ Ending Position _____

Name of Supervisor _____

May we contact? ❏ Yes   ❏ No

Responsibilities _____

_____

Reason for leaving _____

Company Name _____

Address _____ Telephone _____

Date Started _____ Starting Wage _____ Starting Position _____

Date Ended _____ Ending Wage _____ Ending Position _____

Name of Supervisor _____

May we contact? ❏ Yes   ❏ No

Responsibilities _____

_____

Reason for leaving _____

References

List three personal references, not related to you, who have known you for more than one year.

Name _____ Phone _____Years Known_____

Address _____

Name _____ Phone _____ Years Known_____
Address _____

Name _____ Phone _____ Years Known_____
Address _____

Emergency Contact

In case of emergency, please notify:_____

Name _____ Phone _____
Address _____

Name _____ Phone _____
Address _____

Please Read Before Signing:

I certify that all information provided by me on this application is true and complete to the best of my knowledge and that I have withheld nothing that, if disclosed, would alter the integrity of this application.

I authorize my previous employers, schools, or persons listed as references to give any information regarding employment or educational record. I agree that this company and my previous employers will not be held liable in any respect if a job offer is not extended, or is withdrawn, or employment is terminated because of false statements, omissions, or answers made by myself on this application. In the event of any employment with this company, I will comply with all rules and regulations as set by the company in any communication distributed to the employees.

In compliance with the Immigration Reform and Control Act of 1986, I understand that I am required to provide approved documentation to the company that verifies my right to work in the United States on the first day of employment. I have received from the company a list of the approved documents that are required.

I understand that employment at this company is "at will," which means that either I or this company can terminate the employment relationship at any time, with or without prior notice, and for any reason not prohibited by statute. All employment is continued on that basis. I hereby acknowledge that I have read and understand the above statements.

Signature _____ Date _____

Immigration Reform and Control Act Requirement

In compliance with the Immigration Reform and Control Act of 1986, you are required to provide approved documentation that verifies your right to work in the United States prior to your employment with this company. Please be prepared to provide us with the following documentation in the event you are offered and accept employment with our company:

Any one of the following: (These establish both identity and employment authorization.)
1. U.S. Passport.

2. Certificate of U.S. Citizenship (issued by USCIS).
3. Certificate of Naturalization (issued by USCIS).
4. Resident alien card or other alien unexpired endorsement card, with photo or other approved identifying information which evidences employment authorization.
5. Unexpired foreign passport with unexpired endorsement authorizing employment.

Or one from List A and List B:

List A (These establish employment authorization.)
1. Social Security card.
2. Birth Certificate or other documentation that establishes U.S. nationality or birth.
3. Other approved documentation.

List B
1. Driver's license or similar government identification card with photo or other approved identifying information.
2. Other approved documentation of identity for applicants under age 16 or in a state that does not issue an I.D. card (other than a driver's license).

68. Authorization to Release Employment Applicant Information

Employment Applicant:

_____

_____

_____

_____

To:

_____

_____

_____

_____

I have applied for a position with _____.

I have been requested to provide information for their use in reviewing my background and qualifications. Therefore, I authorize the investigation of my past and present work, character, education, military, and employment qualifications.

The release in any manner of all information by you is authorized, whether such information is of record or not, and I do hereby release all persons, agencies, firms, companies, etc., from any damages resulting from providing such information.

This authorization is valid for 90 days from the date of my signature below. Please keep this copy of my release request for your files. Thank you for your cooperation.

Signature_____ Date_____

Note: Medical information is often protected by state laws and civil codes. Consult your attorney if you wish to seek this information.

Note: Many employers are reluctant to provide information on previous employees. If you ask each applicant to distribute this form to his or her references before you contact them, the prior employers may be more willing to release information.

69. Pre-Employment Reference Check via Phone

Applicant's Name_____ Applying for_____

"My name is _____ from _____Company.
_____ has applied for a position with our company.
I would like to verify the information provided us by _____
and _____ has given us permission to contact you."

Person Contacted_____ Company_____

Phone_____ ❏ Personnel Department ❏ Ex-Supervisor ❏ Other _____

Comments: _____
_____

Job Title _____
Employment Date _____
Job Responsibilities _____
Attendance _____
Rehire _____

Person Contacted_____ Company_____
Phone_____ ❏ Personnel Department ❏ Ex-Supervisor ❏ Other _____
Comments: _____
_____

Job Title _____
Employment Date _____
Job Responsibilities _____
Attendance _____
Rehire _____

Person Contacted_____ Company_____
Phone_____ ❏ Personnel Department ❏ Ex-Supervisor ❏ Other _____
Comments: _____
_____

Job Title _____
Employment Date _____
Job Responsibilities _____
Attendance _____
Rehire _____

References Checked by _____ Date _____

Checker's Comments _____
_____
_____

70. Pre-Employment Reference Check via Letter

From:

_____

_____

_____

To:

_____

_____

_____

We would appreciate your assistance in verifying the information listed below regarding an employment application. It is to be understood that all information is confidential and will be treated as such in our company personnel files. Attached, please find an authorization to release information signed by the applicant. A self-addressed, stamped envelope is enclosed for your convenience in replying. We appreciate your assistance in this matter. Thank you.

Yours truly,

Personnel Manager

The following information was provided to us by the applicant. Please make any appropriate corrections:
Name _____ SS # _____
Job Title _____ Final Salary $_____
Date of Employment _____
Reason for Termination

_____

Please complete the following requested information:
Would you rehire this applicant? ❑ Yes   ❑ No
If no, why not? _____

Please review and rate the applicant in these areas:

	Unsatisfactory		Average		Outstanding
Attendance	1	2	3	4	5
Quality of work	1	2	3	4	5
Quantity of work	1	2	3	4	5
Cooperation	1	2	3	4	5
Responsibility	1	2	3	4	5

Signed _____ Title _____ Date _____

71. Applicant Comparison Summary Form

Position_____ Date Interviewed _____

Interviewed
by_____

Candidate
1_____

Candidate
2_____

Candidate
3_____

Candidate
4_____

Critical Job Requirements	Candidate #1	#2	#3	#4	Comments

Legend:
✓ Meets critical job requirements
+ Exceeds critical job requirements
− Does not meet critical job requirements

72. Applicant Rating Form, Part One

Applicant's Name _____

Position and Department _____

Interviewed by _____ Date _____

Critical Job Requirements	Below Average			Average		Above Average			Excellent	
_____	1	2	3	4	5	6	7	8	9	10
_____	1	2	3	4	5	6	7	8	9	10
_____	1	2	3	4	5	6	7	8	9	10
_____	1	2	3	4	5	6	7	8	9	10
_____	1	2	3	4	5	6	7	8	9	10
_____	1	2	3	4	5	6	7	8	9	10
_____	1	2	3	4	5	6	7	8	9	10
_____	1	2	3	4	5	6	7	8	9	10
_____	1	2	3	4	5	6	7	8	9	10
_____	1	2	3	4	5	6	7	8	9	10
_____	1	2	3	4	5	6	7	8	9	10
_____	1	2	3	4	5	6	7	8	9	10
_____	1	2	3	4	5	6	7	8	9	10
_____	1	2	3	4	5	6	7	8	9	10
_____	1	2	3	4	5	6	7	8	9	10
_____	1	2	3	4	5	6	7	8	9	10
_____	1	2	3	4	5	6	7	8	9	10

Comments:

Strong Points _____

_____

Weak Areas _____

_____

Other _____

_____

73. Applicant Rating Form, Part Two

Applicant's Name _____

Position and Department _____

Interviewed by _____ Date _____

Job Experience:	Poor				Outstanding
Relevance to Position	1	2	3	4	5
Accomplishments	1	2	3	4	5
Analytical/Problem Solving	1	2	3	4	5
Leadership	1	2	3	4	5
Career Goals	1	2	3	4	5

Academics:					
Relevance of Studies to Job	1	2	3	4	5
Extent, Variety in Activities	1	2	3	4	5
Abilities as a Student	1	2	3	4	5

Characteristics:					
Grooming	1	2	3	4	5
Bearing	1	2	3	4	5
Initiative	1	2	3	4	5
Grasp of Ideas	1	2	3	4	5
Stability	1	2	3	4	5
Personality	1	2	3	4	5

Preparation for Interview:					
Knowledge of Company	1	2	3	4	5
Relevance of Questions	1	2	3	4	5

Summary of Strength and Shortcomings:

Talent, Skills, Knowledge, Energy _____

_____

Motivation, Interests _____

_____

Personal Qualities, Effectiveness _____

_____

Other Comments _____

_____

74. Offer of Employment and Employment Contract

Date

Employee Name _____

Address _____

_____

Dear _____:

We are pleased to offer you a position with _____ ("Company"). Your start date, manager, compensation, benefits, and other terms of employment will be as set forth below and on EXHIBIT A.

TERMS OF EMPLOYMENT

1. **Position and Duties.** Company shall employ you, and you agree to competently and professionally perform such duties as are customarily the responsibility of the position as set forth in the job description attached as EXHIBIT A and as reasonably assigned to you from time to time by your Manager as set forth in EXHIBIT A.

2. **Outside Business Activities.** During your employment with Company, you shall devote competent energies, interests, and abilities to the performance of your duties under this Agreement. During the term of this Agreement, you shall not, without Company's prior written consent, render any services to others for compensation or engage or participate, actively or passively, in any other business activities that would interfere with the performance of your duties hereunder or compete with Company's business.

3. **Employment Classification.** You shall be a Full-Time Employee and shall not be entitled to benefits except as specifically outlined herein.

4. **Compensation/Benefits.**
   4.1 Wage. Company shall pay you the wage as set forth in the job description attached as EXHIBIT A.
   4.2 Reimbursement of Expenses. You shall be reimbursed for all reasonable and necessary expenses paid or incurred by you in the performance of your duties. You shall provide Company with original receipts for such expenses.
   4.3 Withholdings. All compensation paid to you under this Agreement, including payment of salary and taxable benefits, shall be subject to such withholdings as may be required by law or Company's general practices.
   4.4 Benefits. You will also receive Company's standard employee benefits package (including health insurance), and will be subject to Company's vacation policy as such package and policy are in effect from time to time.

5. **At-Will Employment.** Either party may terminate this Agreement by written notice at any time for any reason or for no reason. This Agreement is intended to be and shall be deemed to be an at-will employment Agreement and does not constitute a guarantee of continuing employment for any term.

6. **Nondisclosure Agreement.** You agree to sign Company's standard Employee Nondisclosure Agreement and Proprietary Rights Assignment as a condition of your employment. We wish to impress upon you that we do not wish you to bring with you any confidential or proprietary material of any former employer or to violate any other obligation to your former employers.

7. **Authorization to Work.** Because of federal regulations adopted in the Immigration Reform and Control Act of 1986, you will need to present documentation demonstrating that you have authorization to work in the United States.

8. **Further Assurances.** Each party shall perform any and all further acts and execute and deliver any documents that are reasonably necessary to carry out the intent of this Agreement.

9. **Notices.** All notices or other communications required or permitted by this Agreement or by law shall be in writing and shall be deemed duly served and given when delivered personally or by facsimile, air courier, certified mail (return receipt requested), postage and fees prepaid, to the party at the address indicated in the signature block or at such other address as a party may request in writing.

10. **Governing Law.** This Agreement shall be governed and interpreted in accordance with the laws of the State of California, as such laws are applied to agreements between residents of California to be performed entirely within the State of California.

11. **Entire Agreement.** This Agreement sets forth the entire Agreement between the parties pertaining to the subject matter hereof and supersedes all prior written agreements and all prior or contemporaneous oral Agreements and understandings, expressed or implied.

12. **Written Modification and Waiver.** No modification to this Agreement, nor any waiver of any rights, shall be effective unless assented to in writing by the party to be charged, and the waiver of any breach or default shall not constitute a waiver of any other right or any subsequent breach or default.

13. **Assignment.** This Agreement is personal in nature, and neither of the parties shall, without the consent of the other, assign or transfer this Agreement or any rights or obligations under this Agreement, except that Company may assign or transfer this Agreement to a successor of Company's business, in the event of the transfer or sale of all or substantially all of the assets of Company's business, or to a subsidiary, provided that in the case of any assignment or transfer under the terms of this Section, this Agreement shall be binding on and inure to the benefit of the successor of Company's business, and the successor of Company's business shall discharge and perform all of the obligations of Company under this Agreement.

14. **Severability.** If any of the provisions of this Agreement are determined to be invalid, illegal, or unenforceable, such provisions shall be modified to the minimum extent necessary to make such provisions enforceable, and the remaining provisions shall continue in full force and effect to the extent the economic benefits conferred upon the parties by this Agreement remain substantially unimpaired.

15. **Arbitration of Disputes.** Any controversy or claim arising out of or relating to this contract, or the breach thereof, shall be settled by arbitration administered by the American Arbitration Association under its National Rules for the Resolution of Employment Disputes, and judgment upon the award rendered by the arbitrator(s) may be entered by any court having jurisdiction thereof.

We look forward to your arrival and the start of a long and mutually satisfying work relationship.

Sincerely,

Company

By: _____

Date: _____

Acknowledged, Accepted, and Agreed

_____

Employee Signature

75. New Employee Announcement

Date _____

To: All Employees

From: _____

Subject: New Employee

I am pleased to announce that _____ (new employee name) has joined our staff as a _____ (job title).

In his/her new position, _____ will report to_____.

Our new employee comes to us from _____ (last employer), where he/she was _____ (job title and major responsibilities) and prior to that was _____ (job title and major responsibilities).

Please join me in welcoming our new employee to our staff and in wishing him/her much success!

76. Employee Master Database

Employee File Information

OF = On File

Current Employee	Name	SS Number	DOB	Home Address	Date Hired	Full/Part Time	Employm't Contract	Stock Opt. Agreement	Emp Hdbk Ack	Signed NDA	W-4 on File	US Dept Just EEV

CHAPTER 9

Contracts and Agreements

S A BUSINESS OWNER, YOU WILL RECEIVE and administer all kinds of contracts and agreements, the most common legal transactions you will be involved in when running a business. Properly executed contracts provide grounds to legally enforce and dispute business matters.

The surest way to maintain clear understandings with your customers and vendors is to document your arrangements in written agreements. We have included here several useful and universal contracts and agreements.

Use the *Bill of Sale* to record the terms of a simple sale of goods or property. The *Unsecured Promissory Note* is a legal document that documents a promise to pay money at a future date. Use this document to memorialize simple business or personal loans. The *Secured Promissory Note and Security Agreement* is a legal document that memorializes a loan, but it goes a step farther: it grants to the lender the right to repossess property in the event the loan is not repaid. The *Secured*

Promissory Note and Security Agreement gives the lender greater rights and power than the *Unsecured Promissory Note*.

The *Consulting Services Agreement* is a general and universal agreement suitable for nearly all types of consulting services firms. Customize the agreement to cover the particular services that you offer.

The *Multimedia Development Contract* is a contract suitable for use by Web developers, programmers, and print and graphic designers. Keep in mind, however, that you'll need to customize the contract to cover the particular services you offer.

The *Mutual Compromise Agreement and Mutual Release* is an agreement to finally and forever settle a dispute between two parties. Use this agreement to finalize the resolution of conflicts and lawsuits between you and third parties.

Use the *Checklist for a Buyer's Purchase Order* for quality assurance, knowing that the final order is correct in its wording as to all terms and conditions. The *Checklist for Modi-*

fying or Extending an Existing Contracts to ensure the changes you make to a signed agreement are compliant and correctly communicate all amendments, redefined terms, and other changes.

If your company is the seller, refer to the *Checklist for Purchase Orders Where Your Company Is the Seller* to confirm you've clearly established the terms and conditions of the sale including pricing, loss assessment, shipping, and delivery dates.

Use the *Checklist for Sales Agreements Where Your Company is the Seller* to ensure the correct legal name of parties, effective dates of the contract are set, the terms, and more.

Refer to the sample *Terms of Purchase* to help you establish the contractual obligations of the buy. In addition, the seller can use the sample *Terms of Sale* form to establish the delivery and payment terms agreed on between your company and the buyer.

If your contract will require legal counsel, refer to the *Examples of Legal "Boilerplate"* for assigning a lawyer, lawyer fees, and venue, and defining the overall legal contract.

The *Lawyer Engagement Letter* can be used as a sample letter to request legal representation from your chosen firm. Once your company is set to work with outside counsel, refer to the *Terms and Conditions for Outside Legal Counsel* to establish the framework of the relationship.

Finally, if your company requires outside service that may involve diagnostic testing and/or the use of specialized equipment, use the sample *Service Evaluation and Repair Agreement* to document the description of work, costs, liability, and warranties.

77. Bill of Sale

BILL OF SALE

This Bill of Sale is made on this _____ day of 20___ between _____ ("Seller") and _____ ("Buyer").

Seller, in exchange for consideration of $_____, the receipt of which funds is acknowledged, hereby do grant, sell, transfer, and deliver to Buyer the following goods: _____.

Buyer shall have full rights and title to the goods described above.

Seller is the lawful owner of the goods and the goods are free from all encumbrances. Seller has good right to sell the goods and will warrant and defend the right against the lawful claims and demands of all persons.

_____

Signature of Seller

_____

Signature of Buyer

78. Unsecured Promissory Note

UNSECURED PROMISSORY NOTE

Amount: $_____

Date: _____

For value received, _____ ("Borrower") hereby covenants and promises to pay to _____ ("Lender") _____ Dollars ($_____.00) in lawful money of the United States of America, together with interest thereon computed from the date hereof at the rate of ten percent (10%) per annum, on an actual day/365 day basis. All interest, principal, and other costs hereunder shall be due and payable to the holder ("Holder") of this Promissory Note (this "Note") on or before _____ (the "Due Date").

Payments of principal and interest will be made in legal tender of the United States of America. Borrower shall have the right to prepay without penalty all or any part of the unpaid balance of this Note at any time. Borrower shall not be entitled to re-borrow any prepaid amounts of the principal, interest, or other costs or charges. All payments made pursuant to this Note will be first applied to accrued and unpaid interest, if any, then to other proper charges under this Note, and the balance, if any, to principal.

This Note shall be paid as follows: monthly payments of $_____ shall be made upon this Note on the first day of each month, commencing with the date of _____, and shall continue until _____ (the "Repayment Date"), at which time all sums due hereunder shall be paid.

Notwithstanding anything in this Note to the contrary, the entire unpaid principal amount of this Note, together with all accrued but unpaid interest thereon and other unpaid charges hereunder, will become immediately all due and payable without further notice at the option of the Holder if Borrower fails to timely make any payment hereunder when such payment becomes first due and such failure continues for a period of ten days after written notice from Holder to Borrower.

If any amount payable to Holder under this Note is not received by Holder on or before the Due Date, then such amount (the "Delinquent Amount") will bear interest from and after the Due Date until paid at an annual rate of interest equal to the greater of (i) fifteen percent (15%) or (ii) the maximum rate then permitted by law (the "Default Rate"). If the maximum rate then permitted by law is lower than 15%, the maximum legal rate shall be the Default Rate.

All rights, remedies, undertakings, obligations, options, covenants, conditions, and agreements contained in this Note are cumulative and no one of them will be exclusive of any other. Any notice to any party concerning this Note will be delivered as set forth in the Financing Agreement.

Borrower for itself and its legal representatives, successors, and assigns expressly waives presentment, protest, demand, notice of dishonor, notice of nonpayment, notice of maturity, notice of protest, presentment for the purpose of accelerating maturity, and diligence in collection, and consents that Holder may extend the time for payment or otherwise modify the terms of payment or any part or the whole of the debt evidenced hereby.

The prevailing party in any action, litigation, or proceeding, including any appeal or the collection of any judgment concerning this Note, will be awarded, in addition to any damages, injunctions, or other relief, and without regard to whether or not such matter be prosecuted to final judgment, such party's costs and expenses, including reasonable attorneys' fees, and Lender shall be entitled to recover all of its attorneys' fees and costs should Lender place this Note in the hands of an attorney for collection.

_____ ("Borrower")

Signature _____

Date _____

79. Secured Promissory Note and Security Agreement

SECURED PROMISSORY NOTE

Amount: $_____

Date: _____

For value received, _____ ("Borrower") hereby covenants and promises to pay to _____ ("Lender") _____ Dollars ($_____) in lawful money of the United States of America, together with interest thereon computed from the date hereof at the rate of ten percent (10%) per annum, on an actual day/365 day basis. All interest, principal, and other costs hereunder shall be due and payable to the holder ("Holder") of this Promissory Note (this "Note") on or before _____ (the "Due Date").

Payments of principal and interest will be made in legal tender of the United States of America. Borrower shall have the right to prepay without penalty all or any part of the unpaid balance of this Note at any time. Borrower shall not be entitled to re-borrow any prepaid amounts of the principal, interest, or other costs or charges. All payments made pursuant to this Note will be first applied to accrued and unpaid interest, if any, then to other proper charges under this Note, and the balance, if any, to principal.

This Note is secured by a security interest in Borrower's assets, as more particularly described in the Security Agreement attached to this Note.

This Note shall be paid as follows: monthly payments of $_____ shall be made upon this Note on the first day of each month, commencing with the date of _____, and shall continue until _____ (the "Repayment Date"), at which time all sums due hereunder shall be paid.

Notwithstanding anything in this Note to the contrary, the entire unpaid principal amount of this Note, together with all accrued but unpaid interest thereon and other unpaid charges hereunder, will become immediately all due and payable without further notice at the option of the Holder if Borrower fails to timely make any payment hereunder when such payment becomes first due and such failure continues for a period of ten days after written notice from Holder to Borrower.

If any amount payable to Holder under this Note is not received by Holder on or before the Due Date, then such amount (the "Delinquent Amount") will bear interest from and after the Due Date until paid at an annual rate of interest equal to the greater of (i) fifteen percent (15%) or (ii) the maximum rate then permitted by law (the "Default Rate"). If the maximum rate then permitted by law is lower than 15%, the maximum legal rate shall be the Default Rate.

All rights, remedies, undertakings, obligations, options, covenants, conditions, and agreements contained in this Note are cumulative and no one of them will be exclusive of any other. Any notice to any party concerning this Note will be delivered as set forth in the Financing Agreement.

Borrower for itself and its legal representatives, successors, and assigns expressly waives presentment, protest, demand, notice of dishonor, notice of nonpayment, notice of maturity, notice of protest, presentment for the purpose of accelerating maturity, and diligence in collection and consents that Holder may extend the time for payment or otherwise modify the terms of payment or any part or the whole of the debt evidenced hereby.

The prevailing party in any action, litigation, or proceeding, including any appeal or the collection of any judgment concerning this Note, will be awarded, in addition to any damages, injunctions, or other relief, and without regard to whether or not such matter be prosecuted to final judgment, such party's costs and expenses, including reasonable attorneys' fees, and Lender shall be entitled to recover all of its attorneys' fees and costs should Lender place this Note in the hands of an attorney for collection.

_____ ("Borrower")

Signature _____

Date _____

This Security Agreement is made on this _____ day of _____ between _____
("Borrower") and _____ ("Lender").

SECURITY AGREEMENT ACCOMPANYING SECURED PROMISSORY NOTE

1. Security Interest. Borrower grants to Lender a "Security Interest" in the following property (the "Collateral"):

_____

_____

_____

_____

_____

The Security Interest shall secure the payment and performance of Borrower's promissory note of given date herewith in the principal amount of _____ Dollars ($_____) and the payment and performance of all other liabilities and obligations of Borrower to Lender of every kind and description, direct or indirect, absolute or contingent, due or to become due, now existing or hereafter arising.

2. Covenants. Borrower hereby warrants and covenants:

   a. The parties intend that the collateral is and will at all times remain personal property despite the fact and irrespective of the manner in which it is attached to realty.

   b. The Borrower will not sell, dispose, or otherwise transfer the collateral or any interest therein without the prior written consent of Lender, and the Borrower shall keep the collateral free from unpaid charges (including rent), taxes, and liens.

   c. The Borrower shall execute alone or with Lender any Financing Statement or other document or procure any document, and pay the cost of filing the same in all public offices wherever filing is deemed by Lender to be necessary.

   d. Borrower shall maintain insurance at all times with respect to all collateral against risks of fire, theft, and other such risks and in such amounts as Lender may require. The policies shall be payable to both the Lender and the Borrower as their interests appear and shall provide for ten (10) days' written notice of cancellation to Lender.

e. The Borrower shall make all repairs, replacements, additions, and improvements necessary to maintain any equipment in good working order and condition. At its option, Lender may discharge taxes, liens, or other encumbrances at any time levied or placed on the collateral, may pay rent or insurance due on the collateral, and may pay for the maintenance and preservation of the collateral. Borrower agrees to reimburse Lender on demand for any payment made or any expense incurred by Lender pursuant to the foregoing authorization.

3. Default. The Borrower shall be in default under this Agreement if it is in default under the Note. Upon default and at any time thereafter, Lender may declare all obligations secured hereby immediately due and payable and shall have the remedies of a Lender under the Uniform Commercial Code. Lender may require the Borrower to make it available to Lender at a place that is mutually convenient. No waiver by Lender of any default shall operate as a waiver of any other default or of the same default on a future occasion. This Agreement shall inure to the benefit of and bind the heirs, executors, administrators, successors, and assigns of the parties. This Agreement shall have the effect of an instrument under seal.

_____ ("Borrower")

Signature _____

Date_____

80. Consulting Services Agreement

CONSULTING SERVICES AGREEMENT

This Consulting Services Agreement (this "Agreement") is hereby made between
_____ ("Client") and _____ ("Consultant"). Consultant agrees to provide the "Services," as more fully defined below, to Client and Client agrees to pay to Consultant the Consultant Services Fee, as more fully defined below.

1. Definitions. The following definitions shall apply to this Agreement.

   a. The "Services Fee Payment Schedule" (if applicable) shall include the compensation outlined in Exhibit A, and shall be paid according to the terms outlined in the table attached to this Agreement as Exhibit B.

   b. The "Agreement Term" shall begin with the Commencement Date and shall end with the Termination Date.

   c. The "Commencement Date" shall be the later of (i) the last date upon which a party executes this Agreement or (ii) the first date upon which Services are rendered.

   d. The "Termination Date" shall be any of the following: (i) the one-year anniversary of the Commencement Date or (ii) the date of receipt by either party of a Termination Notice.

2. Services. Consultant shall perform the duties and tasks outlined in the table attached to this Agreement as Exhibit C (the "Services"). The Services may include a development schedule and milestones.

3. Payment. Client shall pay the "Consulting Services Fee" as outlined in the table attached to this Agreement as Exhibit A, and shall pay such Consulting Services Fee according to the "Services Fee Payment Schedule" (if applicable) as outlined in the table attached to this Agreement as Exhibit B.

4. Termination. Either party may without cause terminate this Agreement by delivering to the other party written notice via U.S. Mail, facsimile, or personal delivery (but not by electronic mail transmission) expressing a desire to terminate this Agreement (a "Termination Notice"). Termination shall be effective immediately upon receipt of a Termination Notice.

5. Representations and Warranties. The parties to this Agreement make the following representations and warranties.

   a. Both parties represent and warrant to the other party that they have the full power to enter into this agreement without restriction.

   b. This Agreement shall not establish an employer/employee relationship between the parties. Consultant shall be an independent contractor and shall not enjoy the benefits normally afforded to employees provided either by Client's policy or by law.

   c. Consultant shall not include in the Material (as defined in Paragraph 5, below) any copyrights, trade secrets, trademarks, service marks, patents, or other property that to the Consultant's knowledge would infringe on the rights of third parties.

   d. Consultant shall not be an agent or representative of Client, except as specifically defined in this Agreement. Consultant shall have no authority to, and shall not attempt to, bind Client to contracts with third parties.

6. Confidential Information. Neither party shall, at any time, either directly or indirectly, use for its own benefit, nor shall it divulge, disclose, or communicate any information received from the other party that has been identified as Confidential. Both parties agree to execute standard nondisclosure agreements in connection with this Agreement.

7. Copyrights. Consultant, in the absence of any agreement to the contrary, agrees to irrevocably assign and convey to Client all rights, title, and interest to the copyrights, trade secrets, trademarks, service marks, patents, or other property created or to be created in connection with the performance of the Services (the "Material"). Client shall be deemed the author of such material and the Material shall be a "work for hire" as defined in 17 U.S.C. § 201 and the cases interpreting it.

8. Limitation of Damages. NEITHER PARTY SHALL BE LIABLE TO THE OTHER PARTY FOR ANY INCIDENTAL, CONSEQUENTIAL, SPECIAL, OR PUNITIVE DAMAGES OF ANY KIND OR NATURE, INCLUDING, WITHOUT LIMITATION, THE BREACH OF THIS AGREEMENT OR ANY TERMINATION OF THIS AGREEMENT, WHETHER SUCH LIABILITY IS ASSERTED ON THE BASIS OF CONTRACT, TORT, OR OTHERWISE, EVEN IF EITHER PARTY HAS BEEN WARNED OR WARNED OF THE POSSIBILITY OF ANY SUCH LOSS OR DAMAGE.

9. General Provisions. This Agreement constitutes the entire agreement of the parties and supersedes all prior understandings and agreements of the parties, whether oral or written. If any provision of this Agreement shall be held to be invalid or unenforceable for any reason, (i) the remaining provisions shall continue to be valid and enforceable; or (ii) if by limiting such provision it would become valid and enforceable, then such provision shall be deemed to be written, construed, and enforced as so limited. This Agreement shall be governed by the laws of the State of California. This Agreement is to be performed in (and venue shall lie exclusively in) _____ County, _____. This Agreement shall not be strictly construed against any party to this Agreement. Any controversy or claim arising out of or relating to this Agreement, or the breach thereof, shall be resolved by either (i) adjudication in a small claims court (subject to jurisdictional limitations) or (ii) in binding arbitration administered under the rules of the American Arbitration Association in accordance with its applicable rules.

Date _____   Date _____

_____   _____
Consultant   Client

Exhibit A: The "Consulting Services Fee" shall include the following payments and shall be according to the terms outlined herein:

The "Consulting Services Fee" shall include:

$_____, payable per hour for the time that Consultant devotes to the performance of the Services and for which written itemization for individual tasks is provided to Client (the "Hourly Rate"). The Hourly Rate shall be recorded in increments of time no greater than 1/10 of an hour (6 minutes). Payment shall be made within 15 days of the receipt of a written invoice by Client.

The "Consulting Services Fee" shall include:

$_____, payable in cash, by negotiable draft(s), or by transfer(s) to Client's bank account, according to the Services Fee Payment Schedule, which appears as Exhibit B.

Exhibit B: The "Services Fee Payment Schedule" shall include the following payments and according to the terms outlined herein:

The "Consulting Services Fee" shall be paid as follows:

$_____ shall accrue to the consultant upon the completion of each calendar month of service. Partial months shall be prorated on a daily basis. Payment shall be made within 15 days following the later of (a) the end of any applicable calendar month or (b) the submission of a written invoice to Client.

Exhibit C: The "Services" to be performed under the Agreement shall include the following:

Describe services to be performed.

81. Multimedia Development Contract

MULTIMEDIA DEVELOPMENT CONTRACT

This agreement is entered into by and between _____("Client") and _____ ("Developer") (together, the "Parties").

The effective date of this agreement is _____ ("Effective Date").

Recitals

WHEREAS, Developer offers the following services and related services: digital media design and development, corporate identity design and development, print design, Web site design and development, interactive kiosk design and development, CD-ROM design and development, logo design and development, computer graphics design and development.

WHEREAS, Client wishes to have Developer provide services for compensation.

NOW, THEREFORE, in consideration of the promises and mutual covenants and agreements set forth herein, Client and Developer agree as follows:

Definitions

"Existing Client Content" means the material provided by Client to be incorporated into the Product.

"Developer Tools" means the software tools of general application, whether owned or licensed to Developer, which are used to develop the Product.

"Development Schedule" shall be, only when applicable, as set forth in Schedule B to this Agreement, which lists the deliverable items contracted for ("Deliverables") and the deadlines for their delivery.

"Error" means, only when applicable, any failure of a Deliverable or Product to (i) meet the Specifications, if any, or (ii) to properly operate.

"Payment Schedule" shall be set forth in Schedule C to this Agreement and is the schedule by which payments under this agreement shall be made.

"Product" means the material that is the subject of this agreement, as further described in paragraph 1.1, below.

"Specifications" for the product, only when applicable, shall be set forth in Schedule A.

DEVELOPMENT AND DELIVERY OF DELIVERABLES, PAYMENT

1.1. Developer agrees to develop, on behalf of Client, the following (the "Product"): (describe what you are making, e.g., interactive Kiosk, educational CD-ROM, Web site, etc.).

1.2. Developer shall use his best efforts to develop each Deliverable and/or Product in accordance with the Specifications, if any.

1.3. All development work will be performed by Developer or his employees or by approved independent contractors who have executed confidentiality agreements, where appropriate.

1.4. Developer shall deliver all Deliverables and/or Product within the times specified in the Development Schedule and in accordance with the Specifications, if any.

1.5. Developer agrees to comply with all reasonable requests of Client as to the manner of delivery of all Deliverables, which may include delivery by electronic means.

1.6. Client agrees to pay according to the Payment Schedule.

1.7. If the Client, following the execution of this Agreement, alters the Specifications, or alters the nature and/or scope of the project as described in paragraph 1.1, or requests additional work, Developer reserves the right, upon notification to the Client, to (i) modify the Payment Schedule or (ii) charge Client on an hourly basis for the additional time at the rate of $_____ per hour.

1.8. Except as expressly provided in this Agreement or in a later writing signed by the Client, Developer shall bear all expenses arising from the performance of its obligations under this Agreement.

1.9. Except as expressly provided in this Agreement, this Agreement does not include any maintenance work on the Product or later enhancements to the product.

TESTING AND ACCEPTANCE

2.1. All Deliverables shall be thoroughly tested by Developer (if applicable) and all necessary corrections as a result of such testing shall be made, prior to delivery to Client.

2.2. When applicable, in the event that a Deliverable or Product delivered to Client has an Error, Client shall notify Developer within 7 days of delivery or shall waive its objections. Upon notification to Developer, Developer shall have 7 days to make a correction to the Deliverable or Product and present the repaired Deliverable or Product to Client. If the Payment Schedule calls for work under this Agreement to be paid by piece rate, time spent correcting Errors is to be included in the amounts in the Payment Schedule. If the Payment Schedule calls for work under this Agreement to be paid by hourly rate, time spent correcting Errors shall be billed to Client according to the hourly rate in the Payment Schedule.

COPYRIGHTS

3.1. Client will retain copyright ownership of Existing Client Content.

3.2. Developer will retain copyright ownership of the following material ("Developer's Components") to be created in the development of the Product and to include any and all of the following:

   a. Developer's existing tools, such as (source code, pre-existing code, scripts, stock images—basically your tools that you bring to the project: these should be non-negotiable items and should appear here in every contract.)

   b. Content created in connection with development of the Product, including: (simply insert the components that you are creating to which you wish to retain the rights—HTML code, source code, Java code, computer code in any language, images, animations, scripts, script code, text, logos).

3.3. Client will retain copyright ownership of, and Developer agrees to irrevocably assign and convey to Client all rights, title, and interest in the same, the following material ("Client's Components") to be created in the development of the Product and to include any and all of the following: (HTML code, source code, Java code, computer code in any language, images, animations, scripts, script code, text, logos—simply insert the components that you are creating to which you wish to give the rights).

3.4. Developer will retain copyright ownership of any copyrights not specifically granted to either party by this Agreement ("Non-specified Components").

3.5. Developer, however, grants to Client a royalty-free, worldwide, perpetual, irrevocable, non-exclusive license, with the right to sublicense through multiple tiers of sub-licensees, to use, reproduce, distribute, modify, publicly perform, and publicly display the Developer's Components and Non-specified Components in any medium and in any manner, unless such rights are specifically limited by this Agreement. This license includes the right to modify such copyrighted material.

3.6. Client, however, grants to Developer a royalty-free, worldwide, perpetual, irrevocable, non-exclusive license, to use, reproduce, distribute, modify, publicly perform, and publicly display its Existing Client Content and Client's Components (if any) for the sole and limited purpose of use in Developer's portfolio as self-promotion and not for direct commercial sale.

3.7. For the purposes of this agreement, "copyright" shall be deemed to include copyrights, trade secrets, patents, trademarks, and other intellectual property rights.

3.8. If any third party content or Developer Tools are used in the development of the Product, Developer shall be responsible for obtaining and/or paying for any necessary licenses to use third party content.

CONFIDENTIALITY

4.1. The terms of this Agreement, Existing Client Content, and other sensitive business information are confidential ("Confidential Information"). Developer and Client agree, except as authorized in writing, not to disclose to any third party Confidential Information. Developer agrees to return to Client promptly, upon completion of the Product, all Existing Client Content.

WARRANTIES, COVENANTS, AND INDEMNIFICATION

5.1. Developer represents and warrants to Client the following: (i) Developer has the full power to enter into this agreement without restriction, (ii) except with respect to Existing Client Content, and properly licensed materials, the performance, distribution, or use of the Product will not violate the rights of any third parties, and (iii) Developer agrees to defend, hold harmless, and indemnify Client and its representatives from and against all claims, defense costs, judgments, and other expenses arising out of the breach of the foregoing warranties.

5.2. Client represents and warrants to Developer the following: (i) Client has the full power to enter into this agreement without restriction, (ii) the performance of this Agreement will not violate the rights of any third parties, and (iii) Client agrees to defend, hold harmless, and indemnify Developer and its representatives from and against all claims, defense costs, judgments, and other expenses arising out of the breach of the foregoing warranties.

TERMINATION

6.1. If Developer fails to correct an Error according to paragraph 2.2 after 3 attempts, Client may terminate this agreement without making any further payments according to the Payment Schedule.

6.2. No termination of this Agreement by any party shall affect Developer's rights to receive his hourly rate for all time spent producing Deliverables and/or Product.

MISCELLANEOUS PROVISIONS

7.1. This Agreement contains the entire understanding and agreement of the parties, supersedes all prior written or oral understandings or agreements, and may not be altered, modified, or waived except in a signed writing.

7.2. EXCEPT AS PROVIDED ABOVE WITH RESPECT TO THIRD PARTY INDEMNIFICATION, NEITHER PARTY SHALL BE LIABLE TO THE OTHER PARTY FOR ANY INCIDENTAL, CONSEQUENTIAL, SPECIAL, OR PUNITIVE DAMAGES OF ANY KIND OR NATURE, INCLUDING, WITHOUT LIMITATION, THE BREACH OF THIS AGREEMENT OR ANY TERMINATION OF THIS AGREEMENT, WHETHER SUCH LIABILITY IS ASSERTED ON THE BASIS OF CONTRACT, TORT, OR OTHERWISE, EVEN IF EITHER PARTY HAS BEEN WARNED OR WARNED OF THE POSSIBILITY OF ANY SUCH LOSS OR DAMAGE.

_____

Developer

_____

Client

Schedule A

Specifications

(This will depend on the job, obviously, and may not apply to all jobs.)

Schedule B

Development Schedule

(This will depend on the job, obviously, and may not apply to all jobs.)

Schedule C

Payment Schedule

(For hourly rate:)

Developer shall be paid on an hourly basis, and his rates and billing procedures are as follows: Charges are $_____ per hour. The minimum billing increment is six minutes or 1/10 of an hour. Time spent on individual tasks is rounded up to the next 10th of an hour.

(For piece rate:)

Deliverables	**Due Date**	**Payment Due**
Down payment (1/3)	_____	$_____
Milestone 1	_____	$_____
Milestone 2	_____	$_____
Final Completion	_____	$_____
Total Payment	_____	$_____

82. Mutual Compromise Agreement and Mutual Release

THIS MUTUAL COMPROMISE AGREEMENT AND MUTUAL RELEASE ("Agreement") is entered into as of _____, by and between _____ ("Debtor") and _____ ("Creditor") (collectively "Parties or Party"). For the purposes of the Agreement, "Party" includes subsidiaries and parents of a Party and includes individuals serving as directors, officers, employees, agents, consultants, and advisors to or of a Party.

A. BACKGROUND

1. Debtor and Creditor entered into an agreement or series of agreements (the "Contract") whereby Debtor provided a series of services to Creditor for an agreed-upon fee.

2. Since the time of entering into the Contract, the Parties have determined that a settlement of the mutual obligations between them is appropriate and would best serve the interests of all of the Parties. This Agreement is intended to express the Parties' intent to equitably settle the obligations arising from or related to the Contract.

B. AGREEMENT

NOW, THEREFORE, IN CONSIDERATION OF THE FOLLOWING, THE FOREGOING, THE MUTUAL COVENANTS, PROMISES, AGREEMENTS, REPRESENTATIONS, AND RELEASES CONTAINED HEREIN, AND IN EXCHANGE FOR OTHER GOOD AND VALUABLE CONSIDERATION, THE RECEIPT, SUFFICIENCY, AND ADEQUACY OF WHICH IS HEREBY ACKNOWLEDGED, THE PARTIES HEREBY AGREE AS FOLLOWS:

1. Settlement.

    a. Debtor shall pay the following amounts to Creditor: _____, such payment to be made no later than _____ date.

    b. Debtor shall owe no further liability or obligation to Creditor in connection with any services.

2. Confidentiality. Debtor and Creditor shall keep the terms of the Agreement confidential and shall not disclose such terms to any other Party except as is necessary for the proper conduct of the disclosing Party's business.

3. No Other Payments. No additional funds shall be required to be paid or transferred by Creditor to Debtor or by Debtor to Creditor.

4. Nature and Effect of Agreement and Conditions Thereon. This Agreement consists of a compromise and settlement by the Parties of claims arising from the Contract described in Section A, Paragraph 2, above, and a release given by the Parties relinquishing their claims against the other. By executing this Agreement, the Parties intend to and do hereby extinguish the obligations heretofore existing between them and arising from that dispute.

    The nature and effect of this agreement, and the enforcement of any of the provisions found herein, is strictly conditioned upon the actions described in Paragraph 1. The shares must bear the medallion guaranteed signature of an authorized officer of the entity whose name appears on the face of the certificate and the shares must be accompanied by a resolution of the board authorizing transfer of the shares.

5. Admissions. This Agreement is not, and shall not be treated as, an admission of liability by either Party for any purpose, and shall not be admissible as evidence before any tribunal or court.

6. Compromise Agreement. The Parties hereby compromise and settle any and all past, present, or future claims, demands, obligations, or causes of action for compensatory or punitive damages, costs, losses, expenses, and compensation, whether based on tort, contract, or other theories of recovery, which the Parties have or which may later accrue to or be acquired by one Party against the other, the other's predecessors and successors in interest, heirs, and assigns, past, present, and future officers, directors, shareholders, agents, employees, parent and subsidiary organizations, affiliates, and partners, arising from the subject matter of the claim described in Section A, Paragraph 2, above, and agree that this compromise and settlement shall constitute a bar to all such claims. The Parties agree that this compromise and settlement shall constitute a bar to all past, present, and future claims arising out of the subject matter of the action described in Section A, Paragraph 2, above.

7. Release and Discharge. The Parties hereby release and discharge the other, the other's predecessors and successors in interest, heirs, and assigns, past, present, and future officers, directors, shareholders, agents, employees, parent and subsidiary organizations, affiliates, and partners from, and relinquish, any and all past, present, or future claims, demands, obligations, or causes of action for compensatory or punitive damages, costs, losses, expenses, and compensation, whether based on tort, contract, or other theories of recovery, which the Parties have or which may later accrue to or be acquired by one Party against the other arising from the subject of the claim described in Section A, Paragraph 2, above.

8. Unknown Claims. The Parties acknowledge and agree that, upon execution of the release, this Agreement applies to all claims for damages or losses that either Party may have against the other, whether those damages or losses are known or unknown, foreseen or unforeseen, and in the event that this Agreement is deemed executed in California, the Parties thereby waive application of California Civil Code Section 1542.

The Parties certify that each has read the following provisions of California Civil Code Section 1542: "A general release does not extend to claims which the creditor does not know or suspect to exist in his favor at the time of executing the release, which if known by him must have materially affected his settlement with the debtor."

The Parties understand and acknowledge that the significance and consequence of this waiver of California Civil Code Section 1542 is that even if one Party should eventually suffer additional damages arising out of the facts referred to in Section A, Paragraph 2, above, that Party will not be able to make any claim for these damages. Furthermore, the Parties acknowledge that they intend these consequences even as to claims for damages that may exist as of the date of this release but that the damaged or harmed Party does not know exist and that, if known, would materially affect that Party's decision to execute this release, regardless of whether the damaged Party's lack of knowledge is the result of ignorance, oversight, error, negligence, or any other cause.

9. Conditions of Execution. Each Party acknowledges and warrants that its execution of this compromise agreement and release is free and voluntary.

10. Representation of Understanding. All Parties and signatories to this Agreement acknowledge and agree that the terms of this Agreement are contractual and not mere recital, and all Parties and signatories

represent and warrant that they have carefully read this Agreement, have fully reviewed its provisions with their attorneys, know and understand its contents, and sign the same as their own free acts and deeds. It is understood and agreed by all Parties and signatories to this Agreement that execution of this Agreement may affect rights and liabilities of substantial extent and degree and, with the full understanding of that fact, they represent that the covenants and releases provided for in this Agreement are in their respective best interests.

11. Construction. The provisions of this Agreement shall not be construed against either Party.

12. Entire Agreement. This Agreement constitutes the entire agreement between the Parties and signatories and all prior and contemporaneous conversation, negotiations, possible and alleged agreements, and representations, covenants, and warranties, express or implied, or written, with respect to the subject matter hereof, are waived, merged herein, and superseded hereby. There are no other agreements, representations, covenants, or warranties not set forth herein. The terms of this Agreement may not be contradicted by evidence of any prior or contemporaneous agreement. The Parties further intend and agree that this Agreement constitutes the complete and exclusive statement of its terms and that no extrinsic evidence whatsoever may be introduced in any judicial or arbitration proceeding, if any, involving this Agreement. No part of this Agreement may be amended or modified in any way unless such amendment or modification is expressed in writing signed by all Parties to this Agreement.

13. Counterparts. This Agreement may be executed in multiple counterparts, each of which shall be deemed an original but all of which together shall constitute one and the same instrument. When all of the Parties and signatories have executed any copy hereof, such execution shall constitute the execution of this Agreement, whereupon it shall become effective.

14. Governing Law. THIS AGREEMENT WILL BE GOVERNED AND CONSTRUED IN ACCORDANCE WITH THE LAW OF THE STATE OF _____ AND THE UNITED STATES OF AMERICA, WITHOUT REGARD TO CONFLICT OF LAW PRINCIPLES. This Agreement shall not be strictly construed against any Party to this Agreement. Any controversy or claim arising out of or relating to this Agreement, or the breach thereof, shall be resolved by arbitration administered under the rules of the American Arbitration Association in accordance with its applicable rules. Such arbitration shall take place within San Mateo County, California, and shall be binding upon all Parties, and any judgment upon or any an award rendered by the arbitrator may be entered in any court having jurisdiction thereof.

15. Binding Effect. The provisions of this Agreement shall be binding upon and inure to the benefit of each of the Parties and their respective successors and assigns. Nothing expressed or implied in this Agreement is intended, or shall be construed, to confer upon or give any person, partnership, or corporation, other than the Parties, their successors and assigns, any benefits, rights, or remedies under or by reason of this Agreement, except to the extent of any contrary provision herein contained.

16. Authority. The Parties hereto represent and warrant that they possess the full and complete authority to covenant and agree as provided in this Agreement and, if applicable, to release other Parties and signatories as provided herein. If any Party hereto is a corporation or limited liability company, the signatory for any such corporation or limited liability company represents and warrants that such signatory possesses the authority and has been authorized by the corporation or limited liability company to enter

into this Agreement, whether by resolution of the board of, upon the instruction by an authorized officer of, as authorized in the bylaws of the corporation on whose behalf the signatory is executing this Agreement, or otherwise.

17. Severability. If any provision of this Agreement is held by a court to be unenforceable or invalid for any reason, the remaining provisions of this Agreement shall be unaffected by such holding.

18. Exchanges by Fax. The exchange of a fully executed Agreement in counterparts or otherwise by fax shall be sufficient to bind the Parties to the terms and conditions of this Agreement.

IN WITNESS WHEREOF, the Parties and signatories execute this Agreement on the dates indicated.

_____, "Debtor"

Date _____

Signature _____

_____, "Creditor"

Date _____

Signature _____

83. Checklist for a Buyer's Purchase Order

❑ Definitions for capitalized terms

❑ Limit right to take actions affecting agreement to authorized buyer and member of management

❑ Order acceptance
- On written acceptance from seller
- On expiration of time period
- On shipment
- Payment not final acceptance
- Acceptance not waiver of latent defects
- Testing and inspection at anytime during and after manufacture

❑ Products
- Must meet specifications
- No substitutions without consent

❑ Seller may not manufacture in advance of buyer's needs

❑ Buyer has right to require progress reports on orders

❑ Product rejection
- At buyer's option may return for credit or replacement, halt at plant for correction, or keep if adjustment in price

❑ Buyer's changes to order
- Process for initiating changes
- Changes at any time
- Changes can be specifications, delivery date, drawings, designs, packaging, destination, schedule, inspection, quantities, and suspension of manufacture
- Notification of additional charges
- Notification of additional time for delivery

❑ Price
- As stated in buyer's PO
- No extra charges
- No greater than lowest prevailing price offered to any customer

❑ Invoices
- What is to be included in invoice detail
- Cash discount and how calculated
- When time period for determining cash discounts begins
- Payment due dates
- Invoice intervals
- Payments in what currency
- Payments to be made by cash, check, electronic funds transfer or other

- ■ Buyer has right to set off any amounts owed by seller
- ❏ Shipping
    - ■ Notification of drop shipment
    - ■ Notification of actual or expected delay
    - ■ Title and risk of loss passes at delivery to buyer

Designation of carrier

- Packaging and labeling requirements

- No advance delivery

- If advance delivery, returned or stored at seller's cost

- Seller to pay rush delivery if needed to meet delivery date

- ❏ Time of essence to buyer only

- ❏ Returns - process

- ❏ Warranty

- Passed on to buyer's customer

- Free from defects in design, workmanship, and materials

- Conforms to specifications, drawings, samples, advertising literature

- Warranty period – period of time, period of use, or period of performance

- Warranty period for repaired products

- Warranty period for refurbished products

- Merchantable

- Fit for intended purpose

- Free of defects in title

- Does not infringe any patent, copyright, mask work or other intellectual property right

- Packaged to protect from damage

- Remedies for breach of warranty at buyer's option

- Remedies include repair, replace, refund or buyer may fix and charge seller

- Remedies not exclusive

- ❏ Buyer expressly objects to any conflicting terms in seller's PO

- ❏ Corrective action plan required on notice by buyer

- ❏ No credit hold without notice

- ❏ Taxes included in price
- ❏ No gratuities to staff or families of staff
- ❏ Patent Infringement
- • Indemnification for all products
- • Includes claims of unfair competition
- • Retain right to defend and settle
- • Seller must procure for buyer right to use product
- • Seller must modify product to become non-infringing
  - ■ Seller must replace product with non-infringing product
  - ■ Seller must refund price
- ❏ Termination provision
  - ■ For cause
- ❏ Any breach or material breach
- ❏ Fails to perform
- ❏ Performs unsatisfactorily
- ❏ Fails to make progress
- ❏ Right to cure period
  - ■ For convenience
- ❏ At any time
- ❏ Work stops immediately
- ❏ If partial cancellation, work continues on remainder of order
- ❏ Amount of payment to seller for cancellation of custom products by period of time between cancellation and delivery date
- ❏ Amount of payment for cancellation of stock products if any
- ❏ Limit on time to claim payment for a cancellation
  - ■ Insolvency
  - ■ Bankruptcy
  - ■ Assignment for benefit of creditors
  - ■ Receiver appointed
  - ■ Initiates reorganization
- ❏ Closes business
- ❏ Stops operating

- ❏ Buyer has right to manufacture if seller ceases business

- ❏ Conflicting language between agreements resolved in what manner

- ❏ Confidential information
  - ▪ How defined
  - ▪ What are acceptable uses and disclosures
  - ▪ Term of confidentiality obligations
  - ▪ Duties towards confidential information
  - ▪ Exceptions to duties of confidentiality

- ❏ No implied licenses to buyer's information or property

- ❏ Alternative dispute resolution
  - ▪ Negotiation
  - ▪ Mediation
  - ▪ Arbitration
  - ▪ If don't want any of these include provision specifically rejecting
  - ▪ Is alternative exclusive or required before litigation
  - ▪ Who pays for alternative
  - ▪ Who specifically is required to participate in alternative
  - ▪ Qualifications of neutral party officiating over the alternative
  - ▪ What is the timeframe for alternative
  - ▪ Where does alternative dispute forum occur
  - ▪ What rules govern alternative dispute forum
  - ▪ If neutral party renders a decision is it binding

- ❏ Indemnity
  - ▪ Seller to provide
  - ▪ To buyer, officers, employees, consultants, directors, agents, parent, subsidiary
  - ▪ Claims, liabilities, losses, damages, costs, charges, attorneys' fees, legal costs, liens, death, personal injury, accidents, property damage.
  - ▪ Arising out of actual or alleged defects in material and workmanship, negligence, gross negligence, breach of the contract, claims of liens or encumbrances

- ❏ Limitation on liability
  - ▪ Consequential damages- special, indirect, incidental, exemplary
  - ▪ Limit on damages

- ❏ Requirement to obtain and maintain insurance
  - ▪ Contract liability, comprehensive, general, automobile liability, workers' compensation, product liability.
  - ▪ Insurance certificates required to be produced
  - ▪ Named insured

- ❏ Compliance with laws
  - ▪ Requirement to obtain permits and licenses

- Comply with OSHA, hazardous materials laws
- ❑ Safety
  - Label hazardous materials
  - Provide material safety data sheet on any chemicals
  - If hazardous materials in products, inform in writing
  - If defects become known must inform buyer

- ❑ Publicity
  - Allow with other party's written consent not to be unreasonably withheld
  - Allow for your company at its discretion
  - Prohibit entirely

- ❑ Choice of law to interpret contract

- ❑ Recovery of prevailing party's expenses in litigation
  - Attorneys fees
  - Legal costs
  - Expert witness fees

- ❑ Investigation costs

- ❑ Severability—illegal or otherwise unenforceable provisions can be severed

- ❑ Waiver—waiver of breach not agreement to waive all breaches

- ❑ Assignment/subcontracting permitted
  - Preclude partial or complete assignment but allow subcontracting
  - Preclude subcontracting but allow partial or complete assignment
  - Allowed with consent not to be withheld unreasonably
  - Allowed with consent at other party's sole discretion
  - Allowed if a party is sold
  - Allowed if a party is transferred to an affiliate or subsidiary
  - If subcontractor's permitted will sub be required to maintain company confidential information

- ❑ Choice of venue for litigation

- ❑ Rights provided in contract are cumulative or exclusive

- ❑ Force Majeure – consider inclusion of fire, accident, acts of public enemy, terrorism, severe weather, acts of God, labor disruption, flood, failure of suppliers to deliver, difficulty obtaining supplies, epidemics, nuclear strike, government intervention, government or freight embargo, quarantine, difficulty obtaining transportation
  - Notice required if event occurs
  - Right to terminate if event lasts specified amount of time
  - Integration (or Entire Agreement) provision
  - All documents making up the agreement referenced

- ❏ Notice provision
  - ▪ Are both parties addresses included
  - ▪ Acceptable delivery methods
- • Time that the other party is deemed to have received the notice specified
- ❏ No joint venture, agency, partnership, trust, or association
- ❏ Successors and assigns – agreement binding on
- ❏ Survival–certain terms of the agreement may survive termination
- ❏ Written modification – all modifications in writing and signed
- ❏ If terms on back of a form, does the front call attention to the terms
- ❏ Will Buyer provide tooling or otherwise have its own property at seller
  - ▪ Seller must insure it, label it as buyers, separate it from other property, return it in good condition, and secure it
  - ▪ Buyer may enter and inspect it at any time

84. Checklist for Modifying or Extending an Existing Contract

❏ Document is numbered in title

❏ Clearly states it is an amendment, modification or supplement

❏ Refers to name and date of original agreement

❏ Refers to parties of original agreement

❏ States parties have received good and valuable consideration for modification

❏ Effective date

❏ States term being deleted and states its replacement

❏ States term being modified and how it is modified

❏ Includes terms to be added

❏ Correct signature blocks and dates

❏ Agreement signed and initialed on all pages by both parties

85. Checklist for Sales Agreements Where Your Company Is the Seller

❑ The checklist for purchase orders is applicable for sales agreements with the addition that a ?sales agreement needs:

❑ Correct legal name of parties

❑ Effective date of contract

❑ Term

❑ No third party beneficiaries

❑ Correct signature blocks

❑ Agreement signed and each page initialed by both parties

86. Terms of Purchase

Indemnification. Each Party shall indemnify and hold harmless the other, its parent, subsidiaries, affiliates, successors, assigns, employees, officers, directors, agents, or subcontractors from and against any and all suits, claims, losses, forfeitures, demands, fees, damages, liabilities, costs, expenses, obligations, proceedings, or injuries, of any kind or nature, including reasonable attorneys fees which that Party may hereafter incur, become responsible for, or pay out as a result of the other Party's breach of any term or provision of this Agreement, or a claim of lien or encumbrances made by third parties.

Assignment. Neither Party may assign or otherwise transfer this Agreement without the prior written consent of the other.

LIMITATION OF LIABILITY. IN NO EVENT SHALL EITHER PARTY BE LIABLE IN CONTRACT, TORT OR OTHERWISE FOR INCIDENTAL OR CONSEQUENTIAL DAMAGES OF ANY KIND, INCLUDING, WITHOUT LIMITATION, ECONOMIC DAMAGE OR LOST PROFITS, REGARDLESS OF WHETHER EITHER PARTY SHALL BE ADVISED, SHALL HAVE OTHER REASON TO KNOW, OR IN FACT SHALL KNOW OF THE POSSIBILITY.

Forum and Legal Fees. Should legal action arise concerning this Agreement, the prevailing party shall be entitled to recover all reasonable attorneys' fees and related costs, in addition to any other relief which may be awarded by any court or other tribunal. The Parties agree that prior to initiating any legal proceedings against the other, the Parties will engage a neutral mediator who will be charged with assisting the parties to reach a mutually agreeable resolution of all contested matters. The mediation shall take place in Ingut, Noodle USA and will be conducted in the English language. The mediator shall be chosen by mutual agreement of the Parties and the mediator's fees shall be borne equally by the Parties. In the event that a mediator cannot be agreed on by the Parties, each Party shall chose a mediator and the two mediators shall together chose a third mediator who will conduct the mediation. The costs of the two mediators chosen to choose the third mediator shall be borne equally by the Parties. The Parties agree to participate in the mediation in good faith.

Severability. If any provision of this Agreement is held by a court of law to be illegal, invalid or unenforceable, that provision shall be deemed amended to achieve as nearly as possible the same economic effect as the original provision, and the legality, validity and enforceability of the remaining provisions of this Agreement shall not be affected or impaired.

Waiver. No term or provision hereof will be considered waived and no breach of this Agreement excused unless such waiver or consent is in writing. The waiver or consent to a breach of any provision of this Agreement shall not operate or be construed as a waiver of, consent to, or excuse of any other or subsequent breach.

Conflicts Between Documents. These terms shall control over any conflicting terms in any other document which might be exchanged related to this transaction.

Force Majeure. Neither Party shall be held responsible for any delay or failure in performance of any part of this Agreement to the extent such delay or failure is caused by fire, flood, explosion, terrorism, war, embargo, government requirement, civil or military authority, act of God, or other similar causes beyond its control and without the fault or negligence of the delayed or non-performing Party. The Party so affected shall notify the non-affected Party in writing within ten (10) days after the beginning of any such cause that would affect the Party's performance.

Successors and Assigns. The Parties intend this Agreement to bind any and all of the Parties' successors, heirs, and assigns.

Survival. All provisions that logically ought to survive termination of this Agreement shall survive.

Entire Agreement. This Agreement supersedes, terminates, and otherwise renders null and void any and all prior written or oral agreements or understandings between the Parties relating to the subject matter of this Agreement. Except as otherwise provided in this Agreement, only a written instrument signed by both Parties may modify this Agreement.

87. Terms of Sale

1. **Order Acceptance.** Acceptance of buyer's order is subject to credit approval.

2. **Price.** Prices shall be those in effect at time of shipment.

3. **Shipping.** Goods shall be shipped F.O.B. shipping point.

4. **Payment.** Invoices are eligible for cash discount if paid by the 10th of the month following the invoice date. All invoices are due on the 15th of the month following the invoice date. Payments not made when due shall incur a monthly service charge of the lesser of 1-1/2 percent or the maximum permitted by law.

5. **Taxes.** Prices do not include sales or other taxes imposed on the sale of goods which shall be separately invoiced unless Buyer provides Seller with an acceptable tax exemption certificate.

6. **Returns.** With Seller's prior approval, goods may be returned for credit against unpaid invoices. The amount of the credit will be reduced by a restocking fee equal to 10% of the price of the returned goods.

7. **Delivery.** Seller shall not be liable for any delay in delivery that is the result of acts not under Seller's control such as weather, strikes, and acts of God. Delivery dates are best estimates only.

8. **WARRANTIES.** SELLER WARRANTS THAT ALL GOODS SOLD ARE FREE OF ANY SECURITY INTEREST. SELLER MAKES NO OTHER EXPRESS OR IMPLIED WARRANTIES, AND SPECIFICALLY MAKES NO IMPLIED WARRANTIES OF MERCHANTABILITY OR FITNESS FOR PURPOSE.

9. **Limitation of Liability.** Seller's liability shall be limited to either repair or replacement of the goods or refund of the purchase price, all at Seller's option, and in no case shall Seller be liable for incidental or consequential damage of any kind for any reason.

10. **Waiver.** The failure of Seller to insist on the performance of any of the terms or conditions of this contract or to exercise any right hereunder shall not be a waiver of such terms, conditions or rights in the future, nor shall it be deemed to be a waiver of any other term, condition, or right under this contract.

11. **Modification of Terms and Conditions.** No terms and conditions other than those stated herein, and no modification of these terms or conditions, shall be binding on Seller without Seller's written consent.

88. Examples of Legal "Boilerplate"

Assignment/Subcontracting: Four Alternatives

Neither party shall have the right to assign or subcontract any part of its obligations under this agreement.

Neither party shall have the right to assign or subcontract any of its obligations or duties under this agreement without the prior written consent of the other party, which consent shall not be unreasonably withheld or delayed.

Neither party shall have the right to assign or subcontract any of its obligations or duties under this agreement, without the prior written consent of the other party, which consent shall be in the sole determination of the party with the right to consent.

Notwithstanding the foregoing, either party may, without the consent of the other party, assign the agreement to an affiliate or subsidiary or to any person that acquires all or substantially all of the assets of a party.

Attorneys Fees

The non-prevailing party in any dispute under this Agreement shall pay all costs and expenses, including expert witness fees and attorneys' fees, incurred by the prevailing party in resolving such dispute.

Choice of Law or Governing Law

This Agreement shall be governed by and construed in accordance with the internal laws of the State of _____ U.S.A., without reference to any conflicts of law provisions.

Choice of Venue

Each party hereby submits to the exclusive jurisdiction of, and waives any venue or other objection against, any federal court sitting in the State of _____, U.S.A., or any _____ state court in any legal proceeding arising out of or relating to this Contract. Each party agrees that all claims and matters may be heard and determined in any such court and each party waives any right to object to such filing on venue, forum non convenient or similar grounds.

Compliance with Laws

Each party shall comply in all respects with all applicable legal requirements governing the duties, obligations, and business practices of that party and shall obtain any permits or licenses necessary for its operations. Neither party shall take any action in violation of any applicable legal requirement that could result in liability being imposed on the other party.

Conflicts

The terms of this Agreement shall control over any conflicting terms in any referenced agreement or document.

Cumulative Rights

Any specific rights or remedy provided in this contract will not be exclusive but will be cumulative of all other rights and remedies.

Force Majeure

Neither Party shall be held responsible for any delay or failure in performance of any part of this Agreement to the extent such delay or failure is caused by fire, flood, explosion, war, embargo, government requirement, civil or military authority, act of God, or other similar causes beyond its control and without the fault or negligence of the delayed or non-performing Party. The affected party will notify the other party in writing within ten (10) days after the beginning of any such cause that would affect its performance. Notwithstanding, if a party's performance is delayed for a period exceeding thirty (30) days from the date the other party receives notice under this paragraph, the non-affected party will have the right, without any liability to the other party, to terminate this agreement.

Indemnity

Each Party shall indemnify, defend and hold the other Party harmless from and against any and all claims, actions, suits, demands, assessments or judgments asserted and any and all losses, liabilities, damages, costs and expenses (including, without limitation, attorneys' fees, accounting fees and investigation costs to the extent permitted by law) alleged or incurred arising out of or relating to any operations, acts or omissions of the indemnifying Party or any of its employees, agents, and invitees in the exercise of the indemnifying Party's rights or the performance or observance of the indemnifying Party's obligations under this Agreement. Prompt notice must be given of any claim, and the Party who is providing the indemnification will have control of any defense or settlement.

Insurance

Each party agrees to maintain insurance in commercially reasonable amounts covering claims of any kind or nature for damage to property or personal injury, including death, made by anyone, that may arise from activities performed or facilitated by this contract, whether these activities are performed by that company, its employees, agents, or anyone directly or indirectly engaged or employed by that party or its agents.

Integration Provision or Entire Agreement

This Agreement sets forth and constitutes the entire agreement and understanding of the parties with respect to the subject matter hereof. This Agreement supersedes any and all prior agreements, negotiations, correspondence, undertakings, promises, covenants, arrangements, communications, representations and warranties, whether oral or written of any party to this Agreement.

Limit of Liability: Two Alternatives

IN NO EVENT SHALL EITHER PARTY BE LIABLE TO THE OTHER OR ANY THIRD PARTY IN CONTRACT, TORT OR OTHERWISE FOR INCIDENTAL OR CONSEQUENTIAL DAMAGES OF ANY KIND, INCLUDING, WITHOUT LIMITATION, PUNITIVE OR ECONOMIC DAMAGES OR LOST PROFITS, REGARDLESS OF WHETHER EITHER PARTY SHALL BE ADVISED, SHALL HAVE OTHER REASON TO KNOW, OR IN FACT SHALL KNOW OF THE POSSIBILITY.

IN NO EVENT SHALL EITHER PARTY BE LIABLE FOR ANY INCIDENTAL OR CONSEQUENTIAL DAMAGES. SELLER'S LIABILITY AND BUYER'S EXCLUSIVE REMEDY FOR ANY CAUSE OF ACTION ARISING IN CONNECTION WITH THIS CONTRACT OR THE SALE OR USE OF THE GOODS, WHETHER BASED ON NEGLIGENCE,

STRICT LIABILITY, BREACH OF WARRANTY, BREACH OF CONTRACT, OR EQUITABLE PRINCIPLES, IS EXPRESSLY LIMITED TO, AT SELLER'S OPTION, REPLACEMENT OF, OR REPAYMENT OF THE PURCHASE PRICE FOR THAT PORTION OF THE GOODS WITH RESPECT TO WHICH DAMAGES ARE CLAIMED. ALL CLAIMS OF ANY KIND ARISING IN CONNECTION WITH THIS CONTRACT OR THE SALE OR USE OF THE GOODS SHALL BE DEEMED WAIVED UNLESS MADE IN WRITING WITHIN SIXTY (60) DAYS FROM THE DATE OF SELLER'S DELIVERY, OR THE DATE FIXED FOR DELIVERY IN THE EVENT OF NONDELIVERY.

Notices

All notices shall be in writing and shall be delivered personally, by United States certified or registered mail, postage prepaid, return receipt requested, or by a recognized overnight delivery service. Any notice must be delivered to the parties at their respective addresses set forth below their signatures or to such other address as shall be specified in writing by either party according to the requirements of this section. The date that notice shall be deemed to have been made shall be the date of delivery, when delivered personally; on written verification of receipt if delivered by overnight delivery; or the date set forth on the return receipt if sent by certified or registered mail.

Relationship of the Parties

The relationship of the parties under this Agreement is that of an independent contractor and the company hiring the contractor. In all matters relating to this Agreement each Party hereto shall be solely responsible for the acts of its employees and agents, and employees or agents of one Party shall not be considered employees or agents of the other Party. Except as otherwise provided herein, no Party shall have any right, power or authority to create any obligation, express or implied, on behalf of any other Party. Nothing in this Agreement is intended to create or constitute a joint venture, partnership, agency, trust or other association of any kind between the Parties or persons referred to herein.

Severability

If any provision of this Agreement shall be declared by any court of competent jurisdiction to be illegal, void, or unenforceable, the other provisions shall not be affected but shall remain in full force and effect. If the non-solicitation or non-competition provisions are found to be unreasonable or invalid, these restrictions shall be shall enforced to the maximum extent valid and enforceable.

Successors and Assigns

This Agreement shall be binding on and inure to the benefit of the parties hereto and their respective heirs, legal or personal representatives, successors and assigns.

Survival

All provisions that logically ought to survive termination of this Agreement shall survive.

Termination for Cause

If either party breaches any provision of this Agreement and if such breach is not cured within thirty (30) days after receiving written notice from the other party specifying such breach in reasonable detail, the non-breaching party shall have the right to terminate this Agreement by giving written notice thereof to the party in breach, which termination shall go into effect immediately on receipt.

Termination for Convenience

This Agreement may be terminated by either party on thirty (30) days advance written notice effective as of the expiration of the notice period.

Termination on Insolvency

Either party has the right to terminate this agreement where the other party becomes insolvent, fails to pay its bills when due, makes an assignment for the benefit of creditors, goes out of business or ceases production.

Waiver

Failure of either party to insist on strict compliance with any of the terms, covenants, and conditions of this Agreement shall not be deemed a waiver of such terms, covenants, and conditions or of any similar right or power hereunder at any subsequent time.

Warranty Disclaimers

EXCEPT AS EXPRESSLY STATED IN THIS AGREEMENT, THE SELLER EXPRESSLY DISCLAIMS AND NEGATES ANY IMPLIED OR EXPRESS WARRANTY OF MERCHANTABILITY, ANY IMPLIED OR EXPRESS WARRANTY OF FITNESS FOR A PARTICULAR PURPOSE, AND ANY IMPLIED OR EXPRESS WARRANTY OF CONFORMITY TO MODELS OR SAMPLES OF MATERIALS.

Written Modification

This Agreement may be amended or modified only by a writing executed by both parties.

89. Lawyer Engagement Letter

Dear _____,

The purpose of this letter ("Engagement Letter") is to confirm the engagement of your firm to represent _____ in the following legal matter: _____.

Our policy regarding retention of legal services is:

1. No expenditure of time or costs should be made without pre-approval of a budget defining the tasks, time, hourly rate and name of staff person conducting the task, or part thereof. I have found that this is the best way for both of us to have the same understanding about what is being done and what it will cost. _____ will not be liable for legal fees or costs exceeding this budget without written pre-approval of such fees and costs.

2. The attached Terms and Conditions, along with this Engagement Letter, comprise the contract governing your firm's provision of legal services to _____. The performance of legal services to _____ signifies your firm's agreement to this contract.

3. Correspondence and bills should be directed to me.

4. I will forward a letter similar to this regarding each matter in which we engage your firm. I have found that this practice clarifies, for both parties, when a discussion rises to the level of legal advice which you expect to be paid for and we expect to be billed for. Please feel free to decline to discuss matters that you expect to be paid for where you have not received an engagement letter.

We look forward to working with you on this and other matters

Sincerely,

90. Terms and Conditions for Engagement of Outside Counsel

I. Introduction

This sets forth the Terms and Conditions ("Terms) for the engagement of outside legal counsel who provide services to _____.

The Legal Department seeks to provide and arrange for the highest quality legal services, provided in an expeditious and cost effective manner, consistent with the values and mission of _____. _____ expects that outside counsel will not only provide high quality, cost effective legal services, but will also offer constructive and forward thinking suggestions regarding the efficient delivery of legal services in each matter for which counsel is engaged.

In evaluating the quality, effectiveness and efficiency of outside counsel's services, _____ will consider the following:

A. How effectively outside counsel works with in-house attorneys and the senior executive staff, with particular emphasis on clear, concise communications;

B. The utilization of a practical, common sense approach to problem solving;

C. Judgment in balancing the need for high quality legal services against the high cost of legal representation generally;

D. Whether innovative, creative approaches to resolving problems are identified, considered and implemented;

E. The reasonableness of the time spent on tasks and projects involved in the representation;

F. The continuity of staffing on matters;

G. Whether personnel are performing work appropriate to the billing rates;

H. The appropriateness and effectiveness of outside resources suggested or used by outside counsel.

II. Working with the _____ Legal Department

The _____ Legal Department has responsibility for the retention and management of outside counsel for _____. As such, the Legal Department expects outside counsel to work closely with the responsible in-house attorney. Assignments, communication with third parties, as well as litigation and transaction strategies should be discussed with _____'s in-house counsel at the commencement of the engagement and regularly throughout its term.

The Legal Department will from time to time involve other outside counsel in transactions or disputes that warrant such involvement. This involvement may require that outside counsel work cooperatively with other attorneys outside _____, although coordination and supervision of all outside counsel remains a Legal Department responsibility. Courtesy and professionalism is expected in connection with all interactions between and among outside counsel and in-house attorneys and _____ executives.

III. Standards of Engagements

All engagements of outside counsel require that attorneys observe the following standards when representing _____:

A. **Confidentiality and Privacy.** _____ is subject to laws requiring the protection of confidential and private information. Outside counsel agree to maintain the confidentiality and privacy of all records and information arising from outside counsel's representation of _____.

B. **Strategy.** Litigation or transaction strategy should be discussed with the responsible _____ attorney and agreed upon at an early stage. Strategy should be reviewed from time to time and should not be changed without prior concurrence of the responsible _____ attorney.

C. **Periodic Reporting.** The responsible _____ attorney should be advised promptly of any unusual adverse or positive developments such as counterclaims, new case law, or affirmative defenses that may apply. While no reporting frequency is universally required, reports should be made at reasonable intervals and whenever specific circumstances warrant. Both _____ and outside counsel are well served by regular communication. Often outside counsel will be expected to communicate both with a responsible _____ attorney and a responsible business executive in the matter for which outside counsel has been engaged.

D. **Prior Document Review.** Although prior review of all documents is not required, certain key documents in litigation or transactions should be submitted in draft form to the Legal Department prior to filing or communicating with clients. For example, contracts, legal opinions, pleadings and appellate briefs should be submitted to the responsible _____ attorney with ample time for review.

E. **Research.** The selection of outside counsel is often based on the expertise and experience of a particular lawyer or lawyers within a firm. As such, basic research should not be billed to _____ without specific authorization from the responsible Legal Department attorney.

F. **Timing.** As time considerations are often a critical element in the selection of outside counsel, any delay or unanticipated complications that may result in delay should be reported to the responsible _____ attorney as soon as possible.

G. **Staffing.** _____ will require that a specific attorney or attorneys be assigned to each particular matter. It is expected that, absent unforeseen circumstances, personnel specified in an engagement letter will be the only attorneys and paralegals to work on any given matter from start to finish. _____ will not be billed for "start up" costs of educating new staff due to personnel changes within the firm. Therefore, it is expected both as a matter of client relations and professional responsibility that attorneys assigned have the requisite skill and expertise necessary to represent _____ effectively. _____ will not be billed for time required for attorneys to become competent in areas outside of their acknowledged expertise. Every effort should be made with regard to maintaining the continuity of staffing a particular matter. The number of different lawyers who work on a particular matter should be held to the minimum number of lawyers needed to handle the matter efficiently. We encourage the use of less experienced attorneys and paralegals where appropriate. Attorneys should not perform a task for which a paralegal is qualified nor should a paralegal perform a task for which an administrative assistant is qualified. We expect only one attorney from the firm to attend meetings, depositions and arguments, unless prior arrangements and approval have been received from the responsible _____ attorney.

H. **Billing Matters.** _____ will not pay for time spent in administrative tasks such as opening a file, clearing conflicts of interest, preparing or reviewing invoices, discussions with in-house counsel regarding the contents of an invoice or time spent on matters solely for the convenience of out-side counsel. Time spent on preparing a strategic plan or budget will be paid for at the agreed upon billing rates. Travel time however is not reimbursed unless the time is actually used in performing serv-ices for _____ or is otherwise arranged with the responsible _____ attorney.

I. **Media Coverage.** _____ has an experienced communications department and does not routinely authorize outside counsel to discuss _____ matters with the media. Any media inquiries relating to _____ or a matter for which outside counsel has been engaged, should be referred to the _____ attorney. In some cases, the _____ Communications Department may request that outside counsel represent _____ with the media, but such arrangements must be made in advance and is solely within the discretion of the responsible _____ attorney.

IV. Consultations

_____ values outside counsel's expertise and advice and is always interested in steps that may be taken by _____ to reduce legal exposure. Therefore outside counsel will periodi-cally meet with the responsible _____ attorney to review complex transactions, or cases in progress and discuss recommendations for a particular matter and for future business planning. Depending upon the circumstances, meetings may be held with General Counsel or other _____ lawyers, management staff, or members of the research staff or board of direc-tors.

V. Client Communications/Representation

All client contact, information and communication should take place through the Legal Department. All requests for _____ or its affiliates' documents, results of internal investigations, data, or interviews should be coordinated through the Legal Department unless the responsible _____ attorney directs otherwise. Outside counsel may be asked to represent _____ affiliate corporations and sometimes the officers, directors and employees of these corporations. Therefore, although outside counsel may have multiple clients through such arrange-ment, the Legal Department will continue to be responsible to coordinate all legal services and communi-cation with all such clients should include the responsible _____ attorney unless conflicts or other considerations necessitate otherwise.

VI. Service of Process/Documents

_____'s statutory agent for Service of Process will insure that any Service of Process, including any summons and complaints or other pleadings that are served on _____ will be forwarded to outside counsel in a timely manner. It is the responsibility of outside counsel to establish a litigation file and docket all pleadings so that timely responses are filed and no default is entered against _____ or any _____ affiliate.

VII. Billing Practices and Format

Use of proper billing practices and billing formats are of critical importance to insure payment for outside counsel services. As such all outside counsel providing services are requested to comply with following standards for billing.

A. **Billing Rates.** Before the commencement of work, an engagement letter must be executed. It will include the hourly rates agreed upon for all attorneys and paralegals providing services on a particular matter. There should be no increase in the hourly rates established for the individuals working on _____ matters during the calendar year. Any proposed increase in hourly rates should be communicated to the Legal Department before January 1.

B. **Billing.** A task-based billing format should be used for all invoices submitted to _____. Task-based billing formats require three elements: First, the outside counsel must record time in a single activity entry. Second, the time records must demonstrate a minimum amount of descriptive detail so that the billing data is intelligible upon review. Third, the time records should organize billing data on a task basis showing exactly what work was done during the billing period, who performed it and how much time was spent on each task and the hourly rate for that individual. Office conferences and third party communications should always identify the other participant to the topic discussed.

C. **No Block Billing.** Counsel should not combine different tasks performed by an attorney during one day that relate to a single billable matter into a single "block" entry. This practice makes it impossible to understand how much time was devoted to each of the several tasks combined in a single entry. _____ will not honor invoices submitted using this format.

D. **Costs and Disbursements.** All costs and disbursements (including lodging, travel, out-of-pocket expenses, copying service, transcripts and the like) must be included in the firm's statements with supporting documentation for all lodging and travel expenses (other than nominal amounts) and for any individual item whose cost is $25 or more. All expenses shall be the reasonable necessary actual net costs incurred and paid by the firm. All expenses are to be billed at cost. Please note that air travel, if any, must be at coach rates, advance purchase discount travel, otherwise expressly authorized by the responsible _____ attorney. Expenses for lodging, meals and transportation shall be at reasonable rates and counsel must exercise prudence at incurring such expenses. Travel time, including time spent traveling from a local office to our facilities, will not be reimbursed unless the time is actually spent performing services for _____. Non-reimbursable expenses include avoidable charges for unused guaranteed hotel reservations and charges for hotel movies and airline headsets, recreation and health club facilities, personal trip insurance, and other personal expenditures.

E. **Overhead Expenses.** Routine overhead costs, including, for example, administrative services, library services, clerical support, office supplies, postage, office copying, telecopying or fax filing, local telephone, file indexing, bill preparations, staff overtime, word processing and meals and snacks (unless while traveling out of town) shall be considered as included in the firm's hourly fees and not charged to

_____. _____ will not pay for time spent in firm administrative tasks, such as opening a file, clearing conflicts of interest, preparing and reviewing invoices, discussion with in-house counsel regarding the contents of an invoice or time spent on matters solely for the convenience of counsel.

VIII. Budgets

_____ expects outside counsel to develop a project budget for each matter. _____ understands the difficulty of predicting the amount of work required in a particular case or transaction; much depends upon the action and reactions of third parties. A request for a budget is a request that outside counsel make a conscientious effort to advise _____ of the various components of work that will be required in any representation and to consider how much work might reasonably cost so that the _____ Legal Department can make an informed decision regarding whether and how to proceed with the matter. Budgets should address the following:

A. **Transaction Matters:**

1. Identify the attorneys proposed to work on the transaction team. This should have been already reflected in the Engagement Letter.

2. Describe the broad paths expected to be required, e.g., key documents to be drafted, issues to be researched. If these are known, identify them specifically and approximate the number of hours required to perform them.

3. Describe the broad tasks that might be required. Even if the particular tasks are only a possibility rather than a likelihood, describe them and approximate the number of hours required in case the need arises.

4. Describe any travel and/or out of town meetings that are to be expected and the approximate cost of each.

5. If you feel that the budgeted numbers reflect an amount that does not adequately address the full range of a firm's work on a particular transaction or case, provide the additional information necessary in order to enable the responsible attorney to obtain a realistic picture of what the costs of the engagement may involve.

B. **Litigation:** Depending on the type of case, a budget will be required either for the complete handling of a case (from assignment through trial) or for particular periods, (e.g., the first 3 months of the case, followed by another budget for the following period; or for a period through discovery; then pretrial motions and then through trial).

IX. Settlement

The Legal Department is responsible to work with outside counsel regarding settlement of any litigation matter. The settlement of any case in litigation requires the approval of the General Counsel. Certain substantial settlements will also require the involvement of _____'s President.

X. Conflicts of Interest

_____ not, as a policy matter, prohibit a lawyer or law firm in all cases from representing clients whose interest have been or could become adverse to _____. However _____ retains the prerogative, where a conflict could arise or has arisen, to object to the representation and require the withdrawal of counsel in accordance with applicable professional rules. _____ requires that outside counsel identify and discuss with the responsible _____ attorney any potential legal conflicts or business conflicts that may arise affecting the engagement of the firm.

91. Service Evaluation and Repair Agreement

Equipment Owner Information:

NAME: _____

ADDRESS: _____

CITY: _____ STATE: _____ ZIP: _____

HOME PHONE: _____ WORK PHONE: _____

Description of Equipment:

MAKE: _____ MODEL: _____

SERIAL NUMBER: _____ COLOR: _____

APPROX. AGE: _____ PROBLEM:

_____

_____

_____

_____

_____

Diagnostic Fee (Must be paid prior to service evaluation)

$_____ Date Paid _____

Agreement

1. **Terms.** The Diagnostic Fee must be paid when the item is checked in for service and is non-refundable. When Company has completed its examination of the equipment, Company will contact the owner listed above to discuss the results of the examination. Owner may be presented with a Repair Price Quote. If a Repair Price Quote is provided, Owner must authorize the repair before Company will proceed to repair the Equipment. If the Repair is authorized the Diagnostic fee paid by Owner will be credited towards the Repair Price Quote

2. **Repair Price Quotes.** The price quoted to repair the Equipment is good for 5 business days from the date the Owner is notified by phone of the Quote. On the expiration of the fifth business day the Quote will no longer be honored and the Equipment must be picked up by Owner within thirty (30) days. Company relies on the Owner to accurately describe all problems in order to properly determine the cost of repair. If the problem description proves to be inaccurate or incomplete, additional charges may apply. Company may not be able to repair your Equipment through no fault of Company's and you will be informed if this is the case.

3. **Warranty.** Company's technicians will use generally recognized commercial practices and standards to resolve all reported issues. Company will re-repair any repair not performed in accordance with the foregoing warranty, provided that Company receives notice from Owner within thirty (30) days after the

Equipment is returned to Owner. If Company is unable within a reasonable time to re-repair the Equipment, Company will refund the Repair Price Quote paid by Owner. These warranties will not apply if Company determines that the re-repair is due to improper or inadequate maintenance or calibration or improper use or operation of the Equipment. THE ABOVE WARRANTIES ARE EXCLUSIVE AND NO OTHER WARRANTY, WHETHER WRITTEN OR ORAL, IS EXPRESSED OR IMPLIED. COMPANY SPECIFICALLY DISCLAIMS THE IMPLIED WARRANTIES OF MERCHANTABILITY AND FITNESS FOR A PARTICULAR PURPOSE.

4. **Abandonment.** Equipment not picked up by the Owner within 30 days of the date the Diagnostic Fee is paid is considered abandoned without notice and becomes the sole property of Company, which may dispose of the Equipment in any manner it chooses without payment or notice to Owner.

5. **Limitation of Liability.** COMPANY'S LIABILITY TO OWNER UNDER THIS AGREEMENT FOR DAMAGES OR LOSSES OF ANY KIND OR NATURE RESULTING FROM COMPANY'S BREACH OF THIS AGREEMENT OR NEGLIGENT CONDUCT SHALL BE LIMITED TO THE AMOUNT PAID TO COMPANY BY OWNER UNDER THIS AGREEMENT.

6. **Complete Agreement.** This agreement constitutes the complete agreement between Company and Owner and supersedes all prior or contemporaneous agreements or representations, written or oral, concerning the subject matter of this agreement. This agreement may not be modified or amended except in writing signed by Company and Owner (no other act, document, usage or custom shall be deemed to amend or modify this agreement).

Acceptance of Terms and Authorization for Evaluation

My signature below indicates that I accept these terms and conditions and authorize Company to conduct any and all evaluations which it, in its sole discretion, determines are necessary to diagnose the condition of the equipment listed above.

Owner: _____ Date: _____

Repair Price Quote

Date of Quote: _____ Technician: _____

Who was contacted: _____ How/At what number:

_____

Repair Authorized: _____ Date Promised:

_____

_____

_____

Acknowledgement of Return of Equipment

I acknowledge that the Equipment referenced above has been returned to me:

Owner: _____ Date: _____

CHAPTER 10

Business Operation Tools

THE FORMS IN THIS CHAPTER ARE DESIGNED to increase your company's sales. The *Sales Call Log* is for use by salespersons; it serves as a record of telephone conversations with customers and prospects. The *Client/Prospect Contact Log* is a related form that summarizes the calls to and contacts made with a particular prospect. The *Sales Prospect File* is the best log for use by salespersons in industries where sales are made through incoming calls and during advertising campaigns.

The *Customer Satisfaction Survey* lets you learn from your most valuable critics—your customers. The *Customer Service Request* helps you effectively gather, track, follow, and respond to customer service inquiries.

Use the *Product Information* form to keep a unified and complete description of all of your products and services. The *Order Card* is a handy and simple card that you can include in mailings and facsimile advertisements. It enables your customers to quickly and easily place orders for your products and services. Use the *Work Order Request for Quote* form when your customers request custom goods and services. The *Sales Order Form* is a familiar receipt/invoice form.

The *Daily Sales Recap* is an internal sales tracking mechanism; it enables you and your staff to see a day-by-day analysis of your company's sales. The *Month-to-Month Sales Comparison Log* enables your staff to compare sales performance on a month-to-month basis.

The *Cash Receipts Control Log* (on the Web) is an effective tracking mechanism for cash-based businesses; the form may also serve to prevent employee theft and loss. Ensure that the cash on hand at the end of each business day reconciles with the amount on the Cash Receipts Control Log.

Controlling business operations is essential to generating a profit and meeting your business expectations. This chapter provides you with a range of worksheets to develop and control key operation issues, production schedules, and costing.

The *Vendor Information Sheet* helps you compile and maintain complete information on current and potential vendors. Use this form initially to confirm approval of new vendors. When deciding among the goods or services of several vendors, use the *Vendor Price and Comparison Analysis* (on the Web) to compare the offerings of each.

If your business conducts manufacturing operations, use the *Daily Production Planning Schedule* to formalize your production goals. Use the *Production Completion Notice* to internally notify departments (sales and billing, especially) of the completion of an order.

The *Marketing Department Budget Recap* helps you analyze the sales, margins, and marketing expenses for your products or services. The *Sales Price Estimate* helps you budget and calculate the expenses you'll incur in the production of goods. This calculation helps you determine a sales price for your production with an adequate profit margin. The *Job Costing Report* helps you budget and calculate the expenses you'll incur in the completion of a job or project; this calculation helps you determine your profit. The *Job Costing Compari-*

son Report (on the Web) is an analytical tool that compares your estimated and actual revenues, material costs, and labor costs.

The *Ratio Analysis Worksheet* is a powerful analytical and budgeting tool. It helps you analyze key financial ratios by comparing your current year ratios with prior year ratios. The Ratio Analysis Worksheet can pinpoint trouble areas in your business and reveal areas where your business operations are improving.

The *Production Efficiency Worksheet* analyzes the hour-by-hour performance of production facilities or production lines.

This chapter offers tools that streamline and control your purchasing procedures. The *Purchase Order* is likely familiar; use it to place orders with vendors. You and your employees can use the *Expense Report* (included in Chapter 11) both internally and in connection with expenses billable directly to clients.

The *Check Requisition* is an internal control and recordkeeping tool; instruct your staff members to use this form to request checks for purchases.

92. Sales Call Log

Number _____ Date_____

Name of Company _____

Contact _____ Phone _____

Type of Call: ❑ Customer ❑ Prospect

Comments

_____

_____

Purpose of Call

_____

_____

Opening Conversation

_____

_____

Sales Story

_____

_____

Benefits to Customer

_____

_____

Objections or Resistance Response

_____

_____

Closing Conversation

_____

_____

When to Follow Up

_____

_____

93. Client/Prospect Contact Log

Sales Representative _____

Company _____

Contact(s) _____

Address _____

Phone _____

Date	Comments	Next Call/Contact?	Sale?
_____	_____	_____	_____
_____	_____	_____	_____
_____	_____	_____	_____
_____	_____	_____	_____
_____	_____	_____	_____
_____	_____	_____	_____
_____	_____	_____	_____
_____	_____	_____	_____
_____	_____	_____	_____
_____	_____	_____	_____
_____	_____	_____	_____
_____	_____	_____	_____
_____	_____	_____	_____
_____	_____	_____	_____
_____	_____	_____	_____
_____	_____	_____	_____
_____	_____	_____	_____
_____	_____	_____	_____
_____	_____	_____	_____
_____	_____	_____	_____

94. Sales Prospect File

❑ New Prospect ❑ Current Client ❑ Follow-up Date _____

Company Name _____

Contact _____

Title _____

Address _____

_____

Phone _____

Source of Initial Contact

❑ Call-in ❑ Direct Mail ❑ Referral–by Whom? _____

Current Supplier _____

Approximate Monthly Sales Volume _____

Action Taken to Follow-up

_____

_____

_____

Sales Calls History

Comments

_____

_____

_____

_____

_____

General Comments

_____

_____

_____

_____

_____

95. Customer Satisfaction Survey

Your input is valuable to us and we are constantly looking for ways to improve the quality of our products and services. Please take a few minutes to fill out the few questions below. Please return this survey by fax at _____ or in the envelope provided.

Please LIST "Outstanding," "Good," "Average," "Needs Improvement," or "Unacceptable" and comment in the area provided:

Products	Outstanding	Good	Average	Needs Improvement	Unacceptable

Services and Support	Outstanding	Good	Average	Needs Improvement	Unacceptable

Delivery	Outstanding	Good	Average	Needs Improvement	Unacceptable

Ordering and Billing	Outstanding	Good	Average	Needs Improvement	Unacceptable

Employees	Outstanding	Good	Average	Needs Improvement	Unacceptable

Comments

_____

_____

Thank you. You are a valued customer!

96. Product Information

Product _____

Brand Name _____

ID # _____

Product Description

_____

_____

_____

Features

_____

_____

_____

Applications

_____

_____

_____

Technical Specifications

_____

_____

_____

Materials Required

_____

_____

_____

Distributors

_____

_____

_____

Required Lead Time _____

Prepared by _____ Date _____

Approved by _____ Date _____

97. Order Card

Yes! I'd like to make an order. Please send me:

Quantity	Item Description	Price per Unit	Extended Price
_____	_____	_____	_____
_____	_____	_____	_____
_____	_____	_____	_____

❏ Payment Enclosed   ❏ Bill Me   Total _____

$_____

Name _____ Phone _____

Address _____

City _____ State _____ZIP

✂···

Yes! I'd like to make an order. Please send me:

Quantity	Item Description	Price per Unit	Extended Price
_____	_____	_____	_____
_____	_____	_____	_____
_____	_____	_____	_____

❏ Payment Enclosed   ❏ Bill Me   Total _____

$_____

Name _____ Phone _____

Address _____

City _____ State _____ZIP

✂···

Yes! I'd like to make an order. Please send me:

Quantity	Item Description	Price per Unit	Extended Price
_____	_____	_____	_____
_____	_____	_____	_____
_____	_____	_____	_____

❏ Payment Enclosed   ❏ Bill Me   Total _____

$_____

Name _____ Phone _____

Address _____

City _____ State _____ZIP

98. Work Order/Request for Quote

Overview

Customer Name _____

Customer Address _____

Contact Person _____

Phone _____

Project Description _____

_____

_____

Specific Instructions

Materials and Quantities to Be Used

_____

_____

_____

Additional Outside Services Required

_____

_____

_____

Comments

_____

_____

_____

Sample of Design or Sketch of Design

Pricing

_____

_____

Submitted by _____ Date _____

99. Sales Order Form

Customer Name _____ Date _____

Phone _____

Address _____

City _____ State_____ ZIP _____

Ship to Address _____

City _____ State_____ ZIP _____

Special Instructions

_____

_____

_____

Item Number	Description	Quantity	Unit Price	Extended Price
_____	_____	_____	_____	_____
_____	_____	_____	_____	_____
_____	_____	_____	_____	_____
_____	_____	_____	_____	_____
_____	_____	_____	_____	_____
_____	_____	_____	_____	_____
_____	_____	_____	_____	_____
_____	_____	_____	_____	_____
_____	_____	_____	_____	_____
_____	_____	_____	_____	_____

Gross Total _____

Tax _____

Freight _____

Labor _____

Total Due _____

Order Taken by _____

100. Daily Sales Recap

For the Month of _____, _____

Date	Taxable Sales	Nontaxable Sales	Total Sales
1			
2			
3			
4			
5			
6			
7			
8			
9			
10			
11			
12			
13			
14			
15			
16			
17			
18			
19			
20			
21			
22			
23			
24			
25			
26			
27			
28			
29			
30			
31			
TOTAL			

101. Month-to-Month Sales Comparison Log

For Year _____

Month	Taxable Sales	Nontaxable Sales	Total Sales
January	_____	_____	_____
February	_____	_____	_____
March	_____	_____	_____
April	_____	_____	_____
May	_____	_____	_____
June	_____	_____	_____
July	_____	_____	_____
August	_____	_____	_____
September	_____	_____	_____
October	_____	_____	_____
November	_____	_____	_____
December	_____	_____	_____

102. Cash Receipts Control Log

Period _____

Date	Check Amount	Customer ID	Reference No.
_____	$_____	_____	_____
_____	$_____	_____	_____
_____	$_____	_____	_____
_____	$_____	_____	_____
_____	$_____	_____	_____
_____	$_____	_____	_____
_____	$_____	_____	_____
_____	$_____	_____	_____
_____	$_____	_____	_____
_____	$_____	_____	_____
_____	$_____	_____	_____
_____	$_____	_____	_____
_____	$_____	_____	_____
_____	$_____	_____	_____
_____	$_____	_____	_____
_____	$_____	_____	_____
_____	$_____	_____	_____
_____	$_____	_____	_____
_____	$_____	_____	_____
_____	$_____	_____	_____
_____	$_____	_____	_____
_____	$_____	_____	_____
_____	$_____	_____	_____
_____	$_____	_____	_____
_____	$_____	_____	_____
_____	$_____	_____	_____

Reconciled to Daily Cash Deposit by _____ Date _____

Authorized by _____ Date _____

103. Vendor Information Sheet

Name of Firm _____ Phone _____

Address _____

_____

Headquarters Office _____

❏ Corporation ❏ Partnership ❏ Individual ❏ Other _____

Date Business Started _____

President/Principal Owner _____

Other Officers _____

_____

Has this company provided products or services to our company before? ❏ Yes ❏ No

If so, when and what type? _____

_____

List current customers and their approximate purchase value _____

_____

List trade references (name, phone) _____

_____

List bank references (name, branch, phone) _____

_____

Completed by _____ Date _____

Approved by _____ Date _____

104. Vendor Price and Comparison Analysis

Item Description _____ Item # _____

Enter quantity here and price per item below.

Vendor Name	_____	_____	_____	_____	Lead Time	Other Factors
_____	$_____	$_____	$_____	$_____	_____	_____
_____	$_____	$_____	$_____	$_____	_____	_____
_____	$_____	$_____	$_____	$_____	_____	_____
_____	$_____	$_____	$_____	$_____	_____	_____
_____	$_____	$_____	$_____	$_____	_____	_____
_____	$_____	$_____	$_____	$_____	_____	_____
_____	$_____	$_____	$_____	$_____	_____	_____
_____	$_____	$_____	$_____	$_____	_____	_____
_____	$_____	$_____	$_____	$_____	_____	_____
_____	$_____	$_____	$_____	$_____	_____	_____
_____	$_____	$_____	$_____	$_____	_____	_____
_____	$_____	$_____	$_____	$_____	_____	_____
_____	$_____	$_____	$_____	$_____	_____	_____
_____	$_____	$_____	$_____	$_____	_____	_____
_____	$_____	$_____	$_____	$_____	_____	_____
_____	$_____	$_____	$_____	$_____	_____	_____
_____	$_____	$_____	$_____	$_____	_____	_____
_____	$_____	$_____	$_____	$_____	_____	_____

Comments

_____
_____
_____
_____
_____
_____
_____
_____

105 Daily Production Planning/Schedule

Date _____ Shift _____ Plant _____

Product Description	Product I.D.#	Quantity
1. _____ _____ _____	_____	_____
2. _____ _____ _____	_____	_____
3. _____ _____ _____	_____	_____
4. _____ _____ _____	_____	_____
5. _____ _____ _____	_____	_____
6. _____ _____ _____	_____	_____
7. _____ _____ _____	_____	_____
8. _____ _____ _____	_____	_____
9. _____ _____ _____	_____	_____
10. _____ _____ _____	_____	_____

106. Production Completion Notice

Customer I.D.# _____ Sales Order # _____ Production Order #
_____

Scheduled Completion Date _____ Actual Date _____

Scheduled Shipping Date _____ Actual Date _____

Signed by _____ Date _____

Description of changes made to original sales order:

_____

_____

_____

_____

_____

_____

_____

_____

_____

_____

_____

_____

_____

_____

_____

107. Marketing Department Budget Recap

For the Reporting Period of _____

Product A _____

Product B _____

Product C _____

Product D _____

		Product A	Product B	Product C	Product D	Total
Gross Sales		$_____	$_____	$_____	$_____	$_____
Discounts & Returns	–	$_____	$_____	$_____	$_____	$_____
Net Sales	=	$_____	$_____	$_____	$_____	$_____
Cost of Goods Sold	–	$_____	$_____	$_____	$_____	$_____
Gross Margin	=	$_____	$_____	$_____	$_____	$_____

Marketing Expenses:

		Product A	Product B	Product C	Product D	Total
Sales Department Expense		$_____	$_____	$_____	$_____	$_____
Delivery	+	$_____	$_____	$_____	$_____	$_____
Warehousing	+	$_____	$_____	$_____	$_____	$_____
Advertising	+	$_____	$_____	$_____	$_____	$_____
Sales Promotion	+	$_____	$_____	$_____	$_____	$_____
Marketing Research	+	$_____	$_____	$_____	$_____	$_____
Development Cost	+	$_____	$_____	$_____	$_____	$_____
Total Marketing Expense	=	$_____	$_____	$_____	$_____	$_____
Gross Margin		$_____	$_____	$_____	$_____	$_____
Total Marketing Expense	–	$_____	$_____	$_____	$_____	$_____
Profit	=	$_____	$_____	$_____	$_____	$_____

108. Sales Price Estimate

For Job #/Name _____

Materials:	Quantity	x Unit Cost	= Extended
Raw Materials - A _____	_____	$_____	$_____
Raw Materials - B _____	_____	$_____	$_____
Raw Materials - C _____	_____	$_____	$_____
Raw Materials - D _____	_____	$_____	$_____

Total Raw Materials
$_____

Labor:	Time	x Rate	= Extended
Set Up Labor	_____	$_____	$_____
Direct Labor	_____	$_____	$_____
Post Labor	_____	$_____	$_____
Benefit Factoring (Add benefit/hour for the hours of employees included in Labor)	_____	$_____	$_____

Total Labor
$_____

Other Costs:		Costs
Outside Services		$_____
Delivery		+ $_____
Burden Rate (Overhead expense directly related to each unit produced)		+ $_____
Other _____		+ $_____
Other _____		+ $_____
Total Other Costs		= $_____

Total Raw Materials + Total Labor + Total Other Costs = Total Job Cost   = $_____

Total Job Cost x Your Desired Profit Margin _____% = Total Price of Job = $_____

109. Job Costing Report

Description _____

Job Number _____

Start Date _____

Completion Date _____

Invoice #	Transaction Description	Amount	Revenues:
_____	_____	_____	$_____
_____	_____	_____	+ $_____
_____	_____	_____	+ $_____
_____	_____	_____	+ $_____
_____	_____	_____	+ $_____
_____	_____	_____	+ $_____

Total Revenues   = $_____

Material and Outside Services Costs:

             _____ $_____

             _____ + $_____

             _____ + $_____

             _____ + $_____

             _____ + $_____

Total Materials and Services   = $_____

Labor Cost:

_____	_____	$_____
_____	_____	+ $_____
_____	_____	+ $_____
_____	_____	+ $_____
_____	_____	+ $_____
_____	_____	+ $_____

Total Labor   = $_____

Total Materials and Services + Total Labor = Total Costs   = $_____

Total Revenues – Total Costs = Profit   = $_____

110. Ratio Analysis Worksheet

For the Month Ending _____

Current Ratio = Current Assets ÷ Current Liabilities

Current Ratio = _____ ÷ _____ = This Year

Current Ratio = _____ ÷ _____ = Last Year

Inventory Turnover = Cost of Goods Sold ÷ Inventory

Inventory Turnover = _____ ÷ _____ = This Year

Inventory Turnover = _____ ÷ _____ = Last Year

Total Asset Turnover = Net Sales ÷ Total Assets

Total Asset Turnover = _____ ÷ _____ = This Year

Total Asset Turnover = _____ ÷ _____ = Last Year

Average Collection Period = Accounts Receivable ÷ Average Credit Sales/Day

Average Collection Period = _____ ÷ _____ = This Year

Average Collection Period = _____ ÷ _____ = Last Year

Long-Term Debt to Equity = Long-Term Debt ÷ Stockholders' Equity

Long-Term Debt to Equity = _____ ÷ _____ = This Year

Long-Term Debt to Equity = _____ ÷ _____ = Last Year

Total Debt to Total Assets = Total Liabilities ÷ Total Assets

Total Debt to Total Assets = _____ ÷ _____ = This Year

Total Debt to Total Assets = _____ ÷ _____ = Last Year

Earnings per Share = Earnings after Tax less Dividends ÷ Number of Common Shares Outstanding

Earnings per Share = _____ ÷ _____ = This Year

Earnings per Share = _____ ÷ _____ = Last Year

111. Production Efficiency Worksheet

Date _____ Shift _____ Supervisor _____

Comments _____

Standard Output is 100% capacity of output for production line.

Actual Output ÷ Standard Output = % Efficient

	Hour									
	1	2	3	4	5	6	7	8	9	10
Line 1 Product										
Actual Output/Hour										
Cumulative Output										
Standard Output/Hour										
Standard Cumulative										
% Efficient/Hour										
Comments										

	Hour									
	1	2	3	4	5	6	7	8	9	10
Line 3 Product										
Actual Output/Hour										
Cumulative Output										
Standard Output/Hour										
Standard Cumulative										
% Efficient/Hour										
Comments										

	Hour									
	1	2	3	4	5	6	7	8	9	10
Line 1 Product										
Actual Output/Hour										
Cumulative Output										
Standard Output/Hour										
Standard Cumulative										
% Efficient/Hour										
Comments										

	Hour									
	1	2	3	4	5	6	7	8	9	10
Line 3 Product										
Actual Output/Hour										
Cumulative Output										
Standard Output/Hour										
Standard Cumulative										
% Efficient/Hour										
Comments										

112. Purchase Order

From:

_____

_____

_____

_____

To:

_____

_____

_____

_____

Purchase Order Number _____

Please supply and deliver the goods or services specified below to the address above. The stated goods or services shall be delivered no later than _____.

This order is subject to the following conditions: _____

_____

Item #	Quantity	Description	Net Unit Price	Total
			Net Total Price	$

Invoices, quoting the order number, should be submitted for payment to:

Signed _____

Name _____

Title _____

This order is not valid unless it is signed.

Please acknowledge receipt of this order.

113. Check Requisition

Requestor		Date of Request		Date Check Needed by	
Make Payable to	**Description of Item Needed**			**Amount**	
	Total Cash Amount		$		
Authorized by			Date		

Requestor		Date of Request		Date Check Needed by	
Make Payable to	**Description of Item Needed**			**Amount**	
	Total Cash Amount		$		
Authorized by			Date		

Requestor		Date of Request		Date Check Needed by	
Make Payable to	**Description of Item Needed**			**Amount**	
	Total Cash Amount		$		
Authorized by			Date		

CHAPTER 11

Accounting 101

THIS SECTION ADDRESSES MONITORING and controlling your entity's general ledger activity, from chart of accounts to general journal. It is essential to maintain the integrity of the general ledger—the source of all of your financial reports. Of course, most businesses today use financial accounting software to record financial transactions. Conveniently, this software maintains the general ledger and general ledger transactions automatically. However, you must still have a sound understanding of underlying accounting principles to operate your financial software properly. If your chart of accounts is improperly created or maintained, your general ledger will be inaccurate.

Keep track of both accounts payable and accounts receivable with forms in this chapter. Use the *Aging of Accounts Payable* form to maintain and track the progress of your accounts payable. For accounts receivable, refer to the *Aging of Accounts Receivable* to track accounts' ages and to identify accounts

in need of collection activities.

The *Chart of Accounts Maintenance* helps you develop your chart of accounts. Classify your most common transactions into short descriptions in a logical order. Classify each chart of accounts entry as one of the following: asset, liability, capital/equity, income, or expense. expense.

Use the sample *Annual Expense Report* to maintain an ongoing summary of a sales territory's and/or product group's annual sales expenses. The sample *Auto Expense Travel Report* coincides with the Annual Expense report and records each employee's transportation-related expenditures.

Keep track of cash flow with the sample *Cash Disbursements Journal*—a form designed to maintain a monthly record of payments and disbursements (checks) that allows for you to track outgoing cash. If your business is cash-based, use the sample *Cash Receipts Control Log* to verify all purchases that would show up in a cash report similar to the sample *Daily Cash Report*, which is used to monitor the daily cash income and expenses in your business.

Keep track of employee expenditures with the sample *Expense Report* that can be given to employees so they can keep a record of daily expenses, such as food, gas, phone, entertainment, etc., while on business trips and be reimbursed when they return. The sample Expense Report is also important to have on file for tax season.

Control and track petty cash flow with the sample *Petty Cash Journal* that shows you how to update and monitor the petty cash flow and to keep a running balance of petty cash. In addition, refer to the sample *Petty Cash Vouchers* for employee use when requesting and receiving approval to use petty cash.

114. Aging of Accounts Payable

Reporting Period
From: To:

Date	Invoice #	Account	Account #	Description	Amount			
					30 Days	60 Days	90 Days	Total

115. Aging of Accounts Receivable

Reporting Period
From: To:

Date	Invoice #	Account	Account #	Description	Amount			
					30 Days	60 Days	90 Days	Total

116. Chart of Accounts Maintenance

Account	Description	Account Type	Ratio Group	Consolidation Account
_____	_____	_____	_____	_____
_____	_____	_____	_____	_____
_____	_____	_____	_____	_____
_____	_____	_____	_____	_____
_____	_____	_____	_____	_____
_____	_____	_____	_____	_____
_____	_____	_____	_____	_____
_____	_____	_____	_____	_____
_____	_____	_____	_____	_____
_____	_____	_____	_____	_____
_____	_____	_____	_____	_____
_____	_____	_____	_____	_____
_____	_____	_____	_____	_____
_____	_____	_____	_____	_____
_____	_____	_____	_____	_____
_____	_____	_____	_____	_____
_____	_____	_____	_____	_____
_____	_____	_____	_____	_____
_____	_____	_____	_____	_____
_____	_____	_____	_____	_____
_____	_____	_____	_____	_____
_____	_____	_____	_____	_____

Account Type: I = Income E = Expense A = Asset L = Liability O = Equity

Ratio Group: For financial ratio relationship groups listed on form 110, *Ratio Analysis Worksheet.*

Consolidation Account: Use to consolidate one or more accounts, such as all cash accounts into one cash account.

Entered by _____ Date _____

Authorized by _____ Date _____

117. Annual Expense Report

Year		Salesperson		
Address				
City		State		ZIP

Territory	Region/Zone	Poduct/Group	Prepared By

Month	Phone	Meals	Travel	Hotel	Enter	Misc	Total
January							
February							
March							
1st Q Total							
April							
May							
June							
2nd Q Total							
July							
August							
September							
3rd Q Total							
October							
November							
December							
4th Q Total							
Annual Totals							

Notes

118. Auto Expense Report

Employee Name:
Employee Phone:
Vehicles (year/make/model, license plate)
Immediate Supervisor Name:
Immediate Supervisor Phone:

Date	Odometer Start	Odometer Stop	Mileage x (amt)	Gas/Oil	Pkg/Tolls	Total
	Totals					

		Less Cash Advance and Charges to Company	
		Balance Due	

If submitted as an expense report, attach receipts and sign below		
Employee Signature	Title	Date
Supervisor Signature	Title	Date

119. Cash Disbursements Journal

Month											
General Ledger Number											
Date	Check #	Payee	Acct Credited	Account #	Cash	Discount	Other	Acct Debited	Account #	Acct Payable	Other

120. Cash Receipts Control Log

Period _____

Date	Check Amount	Customer ID	Reference No.
_____	$_____	_____	_____
_____	$_____	_____	_____
_____	$_____	_____	_____
_____	$_____	_____	_____
_____	$_____	_____	_____
_____	$_____	_____	_____
_____	$_____	_____	_____
_____	$_____	_____	_____
_____	$_____	_____	_____
_____	$_____	_____	_____
_____	$_____	_____	_____
_____	$_____	_____	_____
_____	$_____	_____	_____
_____	$_____	_____	_____
_____	$_____	_____	_____
_____	$_____	_____	_____
_____	$_____	_____	_____
_____	$_____	_____	_____
_____	$_____	_____	_____
_____	$_____	_____	_____
_____	$_____	_____	_____
_____	$_____	_____	_____
_____	$_____	_____	_____
_____	$_____	_____	_____
_____	$_____	_____	_____
_____	$_____	_____	_____
_____	$_____	_____	_____

Reconciled to Daily Cash Deposit by _____ Date _____

Authorized by _____ Date _____

121. Daily Cash Report

Date		Page _____ of _____		
#	Cash Received From	Amount	Cash Paid Out To	Amount
1				
2				
3				
4				
5				
6				
7				
8				
9				
10				
11				
12				
13				
14				
15				
16				
17				
18				
19				
20				
21				
	Total Cash Received		Total Cash Paid Out	
Notes				
			Total Receipts	
			Less Cash Out	
			Balance	

122. Expense Report

Period covered: From _____ To _____

Name		Dept/Sales Office	Report Date	Date of Trip	From / /	To / /

Business Purpose			Account No.			

Day	Date	Transportation (Air, Rail, Taxi, Limousine, Bus, Car Rental, etc.)	Automobile Expense (Gas Mileage, Tolls, Parking) ***	Lodging	Meals (Itemize Business: Breakfast/ Lunch/Dinner)	Entertain-ment	Misc.***	Totals
Sunday								
Monday								
Tuesday								
Wednesday								
Thursday								
Friday								
Saturday								
Totals								

Automobile Expenses*** | Entertainment and Business Meals Only***

Date	Location	Mileage, Gas, Parking, Repairs, Service	Amount	Date	Entertained (name, company, title)	Place	Business Purpose	Amount

Miscellaneous Expenses*** | Expense Summary | Instructions

Date	Detail	Amount	Total Expenses Reported	Amount	Instructions
					Deduct from my advance

Mail to:
_____
_____
_____

Employee Signature	Date
Approved By	Date

123. Petty Cash Voucher

Account	Description	Amount
	Total Cash Amount	$
Received by	Authorized by	

Account	Description	Amount
	Total Cash Amount	$
Received by	Authorized by	

Account	Description	Amount
	Total Cash Amount	$
Received by	Authorized by	

CHAPTER 12

Inventory Movement and Valuation Tools

THIS CHAPTER GUIDES YOU IN MANAGING and evaluating your inventory. Maintaining the accuracy and integrity of your inventory system is important, but so are identifying and correcting all causes of variances.

Use the *In-House Stock Requisition* form to request inventory internally. This form serves as a written record of both the request and the delivery from inventory. When you ship goods to a customer, you should accompany the goods with a *Shipping Verification*. Request that a signed copy of the Shipping Verification be returned to you and instruct your carrier to secure a signed copy on your behalf. This document serves as your proof of delivery of the shipment.

Use the *Physical Inventory Count Sheet* when performing a physical count of your inventory. The *Physical Inventory Gain or Loss* form enables you to track inaccuracies and shrinkage to your inventory by comparing your *book count*—the amount of inventory shown in your records—and your *phys-*

ical count—the amount of inventory shown by an inspection.

Substantial differences between book count and physical count can mean poor recordkeeping, entry errors, and, in some cases, employee theft. The *Raw Material Shrinkage Report* helps calculate and track losses due to shrinkage of inventory. This tool can help you pinpoint problem areas.

The *Physical Inventory Valuation Report* determines your total physical inventory value. Simply enter the quantity of each item based on a physical inventory count and multiply the quantity by the cost per unit to determine the value. The *Book Inventory Valuation Report* works the same way as the Physical Inventory Valuation Report, except that you use the book count of inventory. The advantage of the Book Inventory Valuation Report is that it doesn't require a full physical inventory count. The obvious disadvantage, however, is that book inventory counts are typically less accurate than physical inventory counts. The *Physical vs. Book Inventory Cost*

Variance Report reveals the differences between the book value and the physical value of your inventory.

The *Inventory Status Sheet* helps you maintain an accurate physical count of individual items. Use the *Authorization to Destroy Inventory* to secure approval before disposing of inventory and to notify appropriate personal of the inventory change. Use the *Property Loss Report* whenever your business suffers a loss to its inventory or property. Be sure to fill the form out completely and as soon as possible after the loss. A promptly completed Property Loss Report will carry more evidentiary weight with insurance adjusters.

124. In-House Stock Requisition

Requisition # _____

From _____

Job Reference Number _____ Date Needed _____

Department _____

Location _____

Description of items requested from in-house stock:

Quantity	Item Number	Description	Quantity Issued	Date Issued	Initials

Requested by			Date
Approved by			Date

125. Shipping Verification

From:

_____

_____

_____

_____

Shipper _____   Date _____

Ship to: Carrier

_____   _____

_____   _____

_____   _____

Quantity Shipped	Item Number	Description

Proof of shipment received:

Signature of Receiving Clerk   Date

126. Physical Inventory Count Sheet

Sheet #		Location	
Item Number	Description	Quantity	Location
Counted by		Date	

127. Physical Inventory Gain or Loss

For the Period Ending:

Item Number	Description	Book Count	Physical Count	Difference

| Prepared by | | Date | | |
| Reviewed by | | Date | | |

128. Raw Material Shrinkage Report

For the Period Ending:

Item Number	Description	Cost per Unit	Quantity Lost	Total Value Lost

All shrinkage losses greater than $_____ per item are to be explained below.

_____

_____

Prepared by _____ Date _____

Reviewed by _____ Date _____

129. Physical Inventory Valuation Report

For the Period Ending:

Item Number	Description	Quantity	Cost per Unit	Total Value
			Total Value	$

Prepared by	Date
Reviewed by	Date

130. Book Inventory Valuation Report

For the Period Ending:				
Item Number	Description	Quantity	Cost per Unit	Total Value
			Total Value	$

Prepared by	Date
Reviewed by	Date

131. Physical vs. Book Inventory Cost Variance Report

For the Period Ending:

Item Number	Description	Book Value	Physical Value	Difference
			Total Value	$

Prepared by	Date	
Reviewed by	Date	

132. Inventory Status Sheet

Item Description				Item Number		
Quantity on Hand	Quantity Ordered	Date Ordered	Unit Cost	Quantity Received	Date Received	Usage

Quantity on Hand: The present quantity of inventory per book inventory report
Quantity Ordered: The quantity of item ordered from vendor
Date Ordered: The date item was ordered from vendor
Unit Cost: The unit cost of item per vendor
Quantity Received: The quantity of item received from vendor
Date Received: The date item was received from vendor
Usage: The actual usage of item in production or sales
Add Quantity on Hand to Quantity Received and subtract Usage to get next Quantity on Hand.

133. Authorization to Destroy Inventory

Date _____

Reason for Request to Destroy Inventory:

_____

_____

_____

_____

Item Number	Description	Quantity to Be Destroyed

Prepared by	Date
Reviewed by	Date

Copy to: Inventory Control, Accounting, Warehouse Manager, and Files.

134. Property Loss Report

Department		Date	
Completed by		Date	

Cause of Loss
❏ Theft
❏ Vandalism
❏ Burglary
❏ Tools and Equipment
❏ Fire/Arson
❏ Accident/Damage
❏ Unexplained
❏ Other:

_____
_____
_____

Type of Loss
❏ Property Damage
❏ Inventory
❏ Money/Cash
❏ Tools and Equipment
❏ Employee Time
❏ Business Interruption
❏ Other:

_____
_____
_____

Type of Loss	Description	Value Lost

Date and Time Loss Occurred _____

Date and Time Loss Reported _____

❏ Police Report Made   Report ID # _____

List Police Department Contacts and Notes _____

Besides the property loss, were there any other consequences of the loss? _____

_____

Could this loss have been avoided? ❏ Yes   ❏ No

If Yes, how? _____

_____

Other Comments, Notes: _____

_____

CHAPTER 13

Get Paid: Credit, Billing, and Collection Tools

THE FORMS PRESENTED IN THIS CHAPTER ARE signed to help your company receive payment for the goods and services your company provide. The forms include credit application forms, credit terms documentation, past due reminder and demand letters, and invoices/statements.

Your company will have an easier time with the challenges of billing and collections if it formalizes its credit application process and consistently applies the credit application process for every customer who comes knocking. When a new customer appears, you should begin by asking the customer to complete the *Authorization to Release Credit Information*. This authorization form gives your company the authority to make inquiries with credit reporting bureaus without fear of consequence. Never submit a credit inquiry to a credit-reporting bureau without written authorization. You'll also ask your new customer to complete either the *Business Credit Application* or, if the customer is an individual, the *Personal Credit*

Application. These credit application forms are invaluable. Not only do they help you evaluate your customer for creditworthiness, but also they serve to obtain information that can make the collection process easier in the event that your customer defaults on the credit arrangements. The *Credit Approval Form* is an internal tracking mechanism that collects certain information gleaned from the credit inquiry process and ensures that all necessary staff authorize the approval of credit for each customer.

Once your organization has agreed to extend credit to a customer, you should document the credit terms by having your customer submit a signed copy of the *Credit Terms Agreement*. This is powerful protection that can give you significant leverage if a customer defaults on those credit terms.

Naturally, you can increase the speed at which your customers pay and the reliability with which they pay if you make it fast and easy. The *EasyPay Automatic Payment Agreement* is a notice and agreement signed by your customer that enables you to make automatic withdrawals from either your customer's bank or your customer's credit card. Once this agreement is in place, your customers are far more likely to pay on time and in full.

The *Response to Request for Adjustment of Account* is a letter that your credit or collections department would send to a customer who has formally requested an adjustment to his or her account.

The next four forms in this chapter address the unfortunate but all-too-common circumstance of a late-paying or nonpaying customer. The four letters escalate both in tone and consequences. The *Credit Terms Reminder Letter* is a bland and polite reminder for the habitually late-paying customer. We have included two *Past Due Reminder Letter*s, which you should promptly issue when a customer fails to pay after 30 and 45 days, respectively. You should always endeavor not to let your receivables age: studies show that uncollected customer balances are far less likely to be collected if they are allowed to age beyond 60, 90, and 120 days. A third collection letter is the *Past Due Demand Letter*. This is your last resort when han-

dling a nonpaying customer; the letter terminates the credit privileges of the errant customer and threatens legal and collection action.

It's important to recognize the difference between invoices and statements. *Invoices* are individual billing notices; typically, one invoice is delivered to a customer for each order. *Statements* are billing summaries; typically, a statement is delivered to a customer periodically. The statement summarizes billing and payment activity and references individual invoices. If you invoice your customers, you should issue monthly statements, as well. We have included two forms of invoices. Use the *Job Invoice* when you provide both materials and labor to your customers; use the *Customer Invoice* when you provide only goods or only services. Use the *Customer Statement* to advise your customers of billing and payment activity.

The *Request for Payment* form is a simple invoice best used for a one-time customer for whom you do not wish to set up a full-blown account. Use the *Short Pay Inquiry Form* when a customer fails to pay the full amount of an invoice.

135. Authorization to Release Credit Information

From:

_____

_____

_____

_____

To:

_____

_____

_____

_____

Date _____

Dear _____,

Thank you for your recent interest in establishing credit with our company. Please sign the authorization to release information agreement below and complete the enclosed form. Then send them to us with your most recent financial statements. We will contact your credit and bank references. Then we will contact you regarding your credit terms with our company.

Thank you.

[Signature]

Credit Manager

We have recently applied for credit with _____.
We have been requested to provide information for their use in reviewing our creditworthiness. Therefore, I authorize the investigation of me and my firm, _____, and its related credit information.

The release in any manner of all information by you is authorized whether such information is of record or not.

I do hereby release all persons, agencies, firms, companies, etc. from any damages resulting from providing such information.

This authorization is valid for 30 days from the date of my signature below. Please keep a copy of my release request for your files. Thank you for your cooperation.

Signature _____   Date _____

136. Business Credit Application

From:

_____

_____

_____

Thank you for your interest in our company's products and services. We appreciate your business and look forward to a long and prosperous business relationship.

Please complete the credit application and return it to the above address, attention Credit Department. Please note our credit terms. You will be advised shortly of your credit status with our company. Thank you.

Credit Application

Business Legal Name _____

Business Trade Name _____

Web Site Address _____

Business Address Information

Address _____

City/Town _____

State/Province _____ ZIP _____

Check one:

Sole Proprietorship _____ Partnership _____ Corporation _____ LLC _____ Other _____

Federal Tax ID Number _____

Contact Person _____ Title _____

Contact Person _____ Title _____

Phone (_____)_____ Ext _____ Fax (_____)_____

E-mail Address _____ Dept _____

Hours of Operation _____

Names of Authorized Account Users _____

Do you require an Invoice? Yes _____ No _____

Invoice Preferred?

Weekly invoice and monthly statement _____ Open item statement _____

Billing Address Information (If different from above)

Address _____

City/Town _____

State/Province _____ ZIP _____

Contact Persons _____ Title _____

Phone (_____)_____ Ext _____ Fax (_____)_____

E-mail Address _____ Dept _____

Other Location Information (i.e., local contacts)

Additional Location _____

Address _____

City/Town _____

State/Province _____ ZIP _____

Contact Persons _____ Title _____

Phone (_____)_____ Ext _____ Fax (_____)_____

E-mail Address _____ Dept _____

Hours of Operation _____

Preferred Billing Date _____

Names of Authorized Users _____

Doing Business as (DBA) Names _____

Bank References

Bank Name _____

Account Number _____

City/Town _____

State/Province _____ Phone (_____) _____ Ext _____

Bank Officer _____

Bank Name _____

Account Number _____

City/Town _____

State/Province _____ Phone (_____) _____ Ext _____

Bank Officer _____

Trade or Supplier Credit References (Must provide at least 3)

Name _____

Address _____

Person to Contact _____

City/Town _____

State/Province _____ ZIP _____

Phone (_____)_____ Ext _____ Fax (_____)_____

Name _____

Address _____

Person to Contact _____

City/Town _____

State/Province _____ ZIP _____

Phone (_____)_____ Ext _____ Fax (_____)_____

Name _____

Address _____

Person to Contact _____

City/Town _____

State/Province _____ ZIP _____

Phone (_____)_____ Ext _____ Fax (_____)_____

Names of Principals: Owners, Officers, Partners

Name _____

Address _____

City/Town _____

State/Province _____ ZIP _____

Phone (_____)_____ Ext _____ Fax (_____)_____

Title _____ Social Security # _____-_____-_____

Name _____

Address _____

City/Town _____

State/Province _____ ZIP _____

Phone (_____)_____ Ext _____ Fax (_____)_____

Title _____ Social Security # _____-_____-_____

Please attach additional pages if you have more than two principals.

I certify that I am authorized to sign and submit this application for and on behalf of the applicant. I also certify that the foregoing information is true and correct to the best of my knowledge.

_____   _____
Name (Please Print or Type)   Title

_____   _____
Signature   Date

137. Personal Credit Application

From:

_____

_____

_____

Thank you for your interest in our company's products and services. We appreciate your business and look forward to a long and prosperous business relationship.

Please complete the credit application and return it to the above address, attention Credit Department. Please note our credit terms. You will be advised shortly of your credit status with our company. Thank you.

Credit Application

Personal Information:

Name_____

Address _____

City/Town _____

State/Province _____ ZIP _____

Social Security Number _____-_____-_____

Phone (_____)_____ Ext _____ Fax (_____)_____

E-mail Address _____ Date of Birth_____

Do you ❑ Own? ❑ Rent?   Monthly Housing Payment Amount $_____

Prior Addresses for the Last 5 Years:

Address _____ City, State ZIP

_____

Address _____ City, State ZIP

_____

Employment:

Employer _____

Address _____

Occupation _____

Contact to verify employment _____ Phone # (_____)_____

Length of Employment _____ Monthly Gross Salary _____

Credit References:

Bank Name _____ Account Number
_____

City/Town _____

State/Province _____ Phone (_____) _____ Ext _____

Bank Officer _____

Credit Card Type _____ Number _____ Exp. Date
_____

Credit Card Type _____ Number _____ Exp. Date
_____

I certify that I am authorized to sign and submit this application for and on behalf of the applicant. I also certify that the foregoing information is true and correct to the best of my knowledge.

_____   _____
Name (Please Print or Type)   Date

_____
Signature

138. Credit Approval Form

To be completed by the Credit Department.

Company Name (Applicant) _____

Company Address _____

Contact Name _____

Phone Number _____

Bank References _____

_____

Notes _____

_____

_____

Credit References _____

_____

Notes _____

_____

_____

Approximate Amount of Business Anticipated per Month (as per Sales Manager) $ _____

Credit Terms _____

Credit Limit _____

Any Special Instructions _____

_____

_____

Prepared by _____

Approvals:

Credit Manager _____ Date _____

Sales Manager _____ Date _____

Controller _____ Date _____

General Manager _____ Date _____

139. Credit Terms Agreement

I, the "Applicant," hereby agree to the following credit terms agreement in connection with my application for credit terms from _____ ("Company"). I, Applicant, agree as follows:

1. Applicant represents that the information supplied with the credit application and all associated documentation is in all respects complete, accurate, and truthful. Applicant agrees to notify Company promptly, in writing, of any substantive changes in the information Applicant has provided.

2. Applicant agrees to pay in full for goods and services rendered (without deduction or setoff) on or before the earlier of the 30th day of the month following the date of billing or the due date started on each billing to the order of Company. Any amounts not paid when due shall be assessed a service charge at the rate of _____% per year (_____% per month) or the highest rate allowed by law.

3. If Applicant's account is placed or given to an attorney for collection, Applicant shall pay any and all expenses of collection and attempted collection, court costs, and reasonable attorney's fees in addition to other amounts due. The failure of Company to charge interest on Applicant's account or pursue any other remedy available to it shall not constitute Company's waiver of any rights.

4. The acceptance of this application by Company does not constitute an agreement to extend credit to Applicant or to provide services to Applicant. Company, in its absolute discretion, may set and/or modify credit limits from time to time or terminate credit, with or without notice to Applicant.

5. In the event Applicant or any affiliate of Applicant (i.e., a company or other entity under common control) defaults in the payment of any sums due to Company, all other amounts due from Applicant or any affiliate shall be immediately due and payable, including any amount due for freight in transit. Also, in the event of such default, to the extent allowed under applicable law, Company is hereby authorized by Applicant to take possession of any freight then being shipped by Applicant and hold the same until payment is made, with all the rights of a secured party under the Uniform Commercial Code, as applicable in the State of Company's headquarters.

6. Applicant agrees that Company may set off against monies due it from Applicant or any affiliate any monies owed by Company to Applicant or any affiliate. Applicant agrees that he/she will not set off against any amounts due Company or claimed to be due to Applicant from Company.

7. If any one or more of the above terms becomes invalid or illegal in any respect, such term or terms shall be waived and the validity, legality, and enforceability of the remaining terms shall not be affected.

8. All disputes related to underlying charges must be submitted to Company no later than 30 days following date of billing. Any billing not challenged within 60 days will be deemed accepted and it is agreed will not thereafter be subject to dispute by Applicant. Adjustments must be submitted to Company in writing. All adjustments must reference either an invoice number or an air waybill number, or both numbers, for which the adjustment is being made.

9. I have read, I understand, and I accept the above terms, and I have provided true information to the best of my knowledge. I understand you will rely on the information provided herein in determining

whether to extend credit and the limits thereof and that you may wish to periodically update the information given herein. For the purpose of obtaining credit from Company, Applicant hereby authorizes Company or its agents to investigate the Applicant's personal, partnership, or corporate credit and financial responsibility.

_____

Applicant

_____   _____

Name (Please Print or Type)   Title

_____   _____

Signature   Date

140. EasyPay Automatic Payment Agreement

Here's How It Works:

When you enroll in EasyPay, we deduct funds automatically from your local checking account or credit card account to pay your bill. Your bill will be paid for you on time and automatically. You won't have to worry about missing a payment if you are away on a business trip or vacation. You'll continue to receive your monthly statement and you'll have 15 days from the billing date to review it before your bank pays the amount due. If you feel there is a problem with your bill, simply call us at _____. Of course, you can always dispute a bill with us even if the bill was paid automatically—we are always here to listen. You can notify us if you wish to discontinue EasyPay at any time.

It's Easy to Start EasyPay:

Simply complete the attached form and return it with your next payment. Enclose an original check marked "Void" or a photocopy of a check from the checking account you wish to have debited or, if you wish to have your credit card account billed automatically, just fill out the form below. Your next bill will show "No Payment Due" and your financial institution will show the appropriate debit on your monthly statement.

Why wait? Just fill out the form and send it in with your next payment.

EasyPay Authorization Agreement

I hereby authorize _____ ("Company") to deduct funds from my checking account/credit card account listed below to pay my Company bills. I understand that these automatic payments may be cancelled if I notify Company in writing prior to the next billing date.

_____

Name of Your Bank or Credit Card Company (Please Print)

_____   _____

Your Name as Shown on Financial Institution Records   Your Daytime Phone

_____

Address in Our Records

_____   _____

Your Signature as Shown on Financial Institution Records   Today's Date

To Charge a Bank Account: please attach an original check on which you've written "VOID" or a photocopy of a check from your checking account and return it along with this form with your next payment. Deposit slips cannot be accepted.

To Charge a Credit Card: please fill out the following:

_____   _____

Type: VISA/MasterCard/American Express   Card Number   Exp. Date

_____

Credit Card Billing Address

141. Response to Request for Adjustment of Account

From:

_____

_____

_____

_____

To:

_____

_____

_____

Date _____

Dear Customer:

Thank you for writing us regarding an error or adjustment to your account with our firm.

We have received your request and are currently researching your account and its history. We should complete our research shortly and make any necessary adjustment on your next statement. Understand that the accuracy of your account is of vital importance to us and that we will give this matter our highest attention.

Yours truly,

142. Credit Terms Reminder Letter

From:

_____

_____

_____

_____

To:

_____

_____

_____

_____

Date _____

Dear _____:

Thank you for your recent order with our firm. As a reminder to your Purchasing and Accounts Payable Departments, our credit terms are as follows:

_____. If you have any questions about your credit terms or our policies, please feel free to contact us.

Thank you for adhering to our credit policy. We hope our business relationship is a long and prosperous one.

Thank you again.

143. Past Due Reminder Letter (30 Days)

From:

_____

_____

_____

_____

To:

_____

_____

_____

_____

Date _____

Dear Customer:

Please take note that your account is still past due in the amount of $ _____. We sent you a statement a short time ago, which was not acted upon by you. Please submit payment immediately to avoid further charges to your account. We want to continue our relationship with you, but we need your cooperation and your payment to do so.

Thank you for your attention to this matter.

144. Past Due Reminder Letter (45 Days)

From:

_____

_____

_____

_____

To:

_____

_____

_____

_____

Date _____

Dear Customer:

Please take note that your account is still past due in the amount of $ _____. We sent you a statement a short time ago, which was not acted upon by you. Please submit payment immediately.

Your failure to pay the amount due on your account is a violation of the terms of your credit agreement with us. We therefore will suspend your account in seven days from the date of this letter if we do not receive payment. Once we suspend your account, it is unlikely that we will reactivate credit terms on your account.

We sincerely hope that you submit payment in full.

Thank you.

145. Past Due Demand Letter

From:

_____

_____

_____

_____

To:

_____

_____

_____

_____

Date _____

Dear Customer:

This matter requires your immediate attention. Please take note that your account is still past due in the amount of $_____. We sent you a statement a short time ago, and several reminders, upon which you have not acted. This is our final request for payment and we ask that you submit payment immediately.

We had sincerely hoped that we could continue to do business with you, but your failure to pay your outstanding bill has made that impossible. We have suspended your credit privileges with our company.

Furthermore, if we do not receive payment immediately, we will turn this matter over for collection to a collection agency or attorney, or both. Please review your credit agreement. We will be seeking interest and we may also seek court costs and fees and attorney's fees to the extent permitted by law.

We sincerely hope that you submit payment in full to avoid the course of action that we have outlined here.

Thank you.

146. Job Invoice

Buyer

Date	Your Order #	Our Order #	Sales Rep	FOB	Ship Via	Terms	Tax ID

Materials				Labor			
Quantity	Material	Unit Price	Amount	Date	Hours/Tasks	Rate	Amount
Total Materials					Total Labor		
				Total Materials and Labor			

147. Customer Invoice

Buyer

Date	Your Order #	Our Order #	Sales Rep	FOB	Ship Via	Terms	Tax ID

Quantity	Item	Units	Description	Discount %	Taxable	Unit Price	Total
							Balance

148. Customer Statement

Buyer

Statement Date	Statement #

Reference	Date	Item/Code	Description	Amount	Balance
				Balance	

Codes: C = Credit Memo P = Payment A = Discount Allowed
D = Debit Memo I = Invoice F = Finance Charge

149. Request for Payment

From:

_____

_____

_____

_____

To:

_____

_____

_____

_____

Date _____

Dear Customer:

We have received your order and promptly processed the order according to your instructions. Please send the amount listed below immediately. Payment is expected in the form of a check, money order, VISA, or MasterCard. Please place the reference number on your payment. We appreciate your interest in our product/service and your prompt attention to this matter.

Thank you.

Accounting Department

Amount $ _____ Reference # _____

From:

Check payment $ _____ Check # _____

To Charge a Credit Card: please fill out the following:

_____

Type: VISA/MasterCard/American Express   Card Number   Exp. Date

_____

Credit Card Billing Address

150. Short Pay Inquiry Form

From:

_____

_____

_____

_____

To:

_____

_____

_____

_____

Date _____

Dear Customer:

We recently received payment from you for our invoice # _____. Thank you.

However, the amount that you submitted fell short of the amount of the invoice. We were unable to determine why. Below please tell us the reason for the short pay so that we may review our records and determine if the short pay is acceptable.

Thank you.

Accounting Department

Amount of short-paid $ _____   Reference # _____

From _____

Reason for short payment _____

_____

CHAPTER 14

Financial Reports

THIS CHAPTER OFFERS A FULL RANGE OF financial reports and supporting schedules that will help you produce accurate financial reports for your business. Many of the forms are interactive spreadsheet files that will calculate most of the figures for you.

The *Period-End Closing and Analysis* is a control tool that greatly increases the accuracy and integrity of your financial statements. Use this form to close out the month, the quarter, and the year. The *Actual vs. Budget Income Statement* is an interactive computer spreadsheet file that calculates the variance between budgeted income statement items and actual income statement items. You'll find a copy of the file on the disk included with this volume. Enter the actual and budgeted items and the worksheet calculates the dollar variance for each item.

The seven *Balance Sheet Support Schedules* help you accumulate information for individual balance sheet items. These can be real money-savers; they make it unnecessary for

your accountant or auditor to accumulate the information on his or her own. The *Balance Sheet Support Schedule—Cash Balance* accumulates information on cash accounts. The *Balance Sheet Support Schedule—Marketable Securities* accumulates information on stocks, bonds, and other marketable instruments. The *Balance Sheet Support Schedule—Accounts Receivable* aggregates accounts receivable information. The *Balance Sheet Support Schedule—Inventory* accumulates information on inventory. The *Balance Sheet Support Schedule—Prepaid Expenses* amortizes prepaid expenses and aggregates period-end totals. The *Balance Sheet Support Schedule—Accounts Payable* summarizes and accumulates accounts payable information. The *Balance Sheet Support Schedule—Notes Payable* accumulates information on notes and loan obligations.

The *Cash Flow Forecast—12 Month* is an interactive spreadsheet that forecasts sales, expenses, and available cash for a 12-month period. The *Cash Flow Forecast—Five Year* does the same for a five-year period. The files are on the disk included with this volume. Enter your anticipated sales and expenses, and the worksheet calculates the surplus or deficit and the running cash balance.

The *Income Statement—12 Month* is an interactive spreadsheet that accumulates and totals income statement items for a 12-month period. The *Income Statement—Quarterly* calculates the same data for four quarters. Enter your sales and expenses, and the worksheet records the information and calculates the total annual balance for all items.

The *Quarterly Balance Sheet* is an interactive spreadsheet that accumulates and totals balance sheet items for four quarters. The *Year-End Balance Sheet* calculates the same data at the end of your year. Enter your assets and liabilities and the worksheet records the information and calculates the total balance for all items.

151. Period-End Closing and Analysis

Using this form will increase the level of accuracy and integrity of the financial statements and general ledger. Use to ensure that all month-end tasks have been completed and reviewed.

1. Cash in Banks	Done by	Date	Reviewed by	Date
All bank accounts reconciled from month-end balance per the bank statement to the general ledger balance, with all unusual reconciling items investigated and resolved. (Ensure that, prior to reconciliation, the general ledger balance has been updated to reflect all quarterly entries.)				
Bank reconciliations prepared by an employee who is independent from the cash receipts and disbursements functions.				
Bank reconciliations initialed and dated by the preparer.				
Bank reconciliation reviewed by manager, as evidenced by his/her initials and date.				
2. Accounts Receivable–Trade				
General ledger balance reconciled to balance per detailed accounts receivable aging. All reconciling items investigated and resolved, with journal entries prepared as required.				
All customer account receivable balances have been reviewed for collectibility, giving proper consideration to: ▪ All significant past due accounts ▪ All disputed invoices and erroneous billings ▪ All unissued credits.				
The allowance for doubtful accounts has been determined as the sum of the specific and general reserves and has been treated as an offset of current trade receivables. The journal entry to record the specific reserve for disputed invoices, erroneous credits, and doubtful accounts and the general reserve has been made against bad debt expense: ▪ Debit bad debt expense ▪ Credit allowance for doubtful accounts				
All specific invoices determined to be uncollectible have been written off against the allowance for doubtful accounts by the following entry: ▪ Debit allowance for doubtful accounts ▪ Credit accounts receivables-trade				
The approval for the write-offs of uncollectible accounts has been made by individuals who do not have direct access to incoming cash receipts or to the accounts receivable ledgers.				

3. Other Receivables (including notes)	Done by	Date	Reviewed by	Date
All other receivables are supported by account analyses and have been evaluated as to collectibility. Adjustments have been made as required.				
4. Inventory				
Physical inventory of supplies and materials taken and compared with stock status. Any discrepancies are to be identified, researched, and corrected for the following inventory items: ■ Raw Materials ■ Finished Goods ■ Other				
The physical inventory reconciliation worksheets between physical and stock status report are to be reviewed and approved by manager, as evidenced by his/her initials and date.				
Determine that the stock status report properly reflects month-end quantities on hand and current unit costs.				
Update the inventory cost summary spreadsheet with the following information: ■ Beginning year inventory value by item and category ■ Current month-end inventory value by item and category ■ Determine inventory value difference between beginning inventory values and current month-end values ■ Journal entry prepared to record inventory ■ Reverse the prior period's inventory entry				
Record inventory using the net inventory amount obtained in earlier mentioned step, as follows: ■ Debit/credit inventory account ■ Credit/debit cost of costs sold (If difference between beginning and current month valuations is positive, debit inventory and credit cogs; if difference is negative, debit COGS and credit inventory.)				
Attach supporting schedules to the journal entry sheet.				
5. Prepaid Expenses				
Changes in account balances have been analyzed and composition of account balances listed on support schedules, which agree with general ledger for each account: ■ Prepaid state income taxes? ■ Prepaid IRS ■ Prepaid insurance				

6. Property, Plant, and Equipment	Done by	Date	Reviewed by	Date

Journal entry prepared to record depreciation expense for the current month from prepared detail property records, as follows:
▪ Debit depreciation expense.
▪ Credit accumulated depreciation for each account:
  – Equipment
  – Automobiles
  – Leasehold improvements				

Review and ensure that cost and general ledger agree with detailed records of fixed assets for each account: ▪ Equipment ▪ Automobiles ▪ Leasehold improvements				
Changes in asset costs (additions and disposals) are substantiated by vendor invoices or cash receipts. Gain or loss computed and recorded after taking into account related accumulated depreciation.				
7. Deposits and Other Assets				
Changes in account balances have been analyzed and composition of account balances listed on support schedules, which agree with general ledger for each account.				
8. Accounts Payable				
Accounting department completed matching of invoices received by month-end to open receivers (merchandise received by month-end and included in inventory, for which invoices have not been received), prepared accounts payables vouchers, and processed through A/P system. (Cut-off procedures for accounts payables must coincide with those for inventory.)				
Prepare schedules listing open receivers and other open payables.				
Merchandise recap schedule prepared from accounts payable schedules, listing accruals, returns for credits, merchandise returns, merchandise returns deducted from payments, holding for credit, overage, and freight applicable for the month.				
Journal entry prepared to record above prepared schedules: ▪ Debit applicable cost of sales or expense account. ▪ Credit accounts payables.				
Journal entry prepared reversing prior month accrual for open receivers and other accounts payables adjustments.				

8. Accounts Payable (continued)	Done by	Date	Reviewed by	Date
Check registers issued by accounts payables covering the period between month-end and date of the accounts payable expense. Distribution report reviewed to determine what checks were issued subsequent to month-end.				
Journal entry prepared to record above: ■ Debit cash. ■ Credit accounts payable.				
Accounts payable per detailed listing, reconciled to the general ledger balance. All discrepancies are to be identified, researched, and corrected.				
9. Accrued Expenses				
All accounts analyzed and composition of account balance schedules in agreement with the general ledger balances: ■ Federal tax payable. ■ State income tax payable. ■ Payroll tax payable. ■ Workers comp payable. ■ Sales tax payable. ■ Other taxes payable. ■ City tax payable. ■ Accrued wages payable.				
Inquiries made regarding services received for which invoices not received (e.g. legal, accounting, consulting, etc). Proper journal entries prepared to record such expenses in the month that the services were received, as follows: ■ Debit various expense accounts. ■ Credit various accrued expense accounts.				
Amount of accrued payroll expense determined by obtaining the payroll recap for the first payroll subsequent to month-end and prorating the total to the month prior to and subsequent to month-end. Journal entry prepared as follows: ■ Debit payroll expense by department. ■ Credit accrued wages payable.				
10. Other Liabilities				
General ledger balances in agreement with the detailed support schedules and amortization schedules. Any discrepancies should be identified, researched, and corrected.				
Evaluate propriety of short-term versus long-term general ledger balances and classify accordingly.				

11. Sales	Done by	Date	Reviewed by	Date
Total monthly sales-including gross, sales tax, discounts, and net-have been accumulated from the accounts receivable subsystem into a monthly sales journal, cash receipts, and discounts taken journal.				
12. Other Income				
Interest-bearing investments reviewed and interest earned through month-end but not received is accrued as follows: ■ Debit interest income receivable. ■ Credit interest income.				
13. Work in Progress				
Review open orders file. Prepare list of open orders reflecting all related costs incurred with open orders (jobs).				
Prepare appropriate journal entry to match costs with revenues from above mentioned schedule, as follows: ■ Debit work in progress. ■ Credit various cost of sales, wages, and other related expense accounts.				
Prepare appropriate journal entry to match costs with revenues from above mentioned schedule, as follows: ■ Debit work in progress. ■ Credit various cost of sales, wages, and other related expense accounts.				
Prepare reversing entry of prior month's work in progress entry, as follows: ■ Debit various cost of sales, wages, and other related expense accounts. ■ Credit work in progress.				
14. Commissions				
Review open job orders, ensuring that all closed jobs are recorded closed.				
Review job costing detail reports, ensuring that total revenues and related costs tie out to revenues and costs reflected in preliminary trial balance. If any discrepancies, identify, research, and correct as appropriate.				
Summarize the month's closed job cost detail reports by number of closed jobs, revenues, and related costs from above reconciliation.				
Generate and review commission recap schedule by salesperson, to ensure that closed jobs, revenues less sales tax, and related costs tie out to the summarized job costing detail reports.				

14. Commissions (continued)	Done by	Date	Reviewed by	Date
Extend net sales less related expenses at commission rate ____% for each salesperson by closed job. Total and cross-foot commission recap schedule.				
Accrue commissions expense by the following journal entry: ▪ Debit commission expense. ▪ Credit accrued commissions.				
15. Income Taxes				
Quarterly tax provisions and tax liability calculated based upon pro rata share of annualized net income, giving consideration to tax payments made, net operating loss carry forwards, etc.				

152. Actual vs. Budget Income Statement

For the Period:	Actual	Budget	Variance-$
Sales			
Sales			$0.00
Other			$0.00
Total Sales	$0.00	$0.00	$0.00
Less Cost of Goods Sold			
Materials			$0.00
Labor			$0.00
Overhead			$0.00
Other			$0.00
Total Cost of Goods Sold	$0.00	$0.00	$0.00
Gross Profit	$0.00	$0.00	$0.00
Operating Expenses			
Salaries and wages			$0.00
Employee benefits			$0.00
Payroll taxes			$0.00
Rent			$0.00
Utilities			$0.00
Repairs and maintenance			$0.00
Insurance			$0.00
Travel			$0.00
Telephone			$0.00
Postage			$0.00
Office supplies			$0.00
Advertising/Marketing			$0.00
Professional fees			$0.00
Training and development			$0.00
Bank charges			$0.00
Depreciation			$0.00
Miscellaneous			$0.00
Other			$0.00
Total Operating Expenses	$0.00	$0.00	$0.00
Operating Income	$0.00	$0.00	$0.00
Interest Income (expense)			$0.00
Other Income (expense)			$0.00
Total Nonoperating Income (expense)	$0.00	$0.00	$0.00
Income (Loss) Before Taxes	$0.00	$0.00	$0.00
Income Taxes			$0.00
Net Income (Loss)	$0.00	$0.00	$0.00

153. Balance Sheet Support Schedule–Cash Balance

For the Period:			
Bank Account Detail Description		Balance, This Month, This Year	Balance, This Month, Prior Year
Bank Name	Account		
Total Cash Balances		$	$

Detail totals must agree with Cash on Balance Sheet.

This table reflects bank balances that comprise the cash balance on a company's balance sheet. This is a detailed report often used in CPA review. If management prepares this report before CPA review, CPA fees can be dramatically reduced.

Prepared by _____ Date _____

Reviewed by _____ Date _____

154. Balance Sheet Support Schedule—Marketable Securities

For the Period:			
Marketable Securities Detail Description		Balance, This Month, This Year	Balance, This Month, Prior Year
Investment Type	Description		
Total Marketable Securities Balance		$	$

Detail totals must agree with Marketable Securities on Balance Sheet.

This table reflects bank balances that comprise the marketable securities balance on a company's balance sheet. This is a detailed report often used in CPA review. If management prepares this report before CPA review, CPA fees can be dramatically reduced.

Prepared by _____ Date _____

Reviewed by _____ Date _____

155. Balance Sheet Support Schedule–Accounts Receivable

For the Period:		
Accounts Receivable	Balance, This Month, This Year	Balance, This Month, Prior Year
Balance per Accounts Receivable Detail:		
Current		
Over 30 days		
Over 60 days		
Over 90 days		
Total Accounts Receivable Balance	$	$

Detail totals must agree with Accounts Receivables on Balance Sheet.

Prepared by _____ Date _____

Reviewed by _____ Date _____

156. Balance Sheet Support Schedule–Inventory

For the Period:		
Inventory	Balance, This Month, This Year	Balance, This Month, Prior Year
Balance per Inventory Detail:		
Raw Materials		
Work in Progress		
Finished Goods		
Other		
Total Inventory Balance	$	$

Detail totals must agree with Inventory on Balance Sheet.

Prepared by _____ Date _____

Reviewed by _____ Date _____

157. Balance Sheet Support Schedule—Prepaid Expenses

For the Period:		
Prepaid Expenses	Balance, This Month, This Year	Balance, This Month, Prior Year
Balance per Prepaid Expenses Amortization Schedules:		
Prepaid Insurance		
For the Period _____ / _____ to _____ / _____ Total of Payments Months in Period Monthly Amortized Amount Remaining Periods	÷ = X	
Total Prepaid Insurance Balance	$	$
Prepaid Worker's Compensation		
For the Period _____ / _____ to _____ / _____ Total of Payments Months in Period Monthly Amortized Amount Remaining Periods	÷ = X	
Total Prepaid Worker's Compensation Balance	$	$
Prepaid Other		
Description: For the Period _____ / _____ to _____ / _____ Total of Payments Months in Period Monthly Amortized Amount Remaining Periods	÷ = X	
Total Prepaid Other Balance	$	$
Grand Total All Prepaid Expense Balances	$	$

Detail totals must agree with Prepaid Expenses on Balance Sheet.

Prepared by _____ Date _____

Reviewed by _____ Date _____

158. Balance Sheet Support Schedule—Accounts Payable

For the Period:		
Accounts Payable	Balance, This Month, This Year	Balance, This Month, Prior Year
Beginning Balance		
Purchases		
Disbursements		
Adjustments		
Ending Balance		
Total Accounts Payable Balance	$	$

Detail totals must agree with Accounts Payable on Balance Sheet.

Prepared by _____ Date _____

Reviewed by _____ Date _____

159. Balance Sheet Support Schedule–Notes Payable

For the Period:

Notes Payable	Balance, This Month, This Year	Balance, This Month, Prior Year
Note 1 Description:		
Beginning Balance		
Principal Payments		
Adjustments		
Note 1 Balance	$	$
Note 2 Description:		
Beginning Balance		
Principal Payments		
Adjustments		
Note 2 Balance	$	$
Note 3 Description:		
Beginning Balance		
Principal Payments		
Adjustments		
Note 3 Balance	$	$
Note 4 Description:		
Beginning Balance		
Principal Payments		
Adjustments		
Note 4 Balance	$	$
Total Notes Payable Balance	$	$

Detail totals must agree with Notes Payable on Balance Sheet.

Prepared by _____ Date _____

Reviewed by _____ Date _____

160. Cash Flow Forecast–12-Month

Period/Month:	1	2	3	4	5	6	7	8	9	10	11	12	Total
Receipts													
Cash sales													0
Collections from credit sales													0
Other													0
Total Receipts	0	0	0	0	0	0	0	0	0	0	0	0	**0**
Payments													
Cash purchases													0
Payments to creditors													0
Salaries and wages													0
Employee benefits													0
Payroll taxes													0
Rent													0
Utilities													0
Repairs and maintenance													0
Insurance													0
Travel													0
Telephone													0
Postage													0
Office supplies													0
Advertising													0
Marketing/promotion													0
Professional fees													0
Training and development													0
Bank charges													0
Miscellaneous													0
Owner's drawings													0
Loan repayments													0
Tax payments													0
Capital purchases													0
Other													0
Total Payments	0	0	0	0	0	0	0	0	0	0	0	0	**0**
Cashflow Surplus (+) or Deficit (-)	0	0	0	0	0	0	0	0	0	0	0	0	**0**
Start Cash (Owner's Equity+Loans-Start Up)	0	0	0	0	0	0	0	0	0	0	0	0	**0**
Closing Cash Balance	0	0	0	0	0	0	0	0	0	0	0	0	**0**

161. Cash Flow Forecast–Five-Year

Period/Month:	1	2	3	4	5	Total
Receipts						
Cash sales						0
Collections from credit sales						0
Other						0
Total Receipts	**0**	**0**	**0**	**0**	**0**	**0**
Payments						
Cash purchases						0
Payments to creditors						0
Salaries and wages						0
Employee benefits						0
Payroll taxes						0
Rent						0
Utilities						0
Repairs and maintenance						0
Insurance						0
Travel						0
Telephone						0
Postage						0
Office supplies						0
Advertising						0
Marketing/promotion						0
Professional fees						0
Training and development						0
Bank charges						0
Miscellaneous						0
Owner's drawings						0
Loan repayments						0
Tax payments						0
Capital purchases						0
Other						0
Total Payments	**0**	**0**	**0**	**0**	**0**	**0**
Cashflow Surplus (+) or Deficit (-)	0	0	0	0	0	0
Start Cash (Owner's Equity+Loans-Start Up)	0	0	0	0	0	
Closing Cash Balance	0	0	0	0	0	

162. Income Statement—12-Month

Period/Month:	1	2	3	4	5	6	7	8	9	10	11	12	Total
Sales													
Sales													0
Other													0
Total Sales	0	0	0	0	0	0	0	0	0	0	0	0	0
Less Cost of Goods Sold													
Materials													0
Labor													0
Overhead													0
Other													0
Total Cost of Goods Sold	0	0	0	0	0	0	0	0	0	0	0	0	0
Gross Profit	0	0	0	0	0	0	0	0	0	0	0	0	0
Operating Expenses													
Salaries and wages													0
Employee benefits													0
Payroll taxes													0
Rent													0
Utilities													0
Repairs and maintenance													0
Insurance													0
Travel													0
Telephone													0
Postage													0
Office supplies													0
Advertising/Marketing													0
Professional fees													0
Training and development													0
Bank charges													0
Depreciation													0
Miscellaneous													0
Other													0
Total Operating Expenses	0	0	0	0	0	0	0	0	0	0	0	0	0
Operating Income	0	0	0	0	0	0	0	0	0	0	0	0	0
Interest income (expense)													0
Other income (expense)													0
Total Nonoperating Income (Expense)	0	0	0	0	0	0	0	0	0	0	0	0	0
Income (Loss) Before Taxes	0	0	0	0	0	0	0	0	0	0	0	0	0
Income Taxes	0	0	0	0	0	0	0	0	0	0	0	0	0
Net Income (Loss)	0	0	0	0	0	0	0	0	0	0	0	0	0
Cumulative Net Income (Loss)	0	0	0	0	0	0	0	0	0	0	0	0	0

163. Income Statement—Quarterly

Period/Quarter:	Quarter 1	Quarter 2	Quarter 3	Quarter 4	Total
Sales					
Sales					0
Other					0
Total Sales	0	0	0	0	0
Less Cost of Goods Sold					
Materials					0
Labor					0
Overhead					0
Other					0
Total Cost of Goods Sold	0	0	0	0	0
Gross Profit	0	0	0	0	0
Operating Expenses					
Salaries and wages					0
Employee benefits					0
Payroll taxes					0
Rent					0
Utilities					0
Repairs and maintenance					0
Insurance					0
Travel					0
Telephone					0
Postage					0
Office supplies					0
Advertising/Marketing					0
Professional fees					0
Training and development					0
Bank charges					0
Depreciation					0
Miscellaneous					0
Other					0
Total Operating Expenses	0	0	0	0	0
Opeating Income	0	0	0	0	0
Interest income (expense)					0
Other income (expense)					0
Total Nonoperating Income (Expense)	0	0	0	0	0
Income (Loss) Before Taxes	0	0	0	0	0
Income Taxes					0
Net Income (Loss)	0	0	0	0	0
Cumulative Net Income (Loss)	0	0	0	0	0

164. Quarterly Balance Sheet

	Quarter 1	Quarter 2	Quarter 3	Quarter 4
ASSETS				
Current Assets				
Cash				
Marketable securities				
Accounts receivable, net				
Inventory				
Prepaid expenses				
Other				
Total Current Assets	0	0	0	0
Long-Term Assets				
Property, plant, and equipment				
Less accumulated depreciation				
Net property, plant, and equipment	0	0	0	0
Goodwill				
Other long-term assets				
Total Long-Term Assets	0	0	0	0
Total Assets	0	0	0	0
LIABILITIES AND SHAREHOLDERS' EQUITY				
Current Liabilities				
Short-term debt				
Current maturities of long-term debt				
Accounts payable				
Income taxes payable				
Accrued liabilities				
Other				
Total Current Liabilities	0	0	0	0
Long-Term Liabilities				
Long-term debt less current maturities				
Deferred income taxes				
Other long-term liabilities				
Total Long-Term Liabilities	0	0	0	0
Shareholders' Equity				
Common stock				
Additional paid-in capital				
Retained earnings				
Other				
Total Shareholders' Equity	0	0	0	0
Total Liabilities and Shareholders' Equity	0	0	0	0

165. Year-End Balance Sheet

	Year Ending 20____
ASSETS	
Current Assets	
Cash	
Marketable securities	
Accounts receivable, net	
Inventory	
Prepaid expenses	
Other	
Total Current Assets	0
Long-Term Assets	
Property, plant, and equipment	
Less accumulated depreciation	
Net property, plant, and equipment	0
Goodwill	
Other long-term assets	
Total Long-Term Assets	0
Total Assets	0
LIABILITIES AND SHAREHOLDERS' EQUITY	
Current Liabilities	
Short-term debt	
Current maturities of long-term debt	
Accounts payable	
Income taxes payable	
Accrued liabilities	
Other	
Total Current Liabilities	0
Long-Term Liabilities	
Long-term debt less current maturities	
Deferred income taxes	
Other long-term liabilities	
Total Long-Term Liabilities	0
Shareholders' Equity	
Common stock	
Additional paid-in capital	
Retained earnings	
Other	
Total Shareholders' Equity	0
Total Liabilities and Shareholders' Equity	0

CHAPTER 15

Forms to Protect Your Business

S MALL BUSINESSES SEE THEIR FAIR SHARE OF legal action, whether it stems from employee matters, contractual agreements, or even website jargon. This chapter includes forms that can help small business owners better understand what's legal and what's not, and what to do should a small claims situation occur.

All employees come to a company looking for a job and many leave looking for a job. When an employee is terminated, make sure that all is in order before you part ways. The past few decades have witnessed a significant increase in litigation brought by former employees for wrongful termination. While some suits are valid, others are groundless and abusive and exploit poor recordkeeping by employers. Therefore, secure all documentation necessary to memorialize the separation, and you can more successfully defend a suit brought for wrongful termination.

If an employee chooses to leave voluntarily, have him or her execute the *Voluntary Resignation Form*. This form serves as a nearly

indisputable record of the employee's willing termination of employment. This form may also go a long way to extinguishing an employee's right to charge your business's unemployment insurance for unemployment benefits. *The Employee's Separation Checklist* advises an employee of outstanding issues that must be resolved before separation. *The Manager's Pre-Dismissal Checklist* ensures that all loose ends are well tied before an employee departs. Finally, the *Employee Exit Interview* helps the company and employee communicate their final thoughts before terminating the employment relationship.

With more than 50% of companies in the U.S. operating online in some capacity, it's important to abide by the rules that govern the Web. The *Website Terms of Service* is a strongly worded legal disclaimer for any business that operates a website. In addition, two sample letters are included to use in regard to the Digital Millennium Copyright Act of 1998, which updates U.S. copyright law for the Internet. The act protects online service providers from civil and criminal liability for copyright infringement under some circumstances.

If a copyright holder discovers that his or her content appears on the Internet without proper authorization, the holder may take advantage of the act's "notification and takedown" provisions to have the content removed from the Website where it appears. Those provisions govern the process of notification by copyright holders and the rights and responsibilities of online service providers once they receive notice of infringing material. The copyright owner would deliver to the online service provider the *Notification of Infringement Letter Under the Digital Millennium Copyright Act*. A subscriber who feels his or her material is not infringing then may deliver a *Counter-Notification Letter Under the Digital Millennium Copyright Act* to respond to the notice.

Your company may possess proprietary information or trade secrets that need to be kept confidential. This information may also be your company's bread and butter, whether it includes business plans, marketing strategies, technology, and other information. To protect proprietary information internally and with potential business partners, refer to the *Sample Mutual Nondisclosure Agreement*, that serves to prevent multiple parties from revealing information that pertains to the other parties involved.

Use the *Sample Cease and Desist Letter* to demand in writing that the recipient refrain from a specific action that in a business situation can include debt collections, patent, copyright, or trademark infringement, libel or slander. A sample form of a *Trademark Infringement Cease and Desist Letter* (on the Web) shows how to draft a cease and desist letter for a specific violation, which in this case is when you feel that a party is using a trademark or service mark for which you have priority rights.

As a business owner, you may find yourself in small claims court either as a plaintiff or defendant. This chapter includes forms for both plaintiffs and defendants that help you file, dispute, and settle the matter in a legal framework. As a plaintiff, you may file small claims against the defendant who wrote your business a bad check or have an unpaid promissory note. Defendants can use the forms in this chapter to properly respond and even negotiate claims.

If you have case to state to an opponent or potential opponent, use the *Sample Demand Letter* (on the Web) to construct your argument(s) and send to the opponent before the demand is filed in court (unless your state does not require so).

As a defendant refer to the *Sample Letter by Defendant to Plaintiff in a Collections Matter*, which lays out reasons why the parties should compromise.

Refer to the *Sample Settlement and Compromise Agreement* as an example of how to format the binding agreement if you and the opponent agree on a preliminary settlement.

In the event you settled your claim and received a check that bounced, use the *Bad Check Demand Letter* (on the Web) to mandate proper monies be received within a specified time frame.

Should the need arise to take your case to a small claims court, as a plaintiff you would need to file a small claims complaint form that provides basic facts about your action. A sample *California Small Claims Complaint Form* is included in this chapter as a reference. These forms differ in each state.

Use the *Sample Debtors Order of Examination* (on the Web) to get the debtor to appear in court. The sample *Judgment Debtor's Exam Form* (on the Web) allows a judgment creditor (anyone who is owed money by order of a court) to make the debtor answer questions about his or her assets, like jewelry, cars, stocks, bank accounts, valuable memorabilia, etc.

In some cases you may have need to command a witnesses' testimony to support your case. To command a witness, a written subpoena is the written device used to compel the appearance of a third party at a small claims trial. The law and forms used for subpoenas vary widely from state to state. A *Sample Connecticut Subpoena Form* is included on the Web as a general reference.

If you're a plaintiff and won a judgment, the next step is to collect on it. Depending on your state's requirements, use a form similar to this chapter's *California Debtors Statement of Assets* to inquire on the debtor's personal property in the event he or she has not responded to your other collection efforts.

Depending on your state's requirements, use a form similar to the *Debtors Statement of Assets (California)* to inquire on the debtor's personal property in the event he or she has not responded to your other collection efforts. To garnish a debtor's wages or other assets, refer to the sample *Writ of Execution Form* (on the Web) and the *California Complaint Form*, which you can present to a court clerk for approval and further direction.

As a plaintiff, the ultimate goal is to have your judgment satisfied. If finally the judgment is paid, the plaintiff files a Satisfaction of Judgment with the court. A sample *California Satisfaction of Judgment* is is on the Web as a reference.

166. Voluntary Resignation

Employee Name

_____

Department

_____

I voluntarily resign my employment with

_____

Effective: Month _____ Day _____ Year_____

My reasons for leaving are:

_____

_____

_____

_____

_____

_____

_____

_____

_____

_____

_____

Forwarding Address: _____

_____

_____

Employee Signature _____ Date_____

Manager Signature _____ Date_____

167. Employee's Separation Checklist

Employee Name

_____

Date of Termination

_____

The following items are to have been collected prior to your separation with the company. Please have all these below listed items returned to your manager prior to your separation date. Thank you.

❏ All keys returned.

❏ Company vehicle keys returned.

❏ Company vehicle returned.

❏ Company credit cards returned.

❏ Company phone credit cards returned.

❏ Company equipment (portable phones, beepers, PCs) returned.

❏ COBRA election forms signed and returned.

❏ 401 (k) election forms signed and returned.

❏ Profit-sharing election forms signed and returned.

Your files, desk, and work area will be inventoried for all equipment and work utensils given to you by the company.

❏ Desk and working premises inventoried.

168. Manager's Pre-Dismissal Checklist

Employee Name

_____

Date of Termination

_____

Collect the following items from the employee prior to separation from the company:

❑ All keys returned.

❑ Company vehicle keys returned.

❑ Company vehicle returned.

❑ Company credit cards returned.

❑ Company phone credit cards returned.

❑ Company equipment (e.g., portable phones, beepers, credit cards, laptop computers) returned.

❑ COBRA election forms signed and returned.

❑ 401(k) election forms signed and returned.

❑ Profit-sharing election forms signed and returned.

❑ Company documents and files inventoried.

❑ Desk and working premises inventoried.

❑ Personnel and Payroll Departments notified of departure.

❑ Final expense report received, reviewed, and approved; expense check prepared.

❑ Final check prepared (including all accrued vacation pay, sick pay, accrued wages, bonus, etc.).

❑ Exit interview prepared.

❑ Exit interview given.

❑ Final checks (payroll and expense) given to terminating employee.

All of the above duties have been completed in a satisfactory manner.

Company has no further liability with the terminating employee.

Manager Signature _____ Date _____

169. Employee Exit Interview

Employee Name _____

Title _____

Department _____

Date _____

What did you like best about your current position?

_____

_____

_____

What did you like least about your current position?

_____

_____

_____

What did you like best about the company?

_____

_____

_____

What did you like least about the company?

_____

_____

_____

What are your feelings toward your supervisor?

_____

_____

_____

Why are you leaving the company at this time? What company and position are you going to?

_____

_____

_____

What are your comments about the company's salary and benefits?

_____

_____

_____

What suggestions do you have for improving your current position and other aspects within the company?

_____

_____

_____

Interviewed by _____ Date _____

Interviewer's remarks

_____

_____

_____

_____

_____

_____

170. Web Site Terms of Service

Terms of Service

Some or all of the information on this Web site(s) is provided by _____ ("Company") on one or more Company Web sites. The Company Web sites include the following Web sites: _____. Company provides this service to you, subject to the following Terms of Service ("TOS"), which may be updated by us anytime without notice to you. When using particular Company services, you shall be subject to any posted guidelines or rules applicable to such services that may be posted from time to time. All such guidelines or rules are hereby incorporated by reference into the TOS. For specific services, Company also may put forth specific Terms of Service that differ from this TOS. It is your responsibility to periodically review the TOS. If you do not agree with or understand the TOS, do not use a Company site.

The TOS apply to both "Affiliates" (persons or entities that receive the Service, as defined below, for redistribution and/or republication on a non-Company Web site) and "Users" (all persons, including Affiliates, that make any use whatsoever of any Service, as defined below). Company currently provides Affiliates and Users with several resources, including news feeds, message boards, financial calculators, articles, and stock quotes (the "Service"). Unless expressly stated otherwise, new resources added to the current Service shall be subject to the TOS. You understand and agree that the Service is provided "as is" and that Company assumes no responsibility for the timeliness, deletion, misdelivery, or failure to store any user communications or personalization settings.

In consideration of your use of the Service, you agree to (a) provide true, accurate, current, and complete information about yourself as prompted by the Service's registration form (such information being the "Registration Data") and (b) maintain and promptly update the Registration Data to keep it truthful, accurate, current, and complete. If you provide any information that is untrue, inaccurate, not current, or incomplete, or Company has reasonable grounds to suspect that such information is untrue, inaccurate, not current, or incomplete, Company has the right to suspend or terminate your account and refuse any and all current or future use of the Service (or any portion thereof). You will receive a password and account designation upon completing the registration process for the use of some Services. You are responsible for maintaining the confidentiality of the password and account and are fully responsible for all activities that occur under your password or account. You agree to (a) immediately notify Company of any unauthorized use of your password or account or any other breach of security and (b) ensure that you exit from your account at the end of each session. Company cannot and will not be liable for any loss or damage arising from your failure to comply with this Paragraph.

You understand that all information, data, text, software, music, sound, photographs, graphics, video, messages, or other materials ("Content"), whether publicly posted or privately transmitted, are the sole responsibility of the person from which such Content originated. This means that you, and not Company, are entirely responsible for all Content that you upload, post, e-mail, or otherwise transmit via the Service. Company does not control the Content posted via the Service and thus does not guarantee its accuracy, integrity, or quality. By using the Service, you may be exposed to Content that is offensive, indecent, or objectionable. Under no circumstances will Company be liable in any way for any Content, including, but not limited to, any errors or omissions in any Content, or any loss or damage of any kind incurred as a result of the use of any Content posted, e-mailed, or otherwise transmitted via the Service.

You agree to not use the Service to:

i. upload, post, e-mail, or otherwise transmit any Content that is unlawful, harmful, threatening, abusive, harassing, defamatory, vulgar, obscene, libelous, invasive of another's privacy, hateful, or racially, ethnically, or otherwise objectionable;

ii. impersonate any person or entity or falsely state or otherwise misrepresent your affiliation with a person or entity;

iii. forge headers or otherwise manipulate identifiers in order to disguise the origin of any Content transmitted through the Service;

iv. upload, post, e-mail, or otherwise transmit any Content that you do not have a right to transmit under any law or under contractual or fiduciary relationships;

v. upload, post, e-mail, or otherwise transmit any Content that infringes on any patent, trademark, trade secret, copyright, or other proprietary rights ("Rights") of any party;

vi. upload, post, e-mail, or otherwise transmit any unsolicited or unauthorized advertising, promotional materials, "junk mail," "spam," "chain letters," "pyramid schemes," or any other form of solicitation, except in areas designated for such purpose;

vii. upload, post, e-mail, or otherwise transmit any material that contains software viruses or any other computer code, files, or programs designed to interrupt, destroy, or limit the functionality of any computer software or hardware or telecommunications equipment;

viii. interfere with or disrupt the Service or servers or networks connected to the Service, or disobey any requirements, procedures, policies, or regulations of networks connected to the Service;

ix. intentionally or unintentionally violate any applicable local, state, national, or international law, including, but not limited to, regulations promulgated by the U.S. Securities and Exchange Commission, any rules of any national or other securities exchange, including, without limitation, the New York Stock Exchange, the American Stock Exchange, or the NASDAQ, and any regulations having the force of law; or

x. "stalk" or otherwise harass another or collect or store personal data about other Users.

You acknowledge that Company does not pre-screen Content, but that Company and its designees shall have the right (but not the obligation) in their sole discretion to refuse or move any Content that is available via the Service. Without limiting the foregoing, Company and its designees shall have the right to remove any Content that violates the TOS or is otherwise objectionable. You agree that you must evaluate, and bear all risks associated with, the use of any Content, including any reliance on the accuracy, completeness, or usefulness of such Content. In this regard, you acknowledge that you may not rely on any Content created by Company or submitted to Company, including without limitation information in Company Message Boards and in all other parts of the Service.

You acknowledge and agree that Company may preserve Content and may also disclose Content if required to do so by law or in the good faith belief that such preservation or disclosure is reasonably necessary to (a) comply with legal process; (b) enforce the TOS; (c) respond to claims that any Content violates the rights of third parties; or (d) protect the rights, property, or personal safety of Company, its Users, and the public.

You understand that the technical processing and transmission of the Service, including your Content, may involve (a) transmissions over various networks and (b) changes to conform and adapt to technical requirements of connecting networks or devices.

Recognizing the global nature of the Internet, you agree to comply with all local rules regarding online conduct and acceptable Content. Specifically, you agree to comply with all applicable laws regarding the transmission of technical data exported from the United States or the country in which you reside.

With respect to all Content you elect to post to other publicly accessible areas of the Service, you grant Company the royalty-free, perpetual, irrevocable, non-exclusive, and fully sublicensable right and license to use, reproduce, modify, adapt, publish, translate, create derivative works from, distribute, perform, and display such Content (in whole or part) worldwide and/or to incorporate it in other works in any form, media, or technology now known or later developed.

You agree to indemnify and hold Company and its subsidiaries, Affiliates, officers, agents, co-branders or other partners, and employees harmless from any claim or demand, including reasonable attorneys' fees, made by any third party due to or arising out of Content you submit, post to, or transmit through the Service, your use of the Service, your connection to the Service, your violation of the TOS, or your violation of any rights of another.

You agree not to reproduce, duplicate, copy, sell, resell, or exploit for any commercial purposes any portion of the Service, use of the Service, or access to the Service, except in accordance with the TOS.

You acknowledge that Company may establish general practices and limits concerning use of the Service, including without limitation the maximum number of days Content will be retained by the Service, the maximum number of messages that may be sent from or received by an account on the Service, the maximum size of any message that may be sent from or received by an account on the Service, the maximum disk space that will be allotted on Company's servers on your behalf, and the maximum number of times and the maximum duration for which you may access the Service in a given period of time. You agree that Company has no responsibility or liability for the deletion or failure to store any messages and other communications or other Content maintained or transmitted by the Service. You acknowledge that Company reserves the right to log off accounts that are inactive for an extended period of time. You further acknowledge that Company reserves the right to change these general practices and limits at any time, in its sole discretion, with or without notice.

Company reserves the right at any time and from time to time to modify or discontinue, temporarily or permanently, the Service (or any part thereof), with or without notice. You agree that Company shall not be liable to you or to any third party for any modification, suspension, or discontinuance of the Service.

You agree that Company, in its sole discretion, may terminate your password, account (or any part thereof), or use of the Service and remove and discard any Content within the Service for any reason. Company may also, in its sole discretion and at any time, discontinue providing the Service, or any part thereof, or may change the price for the Service, all with or without notice. You agree that any termination of your access to the Service under any provision of this TOS may be affected without prior notice, and acknowledge and agree that Company may immediately deactivate or delete your account and all related information and files in your account and/or bar any further access to such files or the Service. Further, you agree that Company shall not be liable to you or any third party for any termination of your access to the Service.

Your correspondence or business dealings with, or participation in promotions of, advertisers found on or through the Service, including payment and delivery of related goods or services, and any other terms, conditions, warranties, or representations associated with such dealings, are solely between you and such advertiser. You agree that Company shall not be responsible or liable for any loss or damage of any sort incurred as the result of any such dealings or as the result of the presence of such advertisers on the Service.

The Service or third parties may provide links to other World Wide Web sites or resources. Because Company has no control over such sites and resources, you acknowledge and agree that Company is not responsible for the availability of such external sites or resources and does not endorse and is not responsible or liable for any Content, advertising, products, or other materials on or available from such sites or resources. You further acknowledge and agree that Company shall not be responsible or liable, directly or indirectly, for any damage or loss caused or alleged to be caused by or in connection with use of or reliance on any such Content, goods, or services available on or through any such site or resource.

You acknowledge and agree that the Service and any necessary software used in connection with the Service (the "Software") contain proprietary and confidential information that is protected by applicable intellectual property and other laws. You further acknowledge and agree that Content contained in sponsor advertisements or information presented to you through the Service or advertisers is protected by copyrights, trademarks, service marks, patents, or other proprietary rights and laws. Except as expressly authorized by Company or advertisers, you agree not to modify, rent, lease, loan, sell, distribute, or create derivative works based on the Service or the Software, in whole or in part.

Company grants you a personal, non-transferable, and non-exclusive right and license to use the object code of its Software on a single computer, provided that you do not (and do not allow any third party to) copy, modify, create a derivative work of, reverse engineer, reverse assemble, or otherwise attempt to discover any source code, sell, assign, sublicense, grant a security interest in, or otherwise transfer any right in the Software. You agree not to modify the Software in any manner or form or to use modified versions of the Software, including (without limitation) for the purpose of obtaining unauthorized access to the Service. You agree not to access the Service by any means other than through the interface that is provided by Company for use in accessing the Service.

YOU EXPRESSLY UNDERSTAND AND AGREE THAT:

a. YOUR USE OF THE SERVICE IS AT YOUR SOLE RISK. THE SERVICE IS PROVIDED ON AN "AS IS" AND "AS AVAILABLE" BASIS. COMPANY EXPRESSLY DISCLAIMS ALL WARRANTIES OF ANY KIND, WHETHER EXPRESSED OR IMPLIED, INCLUDING, BUT NOT LIMITED TO, THE IMPLIED WARRANTIES OF MERCHANTABILITY, FITNESS FOR A PARTICULAR PURPOSE, AND NON-INFRINGEMENT.

b. COMPANY MAKES NO WARRANTY THAT (i) THE SERVICE WILL MEET YOUR REQUIREMENTS, (ii) THE SERVICE WILL BE UNINTERRUPTED, TIMELY, SECURE, OR ERROR-FREE, (iii) THE RESULTS THAT MAY BE OBTAINED FROM THE USE OF THE SERVICE WILL BE ACCURATE OR RELIABLE, (iv) THE QUALITY OF

ANY PRODUCTS, SERVICES, INFORMATION, OR OTHER MATERIAL PURCHASED OR OBTAINED BY YOU THROUGH THE SERVICE WILL MEET YOUR EXPECTATIONS, AND (v) ANY ERRORS IN THE SOFTWARE WILL BE CORRECTED.

c. ANY MATERIAL DOWNLOADED OR OTHERWISE OBTAINED THROUGH THE USE OF THE SERVICE IS DONE AT YOUR OWN DISCRETION AND RISK AND THAT YOU WILL BE SOLELY RESPONSIBLE FOR ANY DAMAGE TO YOUR COMPUTER SYSTEM OR LOSS OF DATA THAT RESULTS FROM THE DOWNLOAD OF ANY SUCH MATERIAL.

d. NO ADVICE OR INFORMATION, WHETHER ORAL OR WRITTEN, OBTAINED BY YOU FROM COMPANY OR THROUGH OR FROM THE SERVICE, SHALL CREATE ANY WARRANTY NOT EXPRESSLY STATED IN THE TOS.

YOU EXPRESSLY UNDERSTAND AND AGREE THAT COMPANY SHALL NOT BE LIABLE FOR ANY DIRECT, INDIRECT, INCIDENTAL, SPECIAL, CONSEQUENTIAL, OR EXEMPLARY DAMAGES, INCLUDING BUT NOT LIMITED TO DAMAGES FOR LOSS OF PROFITS, GOODWILL, USE, DATA, OR OTHER INTANGIBLE LOSSES (EVEN IF COMPANY HAS BEEN ADVISED OF THE POSSIBILITY OF SUCH DAMAGES) RESULTING FROM (i) THE USE OR THE INABILITY TO USE THE SERVICE; (ii) THE COST OF PROCUREMENT OF SUBSTITUTE GOODS AND SERVICES RESULTING FROM ANY GOODS, DATA, INFORMATION, OR SERVICES PURCHASED OR OBTAINED OR MESSAGES RECEIVED OR TRANSACTIONS ENTERED INTO THROUGH OR FROM THE SERVICE; (iii) UNAUTHORIZED ACCESS TO OR ALTERATION OF YOUR TRANSMISSIONS OR DATA; (iv) STATEMENTS OR CONDUCT OF ANY THIRD PARTY ON THE SERVICE; OR (v) ANY OTHER MATTER RELATING TO THE SERVICE.

SOME JURISDICTIONS DO NOT ALLOW THE EXCLUSION OF CERTAIN WARRANTIES OR THE LIMITATION OR EXCLUSION OF LIABILITY FOR INCIDENTAL OR CONSEQUENTIAL DAMAGES. ACCORDINGLY, SOME OF THE ABOVE LIMITATIONS OF LIABILITY MAY NOT APPLY TO YOU.

THE SERVICE IS PROVIDED FOR INFORMATIONAL PURPOSES ONLY AND NO CONTENT INCLUDED IN THE SERVICE IS INTENDED FOR TRADING OR INVESTING PURPOSES. COMPANY SHALL NOT BE RESPONSIBLE OR LIABLE FOR THE ACCURACY, USEFULNESS, OR AVAILABILITY OF ANY INFORMATION TRANSMITTED VIA THE SERVICE AND SHALL NOT BE RESPONSIBLE OR LIABLE FOR ANY TRADING OR INVESTMENT DECISIONS MADE BASED ON SUCH INFORMATION.

Company respects the intellectual property of others and we ask our Users to do the same. If you believe that your work has been copied in a way that constitutes copyright infringement, please contact Company:

_____

_____

_____

The TOS constitute the entire agreement between you and Company and govern your use of the Service, superseding any prior agreements between you and Company. You also may be subject to additional terms and conditions that may apply when you use affiliate services, third-party content, or third-party software. The TOS and the relationship between you and Company shall be governed by the laws of the State of California without regard to its conflict of law provisions. You and Company agree to submit to the personal and exclusive jurisdiction of the courts located within the county of _____, _____. The failure of Company to exercise or enforce any right or provision of the TOS shall not constitute a waiver of such right or provision. If any provision of the TOS is found by a court of competent jurisdiction to be invalid, the parties nevertheless agree that the court should endeavor to give effect to the parties' intentions as reflected in the provision and that the other provisions of the TOS remain in full force and effect. You agree that, regardless of any statute or law to the contrary, any claim or cause of action arising out of or related to use of the Service or the TOS must be filed within one (1) year after such claim or cause of action arose or be forever barred.

171. Notification of Infringement Letter Under the Digital Millennium Copyright Act

Date _____

To:

_____

_____

_____

_____

To Whom It May Concern:

I am writing to you to avail myself of my rights under the Digital Millennium Copyright Act (DMCA). This letter is a Notice of Infringement as authorized in § 512(c) of the U.S. Copyright Law. I wish to report an instance or what I feel in good faith is an instance of copyright infringement. The infringing material appears on a service for which you are the designated agent.

You are registered with the U.S. Copyright Office as the Designated Service Provider Agent to receive notifications of alleged Copyright infringement with respect to users of the Service for which you are the Designated Agent.

1. The material that I contend belongs to me and that appears illegally on the service is the following: (describe the infringing material: e.g., "a song entitled "Legal Battle Blues" and a song entitled "A Little Litigation," both performed by Lawyers in Love).

2. The material appears at the Web site address: (provide the full Web site address and a link to the page on which the material appears).

3. My contact information is as follows: (provide your name, address, telephone number, and e-mail address).

4. I have a good-faith belief that the use of the material that appears on the service is not authorized by the copyright owner, by its agent, or by operation of law.

5. The information in this notice is accurate and I am either the copyright owner or authorized to act on behalf of the copyright owner.

I declare under the perjury laws of the United States of America that this notification is true and correct.

_____

Signature

_____

Printed Name

172. Counter-Notification Letter Under the Digital Millennium Copyright Act

Date _____

To:

_____

_____

_____

_____

To Whom It May Concern:

I am writing to you to avail myself of my rights under the Digital Millennium Copyright Act (DMCA). You recently provided me with a copy of Notice of Infringement from (Name the party who submitted the Notice of Infringement). This letter is a Counter-Notification as authorized in § 512(g) of the U.S. Copyright Law. I have a good-faith belief that the material that was removed or disabled as a result of the Notice of Infringement was removed or disabled as a result of mistake or misidentification of the material. I therefore request that the material be replaced and/or no longer disabled.

You are registered with the U.S. Copyright Office as the Designated Service Provider Agent to receive notifications of alleged copyright infringement with respect to users of the Service for which you are the Designated Agent.

1. The material in question formerly appeared at the Web site address:
   (provide the full Web site address and a link to the page on which the material appears).

2. My contact information is as follows:
   (provide your name, address, telephone number, and e-mail address).

3. I consent to the jurisdiction of the Federal District Court for the judicial district in which my address is located (solely for the purposes of the resolution of this dispute) and I agree to accept service of process from the person who provided the Notice of Infringement.

4. I have a good-faith belief that the material removed or disabled following the Notice of Infringement was removed or disabled because of mistake or misidentification of the material. I therefore request that the material be replaced and/or no longer disabled.

I declare under the perjury laws of the United States of America that this notification is true and correct.

_____

Signature

_____

Printed Name

173. Mutual Nondisclosure Agreement

This agreement is made effective on _____ (date) by and between
_____ (first party) and _____ (second party)
(collectively, the "Parties"), to ensure the protection and preservation of the confidential and/or proprietary
nature of information disclosed or made available or to be disclosed or made available to each other. For
the purposes of this agreement, each Party shall be deemed to include any subsidiaries, internal divisions,
agents, and employees. Any signing party shall refer to and bind the individual and the entity that he or
she represents.

Whereas the Parties desire to ensure the confidential status of the information that may be disclosed to
each other.

Now, therefore, in reliance upon and in consideration of the following undertakings, the Parties agree as
follows:

1. Subject to limitations set forth in paragraph 2, all information disclosed to the other party shall be
    deemed to be "Proprietary Information." In particular, Proprietary Information shall be deemed to
    include any information, marketing technique, publicity technique, public relations technique, process,
    technique, algorithm, program, design, drawing, mask work, formula, test data research project, work
    in progress, future development, engineering, manufacturing, marketing, servicing, financing, or per-
    sonal matter relating to the disclosing party, its present or future products, sales, suppliers, clients, cus-
    tomers, employees, investors, or business, whether in oral, written, graphic, or electronic form.

2. The term "Proprietary Information" shall not be deemed to include information that (i) is now, or here-
    after becomes, through no act or failure to act on the part of the receiving party, generally known or
    available information, (ii) is known by the receiving party at the time of receiving such information as
    evidenced by its records, (iii) is hereafter furnished to the receiving party by a third party, as a matter
    of right and without restriction on disclosure, (iv) is independently developed by the receiving party
    without reference to the information disclosed hereunder, or (v) is the subject of a written permission
    to disclose provided by the disclosing party.

    Not withstanding any other provision of this Agreement, disclosure of Proprietary Information shall not
    be precluded if such disclosure:

    a. is in response to a valid order of a court or other governmental body of the United States or any
        political subdivision thereof,

    b. is otherwise required by law, or,

    c. is otherwise necessary to establish rights or enforce obligations under this agreement, but only to
        the extent that any such disclosure is necessary.

    In the event that the receiving party is requested in any proceedings before a court or any other govern-
    mental body to disclose Proprietary Information, it shall give the disclosing party prompt notice of such
    request so that the disclosing party may seek an appropriate protective order. If, in the absence of a pro-
    tective order, the receiving party is nonetheless compelled to disclose Proprietary Information, the receiv-

ing party may disclose such information without liability hereunder, provided, however, that such party gives the disclosing party advance written notice of the information to be disclosed and, upon the request and at the expense of the disclosing party, uses its best efforts to obtain assurances that confidential treatment will be accorded to such information.

3. Each party shall maintain in trust and confidence and not disclose to any third party or use for any unauthorized purpose any Proprietary Information received from the other party. Each party may use such Proprietary Information in the extent required to accomplish the purpose of the discussions with respect to the subject. Proprietary Information shall not be used for any purpose or in any manner that would constitute a violation on law regulations, including without limitation the export control laws of the United States of America. No other rights or licenses to trademarks, inventions, copyrights, or patents are implied or granted under this Agreement.

4. Proprietary Information supplied shall not be reproduced in any form except as required to accomplish the intent of this Agreement.

5. The responsibilities of the Parties are limited to using their efforts to protect the Proprietary Information received with the same degree of care used to protect their own Proprietary Information from unauthorized use or disclosure. Both Parties shall advise their employees or agents who might have access to such Proprietary Information of the confidential nature thereof and that by receiving such information they are agreeing to be bound by this Agreement. No Proprietary Information shall be disclosed to any officer, employee, or agent of either party who does not have a need for such information for the purpose of the discussions with respect to the subject.

6. All Proprietary Information (including all copies thereof) shall remain the property of the disclosing party and shall be returned to the disclosing party after the receiving party's need for it has expired, or upon request of the disclosing party, and in any event, upon completion or termination of this Agreement. The receiving party further agrees to destroy all notes and copies thereof made by its officers and employees containing or based on any Proprietary Information and to cause all agents and representatives to whom or to which Proprietary Information has been disclosed to destroy all notes and copies in their possession that contain Proprietary Information.

7. This Agreement shall survive any termination of the discussion with respect to the subject and shall continue in full force and effect until such time as Parties mutually agree to terminate it.

8. This Agreement shall be governed by the laws of the United States of America and as those laws that are applied to contracts entered into and to be performed in all states. Should any revision of this Agreement be determined to be void, invalid, or otherwise unenforceable by any court or tribunal of competent jurisdiction, such determination shall not affect the remaining provisions of this Agreement, which shall remain in full force and effect.

9. This Agreement contains final, complete, and exclusive agreement of the Parties relative to the subject matter hereof and supersedes any prior agreement of the Parties, whether oral or written. This Agreement may not be changed, modified, amended, or supplemented except by a written instrument signed by both Parties.

10. Each party hereby acknowledges and agrees that, in the event of any breach of this Agreement by the other party, including, without limitations, the actual or threatened disclosure of a disclosing party's Proprietary Information without the prior express written consent of the disclosing party, the disclosing party will suffer an irreparable injury such that no remedy at law will afford it adequate protection against or appropriate compensation for such injury. Accordingly, each party hereby agrees that the other party shall be entitled to specific performance of a receiving party's obligations under this Agreement as well as further injunctive relief as may be granted by a court of competent jurisdiction.

11. The term of this agreement is for two (2) years, commencing on the "Effective Date."

AGREED TO:

Signature _____

Printed Name _____

Date _____

AGREED TO:

Signature _____

Printed Name _____

Date _____

174. Sample Cease and Desist Letter

Your Name

Address
City, State Zip

Debt Collector's Name
Address
City, State Zip

Re: (account #)

Dear (Name of Debt Collection Company or Employee):

Pursuant to my rights under federal debt collection laws, I am requesting that you cease and desist communication with me, in addition to my family and friends. This request in response to the
_____(alleged debts) you claim I owe.

This letter servers as notification that should your and (insert name of debt collection company) not comply with this request, I will immediately file a complaint with the Federal Trade Commission and the [your state] Attorney General's office. Civil and criminal claims will be pursued.

Sincerely,

(your name)

175. Sample Letter by Defendant to Plaintiff in a Collections Matter

December 1, 2010

Joe Plaintiff
Ace Collection Agency
1000 Collection Avenue
NY, NY 10001

Dear Joe,

I received your demand letter. While I sympathize with your position, I strongly suggest that you compromise this claim. Otherwise you are likely to receive nothing, even if you go to court. I am making this offer as a good-faith gesture to you.

I hope to spare us both the hassle and time of preparing paperwork, serving each other with papers, serving witnesses with subpoenas, going to court, and then the substantial efforts that you'll need to expend to collect on any judgment you might get.

We have already talked about my defenses and counterclaims. But I wish to remind you that I am steadfast in pursuing my side of the case. Small claims decisions are not reliable, so really neither of us truly know what is going to happen in court. In light of all this risk, I hope you accept my offer.

But really the main point is that even if you win a judgment for the full amount that you are seeking, you'll still need to expend a lot of effort to collect the debt. Unfortunately, I cannot and will not offer you my cooperation to collect on the judgment if you take me to court, but I do offer my cooperation to settle this case today. While I am now employed, I am considering leaving my job and moving out of state. If I do, you'll need to take the judgment to my new home state to collect. As far as assets, I don't have much, so I can't offer you much.

In order to settle the case, and without admitting any fault or waiving any evidentiary objections, I will agree to settle this case for 25% of what you are seeking, or $250. This is the most I can afford to pay, so this is my final offer.

Please let me know within three days if you accept this offer of settlement.

Yours very truly,

John Debtor

176. Sample Settlement and Compromise Agreement

MUTUAL RELEASE AND WAIVER AGREEMENT

THIS MUTUAL WAIVER AGREEMENT AND MUTUAL RELEASE ("Agreement") is entered into as of March _____, 2008, by and between Muirfield Furniture Company, Inc. ("Debtor") and Elizabeth Berkey, d/b/a Berkey Design ("Creditor") (collectively "Parties or Party"). For the purposes of the Agreement, "Party" includes subsidiaries and parents of a Party and includes owners as well as individuals serving as directors, officers, employees, agents, consultants, and advisors to or of a Party.

A. BACKGROUND

1. Debtor and Creditor entered into an agreement or series of agreements (the "Contract") whereby creditor provided graphic design, marketing, and other creative services to debtor.

2. Since the time of entering into the Contract, the Parties have determined that a settlement of the mutual obligations between them is appropriate and would best serve the interests of all of the Parties, and this Agreement is intended to express the Parties' intent to equitably settle the obligations arising from or related to the Contract.

B. AGREEMENT

NOW, THEREFORE, IN CONSIDERATION OF THE FOLLOWING, THE FOREGOING, THE MUTUAL COVENANTS, PROMISES, AGREEMENTS, REPRESENTATIONS AND RELEASES CONTAINED HEREIN, AND IN EXCHANGE FOR OTHER GOOD AND VALUABLE CONSIDERATION, THE RECEIPT, SUFFICIENCY AND ADEQUACY OF WHICH IS HEREBY ACKNOWLEDGED, THE PARTIES HEREBY AGREE AS FOLLOWS:

1. **Payment to Creditor.**
   a. Debtor shall pay $4,000.00 to Creditor, such payment to be made no later than 72 hours following the execution of this Agreement. Payment under this paragraph is a precondition to the effectiveness of this Agreement.
   b. Debtor shall owe no further liability or obligation to Creditor in connection with any services.

2. **No other Payments.** No additional funds shall be required to be paid or transferred by Creditor to Debtor, or by Debtor to Creditor.

3. **Nature and Effect of Agreement and Conditions Thereon.** By executing this Agreement, the Parties intend to and do hereby extinguish the obligations heretofore existing between them and arising from the Contract.

4. **Admissions.** This Agreement is not, and shall not be treated as, an admission of liability by either Party for any purpose, and shall not be admissible as evidence before any tribunal or court.

5. **Release and Discharge.** The Parties hereby compromise and settle any and all past, present, or future claims, demands, obligations, or causes of action for compensatory or punitive damages, costs, losses, expenses, and compensation whether based on tort, contract, or other theories of recovery, which the Parties have or which may later accrue to or be acquired by one Party against the other, the other's predecessors and successor in interest, heirs, and assigns, past present and future officers, directors, shareholders, agents, employees, parent and subsidiary organizations, affiliates, and partners, arising

from the subject matter of the Contract.

6. **Unknown Claims.** The Parties acknowledge and agree that upon execution of the release, this Agreement applies to all claims for damages or losses either Party may have against the other whether those damages or losses are known or unknown, foreseen or unforeseen.

[Note: the remainder of Paragraph 6 is only for use in the State of California]

In the event that this Agreement is deemed executed in California, the Parties thereby waive application of California Civil Code Section 1542.

The Parties certify that each has read the following provisions of California Civil Code Section 1542:

"A general release does not extend to claims which the Debtor does not know or suspect to exist in his favor at the time of executing the release, which if known by him must have materially affected his settlement with the debtor."

The Parties understand and acknowledge that the significance and consequence of this waiver of California Civil Code Section 1542 is that even if one Party should eventually suffer additional damages arising out of the facts referred to in Section A, above, it will not be able to make any claim for these damages. Furthermore, the Parties acknowledge that they intend these consequences even as to claims for damages that may exist as of the date of this release but which the damaged or harmed Party does not know exists, and which, if known, would materially affect that Party's decision to execute this release, regardless of whether the damaged Party's lack of knowledge is the result of ignorance, oversight, error, negligence, or any other cause.

7. **Conditions of Execution.** Each Party acknowledges and warrants that its execution of this compromise agreement and release is free and voluntary. All Parties and signatories to this Agreement acknowledge and agree that the terms of this Agreement are contractual and not mere recital, and all Parties and signatories represent and warrant that they have carefully read this Agreement, have fully reviewed its provisions with their attorneys and know and understand its contents. It is understood and agreed by all Parties and signatories to this Agreement that execution of this Agreement may affect rights and liabilities of substantial extent and degree and with the full understanding of that fact, they represent that the covenants and releases provided for in this Agreement are in their respective best interests.

8. **Entire Agreement.** This Agreement constitutes the entire agreement between the Parties and signatories and all prior and contemporaneous conversation, negotiations, possible and alleged agreements, and representations, covenants, and warranties, express or implied, or written, with respect to the subject matter hereof, are waived, merged herein and superseded hereby. There are no other agreements, representations, covenants or warranties not set forth herein. The terms of this Agreement may not be contradicted by evidence of any prior or contemporaneous agreement. The Parties further intend and agree that this Agreement constitutes the complete and exclusive statement of its terms and that no extrinsic evidence whatsoever may be introduced in any judicial or arbitration proceeding, if any, involving this Agreement. No part of this Agreement may be amended or modified in any way unless such amendment or modification is expressed in writing signed by all Parties to this Agreement.

9. **Counterparts.** This Agreement may be executed in multiple counterparts, each of which shall be deemed an original but all of which together shall constitute one and the same instrument. When all of the Parties and signatories have executed any copy hereof, such execution shall constitute the execution of this Agreement, whereupon it shall become effective.

10. **Governing Law.** THIS AGREEMENT WILL BE GOVERNED AND CONSTRUED IN ACCORDANCE WITH THE LAW OF THE STATE OF CALIFORNIA AND THE UNITED STATES OF AMERICA, WITHOUT REGARD TO CONFLICT OF LAW PRINCIPLES. This Agreement shall not be strictly construed against any Party to this Agreement. Any controversy or claim arising out of or relating to this Agreement, or the breach thereof, shall be resolved by arbitration administered under the rules of the American Arbitration Association in accordance with its applicable rules. Such arbitration shall take place within Marin County, California, and shall be binding upon all Parties, and any judgment upon or any an award rendered by the arbitrator may be entered in any court having jurisdiction thereof.

IN WITNESS WHEREOF, the Parties and signatories execute this Agreement on the dates indicated.

Muirfield Furniture Company, Inc., Debtor: Elizabeth Berkey/Berkey Design, Creditor:

_____   _____

Donald LeBuhn, President   Elizabeth Berkey

177. California Complaint Form

Case Number:

Plaintiff *(list names):* _____

(1) The Plaintiff (the person, business, or public entity that is suing) is:

Name: _____ Phone: (___) _____

Street address: _____
Street   City   State   Zip

Mailing address *(if different):* _____
Street   City   State   Zip

If more than one Plaintiff, list next Plaintiff here:

Name: _____ Phone: (___) _____

Street address: _____
Street   City   State   Zip

Mailing address *(if different):* _____
Street   City   State   Zip

☐ *Check here if more than 2 Plaintiffs and attach Form SC-100A.*

☐ *Check here if either Plaintiff listed above is doing business under a fictitious name. If so, attach Form SC-103.*

(2) The Defendant (the person, business, or public entity being sued) is:

Name: _____ Phone: (___) _____

Street address: _____
Street   City   State   Zip

Mailing address *(if different):* _____
Street   City   State   Zip

If more than one Defendant, list next Defendant here:

Name: _____ Phone: (___) _____

Street address: _____
Street   City   State   Zip

Mailing address *(if different):* _____
Street   City   State   Zip

☐ *Check here if more than 2 Defendants and attach Form SC-100A.*

☐ *Check here if any Defendant is on active military duty, and write his or her name here:* _____

(3) The Plaintiff claims the Defendant owes $ _____. *(Explain below):*

a. Why does the Defendant owe the Plaintiff money? _____

_____

b. When did this happen? *(Date):* _____
If no specific date, give the time period: *Date started:* _____ *Through:* _____

c. How did you calculate the money owed to you? *(Do not include court costs or fees for service.)* _____

☐ *Check here if you need more space. Attach one sheet of paper or Form MC-031 and write "SC-100, Item 3" at the top.*

Revised January 1, 2007

Plaintiff's Claim and ORDER to Go to Small Claims Court (Small Claims)

SC-100, Page 2 of 5 →

Case Number:

Plaintiff *(list names):*_____

(4) **You must ask the Defendant (in person, in writing, or by phone) to pay you before you sue. Have you done this?** ☐ Yes ☐ No

*If no, explain why not:*_____

(5) **Why are you filing your claim at this courthouse?**
This courthouse covers the area *(check the one that applies):*

a. ☐ (1) Where the Defendant lives or does business. (4) Where a contract (written or spoken) was made,
      (2) Where the Plaintiff's property was damaged.   signed, performed, or broken by the Defendant *or*
      (3) Where the Plaintiff was injured.   where the Defendant lived or did business when
                                        the Defendant made the contract.

b. ☐ Where the buyer or lessee signed the contract, lives now, or lived when the contract was made, if this claim is about an offer or contract for personal, family, or household goods, services, or loans. *(Code Civ. Proc., § 395(b).)*

c. ☐ Where the buyer signed the contract, lives now, or lived when the contract was made, if this claim is about a retail installment contract (like a credit card). *(Civil Code, § 1812.10.)*

d. ☐ Where the buyer signed the contract, lives now, or lived when the contract was made, or where the vehicle is permanently garaged, if this claim is about a vehicle finance sale. *(Civil Code, § 2984.4.)*

e. ☐ Other *(specify):*_____

(6) **List the zip code of the place checked in ⑤ above** *(if you know):*_____

(7) **Is your claim about an attorney-client fee dispute?** ☐ Yes ☐ No
If yes, and if you have had arbitration, fill out Form SC-101, attach it to this form, and check here: ☐

(8) **Are you suing a public entity?** ☐ Yes ☐ No
If yes, you must file a written claim with the entity first. ☐ A claim was filed on *(date):*_____
If the public entity denies your claim or does not answer within the time allowed by law, you can file this form.

(9) **Have you filed more than 12 other small claims within the last 12 months in California?**
☐ Yes ☐ No   *If yes, the filing fee for this case will be higher.*

(10) **I understand that by filing a claim in small claims court, I have no right to appeal this claim.**

(11) I have not filed, and understand that I cannot file, more than two small claims cases for more than $2,500 in California during this calendar year.

I declare, under penalty of perjury under California State law, that the information above and on any attachments to this form is true and correct.

Date:_____   _____   ▶ _____
               Plaintiff types or prints name here   *Plaintiff signs here*

Date:_____   _____   ▶ _____
               Second Plaintiff types or prints name here   *Second Plaintiff signs here*

Requests for Accommodations
Assistive listening systems, computer-assisted, real-time captioning, or sign language interpreter services are available if you ask at least 5 days before the trial. Contact the clerk's office for Form MC-410, *Request for Accommodations by Persons With Disabilities and Order. (Civil Code, § 54.8.)*

Revised January 1, 2007

**Plaintiff's Claim and ORDER
to Go to Small Claims Court**
(Small Claims)

SC-100, Page 3 of 5
→

179. Debtor's Statement of Assets (California)

MAIL TO THE JUDGMENT CREDITOR
DO NOT FILE WITH THE COURT

SC-133

JUDGMENT CREDITOR (the person or business who won the case) *(name):*

JUDGMENT DEBTOR (the person or business who lost the case and owes money) *(name):*

SMALL CLAIMS CASE NO.:

NOTICE TO JUDGMENT DEBTOR: You *must* (1) pay the judgment or (2) appeal or (3) file a motion to vacate. If you fail to pay or take one of the other two actions, you must complete and mail this form to the judgment creditor. If you do not, you may have to go to court to answer questions and may have penalties imposed on you by the court.	**AVISO AL DEUDOR POR FALLO JUDICIAL: Usted debe (1) pagar el monto del fallo judicial, o (2) presentar un recurso de apelación o (3) presentar un recurso de nulidad.** Si usted no paga el fallo o presenta uno de estos dos recursos, deberá llenar y enviar por correo este formulario a su acreedor por fallo judicial. Si no lo hace, es posible que deba presentarse ante la corte para contestar preguntas y pagar las multas que la corte le pueda imponer.

INSTRUCTIONS

The small claims court has ruled that you owe money to the judgment creditor.

1. You may appeal a judgment against you only on the other party's claim. You may *not* appeal a judgment against you on *your* claim.

   a. If you appeared at the trial and you want to appeal, you must file a *Notice of Appeal* (form SC-140) within 30 days after the date the *Notice of Entry of Judgment* (form SC-130) was mailed or handed to you by the clerk.

   b. If you did not appear at the trial, before you can appeal, you must first file a *Notice of Motion to Vacate Judgment and Declaration* (form SC-135) and pay the required fee within 30 days after the date the *Notice of Entry of Judgment* was mailed or handed to you. The judgment cannot be collected until the motion is decided. If your motion is denied, you then have 10 days after the date the notice of denial was mailed to file your appeal.

2. Unless you **pay the judgment or appeal the judgment or file a motion to vacate, you must fill out this form and mail it to the person who won the case** within **30 days** after the *Notice of Entry of Judgment* was mailed or handed to you by the clerk. Mailing this completed form does not stay enforcement of the judgment.

3. If you lose your appeal or motion to vacate, you must pay the judgment, including postjudgment costs and interest. As soon as the small claims court denies your motion to vacate and the denial is not appealed, or receives the dismissal of your appeal or judgment from the superior court after appeal, the judgment is no longer suspended and may be immediately enforced against you by the judgment creditor.

4. Unless you have paid the judgment, complete and mail this form to the judgment creditor within **30 days** after the date the clerk mails or delivers to you (a) the denial of your motion to vacate, or (b) the dismissal of your appeal, or (c) the judgment against you on your appeal.

If you were sued as an individual, skip this box and begin with item 1 below. Otherwise, check the applicable box, attach the documents indicated, and complete item 15 on the reverse.

a. ☐ *(Corporation or partnership)* Attached to this form is a statement describing the nature, value, and exact location of all assets of the corporation or the partners, and a statement showing that the person signing this form is authorized to submit this form on behalf of the corporation or partnership.

b. ☐ *(Governmental agency)* Attached to this form is the statement of an authorized representative of the agency stating when the agency will pay the judgment and any reasons for its failure to do so.

JUDGMENT DEBTOR'S STATEMENT OF ASSETS

EMPLOYMENT

1. What are your sources of income and occupation? *(Provide job title and name of division or office in which you work.)*

2. a. Name and address of your business or employer *(include address of your payroll or human resources department, if different):*

   b. If not employed, names and addresses of all sources of income *(specify):*

3. How often are you paid?
   ☐ daily ☐ every two weeks ☐ monthly
   ☐ weekly ☐ twice a month ☐ other *(explain):*

4. What is your gross pay each pay period? $

5. What is your take-home pay each pay period? $

6. If your spouse earns any income, give the name of your spouse, the name and address of the business or employer, job title, and division or office *(specify):*

Form Adopted for Mandatory Use
Judicial Council of California
SC-133 [Rev. January 1, 2004]

JUDGMENT DEBTOR'S STATEMENT OF ASSETS
(Small Claims)

Page 1 of 2
Code of Civil Procedure,
§§ 116.620(a), 116.830

American LegalNet, Inc.
www.USCourtForms.com

CASH, BANK DEPOSITS

7. How much money do you have in cash? . . . . $

8. How much other money do you have in banks, savings and loans, credit unions, and other financial institutions either in your own name or jointly *(list)*:

Name and address of financial institution	Account number	Individual or joint?	Balance
a.			$
b.			$
c.			$

PROPERTY

9. List all automobiles, other vehicles, and boats owned in your name or jointly:

Make and year	License and vehicle identification (VIN) numbers	Value	Legal owner if different from registered owner	Amount owed
a.		$		$
b.		$		$
c.		$		$
d.		$		$

10. List all real estate owned in your name or jointly:

Address of real estate	Fair market value	Amount owed
a.	$	$
b.	$	$

OTHER PERSONAL PROPERTY (*Do not list household furniture and furnishings, appliances, or clothing.*)

11. List anything of value not listed above owned in your name or jointly *(continue on attached sheet if necessary)*:

Description	Value	Address where property is located
a.	$	
b.	$	
c.	$	

12. Is anyone holding assets for you? ☐ Yes. ☐ No. If yes, describe the assets and give the name and address of the person or entity holding each asset *(specify)*:

13. Have you disposed of or transferred any asset within the last 60 days? ☐ Yes. ☐ No. If yes, give the name and address of each person or entity who received any asset and describe each asset *(specify)*:

14. If you are not able to pay the judgment in one lump sum, you may be able to make payment arrangements with the person or business who won the case (the judgment creditor). State the amount that you can pay each month: $, beginning on *(date)*: . If you are unable to agree, you may also ask the court for permission to make installment payments by filing a *Request to Pay Judgment in Installments* (form SC-106).

15. I declare under penalty of perjury under the laws of the State of California that the foregoing is true and correct.

Date:

▶

_____ (TYPE OR PRINT NAME)   _____ (SIGNATURE)

Mail or deliver this completed form to the judgment creditor at the address shown on the **Notice of Entry of Judgment** *form.*

SC-133 [Rev. January 1, 2004]   **JUDGMENT DEBTOR'S STATEMENT OF ASSETS** (Small Claims)   Page 2 of 2

CHAPTER 16

Forms for Tax Rebates

EVERAL STATE AND FEDERAL FINANCIAL reprieves are available to small business owners, providing rebates and tax breaks for those companies that qualify.

There are a variety of federal programs available that provide rebates and other savings. The American Recovery and Reinvestment Act of 2009 has made the IRS responsible for implementing several tax changes that provide tax incentives for businesses designed to increase green energy investment and spur job growth. While some of these are forms that most businesses can use, some are industry-specific and dependent on the purpose of your business.

Cash or rebates are available to businesses that qualify for renewable energy grants provided by the U.S. Department of Treasury. The specific form you'll see in this chapter is *Application for Section 1603—Payments for Specified Renewable Energy Property in Lieu of Tax Credits*. In addition, corporations can file *Form 3468 Business Energy Investment Tax Credits* for investment credits, including the rehabilitation credit, the energy credit, and the reforestation credit. For example, if your company used solar energy, you may be eligible for commercial solar incentives.

Corporations can also file for the *Energy-Efficient Commercial Buildings Tax Deduction* on form 1120 (on the Web). Include the amount of the deduction in the "Other deductions" line of the tax return.

Energy Star is a joint program of the U.S. Environmental Protection Agency and the U.S. Department of Energy that aims to protect the environment and save people money through its promotion of energy-efficient products and practices. Energy Star programs assist businesses as well as individuals. For example, your company may be eligible for tax credits if it uses alternative fuel vehicles. If alternative fuel vehicles are part of your business model, complete Form 8910 Alternative Motor Vehicle Credit when you file your taxes.

Individual states will have their own applicable tax credits as well. As an example, we include the *Alternative Energy Product Manufacturers Tax Credit* form offered in the state of New Mexico. In addition, the *Oregon Business Energy Tax Credit Application* offered in the state of Oregon is pro-

vided as an alternative example. Several states offer a similar tax credits that small business owners can take advantage of using or manufacturing alternative energy products and components.

179. Section 1603: Payments for Specified Renewal Energy Property in Lieu of Tax

Application for Section 1603:
Payments for Specified Renewable Energy Property in Lieu of Tax Credits

This is one of two parts of the application package for payment under the Section 1603 program. The other document is the signed Terms and Conditions. All applicants must submit this application form before October 1, 2011. Applicants who place a qualified property in service during 2009 or 2010 should submit the application form and the Terms and Conditions form at the same time after the property has been placed in service. Applicants who have begun construction of a qualified property during 2009 or 2010 and have not yet placed the property in service by the date of application, should submit only this application (not the Terms and Conditions) before October 1, 2011 to demonstrate that construction began during 2009 or 2010. Once the qualified property is placed in service, the applicant should submit both an updated application form and the signed Terms and Conditions document, indicating the identification number (issued by Treasury) of the applicant's preliminary submission.

While there are directions in this application, they are not a substitute for reading and understanding the Program Guidance, Terms and Conditions, Section 1603 of the American Recovery and Reinvestment Tax Act of 2009, and Sections 45 and 48 of the Internal Revenue Code.

Section 1: Applicant Eligibility

1A. Type of Applicant – indicate which choice best describes the applicant. Governments, 501(c) organizations, 54(j)(4) entities, partnership or pass-thru entities with any government /501(c)/54(j)(4) entity as a partner (or other holder of an equity or profits interest), and in some cases foreign persons and entities are not eligible for Section 1603 payments.

	Federal, State, or local government or any political subdivision, agency, or instrumentality thereof – do not continue with application
	Organization described in section 501(c) of the Internal Revenue Code and exempt from tax under section 501(a) of such Code – do not continue with application
	Entity referred to in paragraph (4) of section 54(j) of the Internal Revenue Code – do not continue with application
	Partnership or pass-thru entity with a government or any political subdivision, agency, or instrumentality thereof, 501(c) organization, or 54(j)(4) entity as a direct or indirect partner (or other direct or indirect holder of an equity or profits interest) - do not continue with application [Note: If such entity only owns an indirect interest in the applicant through a taxable C corporation – do not choose this selection.]
	Foreign person or entity <u>not</u> qualifying for the exception in section 168(h)(2)(B) of the Internal Revenue Code with respect to the property – do not continue with application
	Foreign person or entity qualifying for the exception in section 168(h)(2)(B) of the Internal Revenue Code with respect to the property
	Sole proprietorship
	Joint venture
	Partnership
	Domestic C corporation
	Domestic S corporation
	Cooperative organization described in section 1381 of the Internal Revenue Code
	Real Estate Investment Trust (REIT)
	Other (specify here):

1B. Applicant's Interest in the Property – check the appropriate box.

	Applicant is owner of the property.
	Applicant is lessee of the property (include waiver from owner as described in the Program Guidance and in Section 6 of this Application).
	Applicant is not the owner or lessee of the property – do not continue with application.

Section 2: Property Information

2A. Depreciation and Use of Property – check the box or boxes which describe the property.

	Property is not depreciable or amortization is not allowed – do not continue with application.
	Property is depreciable or amortization is allowed in lieu of depreciation.
	Property is both depreciable or amortization is allowed in lieu of depreciation and is a public utility property within the meaning of section 168(i)(10) of the Internal Revenue Code.

2B. Property Identification – enter information about the location of the property. * Either a City or County is required.

	Property is located outside of the United States during more than 50% of the year – do not continue with application. [Note: If such property meets the requirements described in section 168(g)(4) of the IRC, do not choose this selection]
	Property is located predominately within the United States.

Name:		Street Address 1	
*City:		State Address 2 (optional)	
*County:		State	
Zip Code:			

2C. Property Placed in Service – enter the date on which the property was placed in service. See Program Guidance for a definition of placed in service date. If applying for multiple units of property that the applicant is treating as a single, larger unit of property and the units have different placed in service dates, enter the date the first and last units were placed in service. If property is not yet placed in service, skip to Section 2D below.

	Property has been placed in service – enter date(s) then skip to Section 3 below. Date (for multiple units, first property): Date (optional – for multiple units, last property):
	Property has not yet been placed in service – skip to Section 2D below.

2D. Date Construction Began – for properties not yet placed in service, enter the date on which construction began. See Program Guidance for a definition of beginning of construction and the credit termination date by which time the project must be placed in service.

	Construction of the property began on this date.
	Construction of the property has not begun – do not continue with this application.

2E. Expected Placed in Service Date – for properties not yet placed in service, enter the anticipated date when the property will be placed in service. See Program Guidance for dates by which specific properties must be placed in service to be eligible for Section 1603 funds. Do not continue with this application if the property will be placed in service within 90 days; rather, return after the property is placed in service and choose "Property has been placed in service" under Section 2C.

	Anticipated date the property will be placed in service.

2F. Narrative Description of Beginning of Construction– for properties not yet placed in service, describe what construction activities have taken place. Limit to 2,500 characters.

Section 3: Applicant Information

3A. Applicant – enter information about the entity that placed the property in service/began construction. If applicant did not or will not originally place the property in service do not continue with this application.

Business name:		Street address 1:	
Phone number:		Street address 2:	
Employer Identification Number (EIN): (do not enter a Social Security number)		City:	
DUNS number:		State:	
Website address (optional):		Zip Code:	

3B. Contact Person – enter information for the person to be contacted about this application.

First Name:		Last Name :	
Organizational affiliation:		E-mail address:	
Phone:		Fax:	

3C. Previous Applications – check the box indicating whether an application has previously been submitted for Section 1603 payments for this property or property at this same location.

	No application(s) submitted previously for Section 1603 payments for this property.
	Application(s) has been submitted previously for this property or property at this same location; enter Treasury application number (TAN) from previously submitted any application(s).

Section 4: Property Description

4A. Specified Energy Property – check the box or boxes which best describes the type of specified energy property. See Program Guidance for a further explanation of each type.

Specified properties eligible under Section 45 of Internal Revenue Code	
	Wind facility – uses wind to produce electricity (wind turbines with capacity of 100kW or less may also qualify below as small wind energy property but only one payment is allowed with respect to the property).
	Closed-loop biomass facility (other than a facility described in the box below) – uses organic material from a plant grown exclusively for purposes of being used to generate electricity. If a portion of fuel is not closed-loop biomass, give the percentage of fuel, on an annual basis, that is closed-loop biomass: _____%.

	Facility modified to use closed-loop biomass to co-fire with coal, other biomass, or both. Modification must be approved under the Biomass Power for Rural Development Program <u>or</u> be part of a pilot project of the Commodity Credit Corporation. Give the percentage of fuel, on an annual basis, that is closed-loop biomass: _____%.
	Open-loop biomass facility (cellulosic waste material) – uses solid, non-hazardous, cellulosic waste material or any lignin material derived from qualified sources described in section 45(c)(3)(ii) of the Internal Revenue Code to produce electricity. If a portion of fuel is not open-loop biomass of this type, give the percentage of fuel, on an annual basis, that is open-loop biomass of this type: _____%.
	Open-loop biomass facility (livestock waste nutrients) – uses agricultural livestock waste nutrients to produce electricity and has a nameplate capacity rating of not less than 150 kW. If a portion of fuel is not agricultural livestock waste nutrients, give the percentage of fuel, on an annual basis, that is agricultural livestock waste nutrients: _____%.
	Geothermal facility – uses geothermal energy to produce electricity.
	Landfill gas facility – uses gas derived from the biodegradation of municipal solid waste to produce electricity.
	Trash facility – uses municipal solid waste to produce electricity and is not a landfill gas facility.
	Hydropower facility (incremental hydropower) – produces incremental hydropower production as a result of efficiency improvements and additions to capacity to which the incremental hydropower production is attributable. The baseline and incremental increase in energy production must be certified by FERC.
	Hydropower facility – hydropower producing facility installed on a qualifying nonhydroelectric dam. The property must be licensed by FERC and meet all other applicable environmental, licensing, and regulatory requirements.
	Marine and hydrokinetic renewable energy facility – uses marine and hydrokinetic renewable energy to produce electricity and has a nameplate capacity rating of at least 150 kW.
Specified properties eligible under Section 48 of Internal Revenue Code	
	Solar electricity property – uses solar energy to generate electricity.
	Solar thermal property – uses solar energy to heat or cool (or provide hot water for use in) a structure, or to provide solar process heat (property used to generate energy for heating a swimming pool ineligible).
	Solar lighting property – uses solar energy to illuminate the inside of a structure using fiber-optic distributed sunlight.
	Geothermal property – equipment used to produce, distribute, or use energy derived from a geothermal deposit.
	Fuel cell property – fuel cell power plant that has a nameplate capacity of at least 0.5 kW of electricity using an electrochemical process <u>and</u> an electricity-only generation efficiency greater than 30%.
	Microturbine property – stationary microturbine power plant that has a nameplate capacity of less than 2,000 kW <u>and</u> an electricity-only generation efficiency of not less than 26% at International Standard Organization conditions

	Combined heat and power system property – system that uses the same energy source for the simultaneous or sequential generation of electrical power, mechanical shaft power, or both, in combination with the generation of steam or other form of useful thermal energy and that meets all of the following requirements:
	1. System produces at least 20% of total useful energy in the form of thermal energy which is not used for electrical or mechanical power (report thermal production in section 4D of this application)
	2. System produces at least 20% of total useful energy in the form of electrical or mechanical power (or combination) (report electrical and/or mechanical production in section 4D of this application).
	3. System energy efficiency percentage exceeds 60% [unless system uses open or closed loop biomass (see Guidance) for at least 90% of the energy source]. Specify energy efficiency percentage:_____% and, if applicable, percentage of energy source from open or closed loop biomass:_____%.
	4. System does not exceed 50 MW or a mechanical energy capacity in excess of 67,000 horsepower or an equivalent combination of electrical and mechanical energy capacities (report system capacity in section 4D of this application).
	Small wind energy property – uses a turbine with nameplate capacity of not more than 100 kW to generate electricity.
	Geothermal heat pump property – uses the ground or ground water as a thermal energy source to heat a structure or as a thermal energy sink to cool a structure.

4B. Narrative Description of Property – give a summary description of the property that is suitable for publication. Limit the summary to 2,500 characters. If applying for multiple units of property that are being treated as a single, larger property, so indicate in the narrative.

4C. Use of Energy - enter information in one of the two boxes to describe how the energy produced is being/will be used.

Energy produced has been/will be sold. Enter the name and address of the buyer. Limit to 500 characters.	
Energy produced has not been/will not be sold. Describe how it is/will be used. Limit to 2,500 characters.	

4D. Energy Generated by the Property – fill in the appropriate column depending on whether the property generates electrical, mechanical, or thermal energy (or combination) for the capacity and production of the property. This section is not applicable to solar illumination properties and geothermal heat pump properties. For properties not yet placed in service or that have not operated for a full year, enter the estimated production. kW=kilowatt(s), kWh=kilowatt hour(s), MMBTU=one-million British Thermal Units, hp=horsepower.

	Electrical	Mechanical	Thermal
Installed nameplate capacity	kW	must specify whether kW, MMBTU/hr, or hp	MMBTU/hr
Estimated annual production	kWh	must specify whether kWh, MMBTU, or hp	MMBTU

4E. Jobs Created/Retained by the Property – enter the estimated number of direct jobs created/retained by the property. Direct jobs are those created/retained in the project, not by suppliers who make the materials used in the project.

	Construction stage	Operational stage
Full-time jobs (at least 35 hours per week)		
Part-time jobs (less than 35 hours per week)		

Section 5. Cost Basis and Request for Payment

5A. Cost Basis and Applicable Percentage – enter the qualified cost basis of the property and the applicable percentage to calculate the request for payment. The applicable percentage is either 10% or 30% depending on the type of energy property. See Program Guidance to determine the correct percentage to apply. For properties not yet placed in service, skip to Section 6B. Fuel cell property formula – if the applicable percentage times the qualified cost basis exceeds an amount equal to $1,500 for each 0.5 kW of capacity, enter an amount equal to $1,500 times each 0.5 kW of capacity. Microturbine property formula – if the applicable percentage times the qualified cost basis exceeds an amount equal to $200 for each kW of capacity, enter an amount equal to $200 times the number of kW of capacity

	Qualified cost basis as shown in supporting documentation
	Applicable percentage (enter either 30% or 10%)
	For fuel cell property: If property has less than _____ kW of capacity enter capacity here:
	For microturbine property: If property has less than _____ kW of capacity, enter capacity here:

5B. Request for Payment – from the calculation in 5A, enter the amount of request for payment. For properties not yet placed in service, skip to Section 6B.

	Amount of request for payment

5C. Assignment – indicate if the 1603 payment has been assigned to a financial institution in accordance with Federal Assignment of Claims Act (31 U.S.C. 3727)

	The 1603 payment has not been assigned to a financial institution.
	The 1603 payment has been assigned to a financial institution.

Section 6. Documentation

6A. Documentation for Properties Placed In Service – for properties placed in service attach documentation: to establish that the property has been placed in service as claimed in Section 2C of this application; to demonstrate that the property has met the requirements shown in Section 4 of this application; and to support costs claimed in Section 5 of this application. See Program Guidance for information on acceptable documentation to establish that a property is placed in service and meets the eligibility requirements and to support costs. If the applicant is a lessee (as indicated in Section 1B), attach a waiver, as described in the Program Guidance, from the owner. For properties not yet placed in service, skip to Section 6B. Note: An applicant may add additional documents or replace documents as needed using the "Add/modify supporting documentation" option in the main menu of the on-line application for up to 3 days after submitting the application.

ACCEPTED FILE TYPES: Office (pre-2007 doc, xls), postscript (pdf), and plain text (txt) formats. Limit total size of all files to 100 MB or less.

Supporting documents requested for properties placed in service (This is provided as guidance for all applicants. However, eligibility decisions by the Department of Treasury will be based ultimately on applicant's eligibility under Section 45 or Section 48 of the US Tax Code.)
ELIGIBLE PROPERTY:
- Design plans – final engineering design documents, stamped by a licensed professional engineer.
- Nameplate capacity – design plans, commissioning reports, or OEM/equipment vendor specification sheets demonstrating that the pproperty meets the required minimum or maximum nameplate capacity (see Section 4A of the Application for properties with minimum or maximum nameplate capacity requirements).

PLACED IN SERVICE:
- Commissioning report – report provided by the project engineer, equipment vendor, or independent third party that certifies that the equipment has been installed, tested, and is ready and capable of being used for its intended purpose.
- Interconnection agreement – a formal document between the applicant and the local utility that establishes the terms and conditions under which the utility agrees to interconnect with the applicant's system. Applicants must also submit any subsequent documentation to demonstrate that the interconnection agreement has been placed in effect. Systems not connected to a utility are required to submit additional documentation, including approval from a building department official or other local agency with jurisdiction.

COST BASIS:
- Detailed breakdown of all costs included in the cost basis – a detailed cost breakdown should separately itemize costs for equipment, labor, installation, engineering, permits, and other project cost items to be included as the eligible cost basis.
- For properties that have a cost basis in excess of $500,000 attach the Independent Accountant Certification attesting to the accuracy of all costs claimed as part of the basis of the property.

APPLICANT THAT IS A LESSEE:
- If applicant is a lessee, attach the Owner's Waiver containing all six elements described on page 17 of the Program Guidance.

APPLICANT THAT IS A LESSEE, LLC, PARTNERSHIP, or PASS-THROUGH ENTITY:
- If the applicant is a lessee, LLC of a parent company, partnership, or a pass-through entity, please attach supporting documentation indicating the applicant's interest in the property which indicates the business structure as well as the applicant's relationship to any other parties with a direct interest in the property (i.e., property owner or parent company).

OTHER:
- Please attach any additional documents to support your application. If you require more uploads than this form provides, supplement these with the "Add/Modify Supporting Documentation" function under the Application Package Control Panel for this application when finished.

	Attached is documentation to support eligibility of the specified energy property is attached.
	Attached is documentation to support costs:
	Attached is documentation to establish that property is placed in service:

	Attached is owner's waiver, if applicant is a lessee (as indicated in Section 1B):

6B. Documentation for Properties Not Yet Placed In Service – for properties not yet placed in service attach documentation to establish that construction has begun.   See Program Guidance for information on acceptable documentation to establish that construction has begun.

ACCEPTED FILE TYPES: Office (pre-2007 doc, xls), postscript (pdf), and plain text (txt) formats. Limit total size of all files to 100 MB or less.

Supporting documents requested for properties not yet placed in service (This is provided as guidance for all applicants. However, eligibility decisions by the Department of Treasury will be based ultimately on applicant's eligibility under Section 45 or Section 48 of the US Tax Code.)

UNDER CONSTRUCTION BUT NOT YET PLACED IN SERVICE:
- Paid invoices and/or other financial documents demonstrating that physical work of a significant nature has begun on the property.
- Binding contract for the manufacture, construction or production of the property as described in Section IV.C of the Program Guidance (required for property not yet placed in service that is being manufactured, constructed, or produced for the applicant by another person).
- Safe harbor – if beginning construction is based on the safe harbor, the financial documents must demonstrate that more than 5 percent of the total cost of the property (excluding the cost of any land and preliminary activities such as planning, designing, securing financing, exploring, or researching) has been incurred or paid by the applicant.

OTHER:
- Please attach any additional documents to support your application. If you require more uploads than this form provides, supplement these with the "Add/Modify Supporting Documentation" function under the Application Package Control Panel for this application when finished.

	Attached is documentation to establish that construction has begun.

Section 7. Signature of Applicant

Under penalties of perjury, I declare that I have examined this application and to the best of my knowledge and belief, it is true, correct, and complete. I declare that I am the applicant or an authorized official for the applicant. Further, I agree the information in this application can be disclosed to the Internal Revenue Service.

First Name		Last Name	
Title		Phone	
Email		Signature*	

*In the on-line application, entering the applicant's password to the on-line application has the same legal effect as the applicant's handwritten signature.

180. Form 3468 Business Energy Tax Credit

Form **3468**	**Investment Credit**	OMB No. 1545-0155

Department of the Treasury
Internal Revenue Service   (99)

► Attach to your tax return. See instructions.

200**8**

Attachment
Sequence No.   52

Name(s) shown on return

Identifying number

Part I Information Regarding the Election To Treat the Lessee as the Purchaser of Investment Credit Property

If you are claiming the investment credit as a lessee based on a section 48(d) (as in effect on November 4, 1990) election, provide
the following information. If you acquired more than one property as a lessee, attach a statement showing the information below.

1   Name of lessor _____

2   Address of lessor _____

3   Description of property _____

4   Amount for which you were treated as having acquired the property   . . . . ► $ _____

Part II Energy Credit (For Tax Years Beginning Before October 4, 2008), Qualifying Advanced Coal Project
Credit, Qualifying Gasification Project Credit, and Qualifying Advanced Energy Project Credit

5   Energy credit:

a Basis of property using geothermal energy placed in service during
the tax year (see instructions) $ _____ × 10% (.10)   **5a**

b Basis of property using solar illumination or solar energy placed in service
during the tax year (see instructions) $ _____ × 30% (.30)   **5b**

Qualified fuel cell property (see instructions):

c Basis of property installed before October 4, 2008
. . . $ _____ × 30% (.30)   **5c**

d Kilowatt capacity of property in   c
above   . . . ► _____ × $1,000   **5d**

e Enter the lesser of line 5c or 5d **5e**

f Basis of property installed after October 3, 2008
. . . $ _____ × 30% (.30)   **5f**

g Kilowatt capacity of property in   f
above   . . . ► _____ × $3,000   **5g**

h Enter the lesser of line 5f or 5g **5h**

Qualified microturbine property (see instructions):

i Basis of property installed during the tax
year $ _____ × 10% (.10)   **5i**

j Kilowatt capacity of property in   i
above   . . . ► _____ × $200   **5j**

k Enter the lesser of line 5i or 5j **5k**

Combined heat and power system property (see instructions):

Caution: You cannot claim this credit if the electrical capacity of the property is more than 50
megawatts or 67,000 horsepower.

l Basis of property installed after October 3, 2008
. . . $ _____ × 10% (.10)   **5l**

m If the electrical capacity of the property is measured in:

• Megawatts, divide 15 by the megawatt capacity.
Enter 1.0 if the capacity is 15 megawatts or less.

• Horsepower, divide 20,000 by the
horsepower. Enter 1.0 if the capacity is
20,000 horsepower or less **5m**

n Multiply line 5l by 5m **5n**

Qualified small wind energy property (see instructions):

o Basis of property installed after
October 3, 2008, and before 2009
. $ _____ × 30% (.30)   **5o**

p Enter the smaller of line 5o or $4,000   . . . .   **5p**

q Basis of property installed after 2008 $ _____ × 30% (.30)   **5q**

Geothermal heat pump systems (see instructions):

r Basis of property installed after October 3, 2008 $ _____ × 10% (.10)   **5r**

Qualified investment credit facility property (see instructions):

s Basis of property installed after 2008 $ _____ × 30% (.30)   **5s**

t **Total.** Add lines 5a, 5b, 5e, 5h, 5k, 5n, 5p, 5q, 5r, and 5s **5t**

For Paperwork Reduction Act Notice, see instructions.

Cat. No. 12276E

Form **3468** (2008)

Form 3468 (2008)   Page **2**

Part II   Energy Credit (For Tax Years Beginning Before October 4, 2008), Qualifying Advanced Coal Project Credit, Qualifying Gasification Project Credit, and Qualifying Advanced Energy Project Credit   (continued)

6   Qualifying advanced coal project credit (see instructions):

a   Basis of qualified investment in integrated gasification combined cycle property placed in service during the tax year for projects described in section 48A(d)(3)(B)(i)   . . $ _____ × 20% (.20)   **6a**

b   Basis of qualified investment in advanced coal-based generation technology property placed in service during the tax year for projects described in section 48A(d)(3)(B)(ii)   . . . $ _____ × 15% (.15)   **6b**

c   Basis of qualified investment in advanced coal-based generation technology property placed in service during the tax year for projects described in section 48A(d)(3)(B)(iii)   . . . $ _____ × 30% (.30)   **6c**

d   Total. Add lines 6a, 6b, and 6c **6d**

7   Qualifying gasification project credit (see instructions):

a   Basis of qualified investment in qualified gasification property placed in service during the tax year for which credits were allocated or reallocated after October 3, 2008, and that include equipment that separates and sequesters at least 75% of the project's carbon dioxide emissions   . . . . . . $ _____ × 30% (.30)   **7a**

b   Basis of qualified investment in property other than in   a above placed in service during the tax year $ _____ × 20% (.20)   **7b**

c   Total. Add lines 7a and 7b **7c**

8a   Qualifying advanced energy project credit (see instructions): Basis of qualified investment in advanced energy project property placed in service after February 17, 2009 $ _____ × 30% (.30)   **8a**

8b   Credit from cooperatives. Enter the unused investment credit from cooperatives **8b**

9   Add lines 5t, 6d, 7c, 8a, and 8b. Report this amount on Form 3800, line 1a **9**

Part III   Rehabilitation Credit (For Tax Years Beginning in 2008) and Energy Credit (For Tax Years Beginning After October 3, 2008)

10   Rehabilitation credit (see instructions for requirements that must be met):

a   Check this box if you are electing under section 47(d)(5) to take your qualified rehabilitation expenditures into account for the tax year in which paid (or, for self-rehabilitated property, when capitalized). See instructions.   Note. This election applies to the current tax year and to all later tax years. You may not revoke this election without IRS consent   . . . . . ▶ ☐

b   Enter the date on which the 24- or 60-month measuring period begins   ___/___/___ and ends   ___/___/___

c   Enter the adjusted basis of the building as of the beginning date above (or the first day of your holding period, if later) $ _____

d   Enter the amount of the qualified rehabilitation expenditures incurred, or treated as incurred, during the period on line 10b above   . . . $ _____

Enter the amount of qualified rehabilitation expenditures and multiply by the percentage shown:

e   Pre-1936 buildings located in the Gulf Opportunity Zone $ _____ × 13% (.13)   **10e**

f   Pre-1936 buildings affected by a Midwestern disaster $ _____ × 13% (.13)   **10f**

g   Other pre-1936 buildings   . . . . $ _____ × 10% (.10)   **10g**

h   Certified historic structures located in the Gulf Opportunity Zone   . . . . . . $ _____ × 26% (.26)   **10h**

i   Certified historic structures affected by a Midwestern disaster   . . . . . . $ _____ × 26% (.26)   **10i**

j   Other certified historic structures   . . . . . $ _____ × 20% (.20)   **10j**

For properties identified on lines 10h, 10i, or 10j, complete lines 10k and 10l

k   Enter the assigned NPS project number or the pass-through entity's employer identification number (see instructions)   . . .   _____

l   Enter the date that the NPS approved the Request for Certification of Completed Work (see instructions)   . . . .   ___/___/___

m   Rehabilitation credit from an electing large partnership (Schedule K-1 (Form 1065-B), box 9)   .   **10m**

Form **3468** (2008)

Form 3468 (2008)   Page **3**

Part III	Rehabilitation Credit (For Tax Years Beginning in 2008) and Energy Credit (For Tax Years Beginning After October 3, 2008) (continued)

11   Energy credit:

a   Basis of property using geothermal energy placed in service during the tax year (see instructions)   .   . $ _____ × 10% (.10) | **11a** |

b   Basis of property using solar illumination or solar energy placed in service during the tax year (see instructions)   . $ _____ × 30% (.30) | **11b** |

Qualified fuel cell property (see instructions):

c   Basis of property installed during the tax year   . $ _____ × 30% (.30) | **11c** |

d   Kilowatt capacity of property in   c above .   .   . ▶ _____ × $3,000 | **11d** |

e   Enter the lesser of line 11c or 11d   .   .   .   . | **11e** |

Qualified microturbine property (see instructions):

f   Basis of property installed during the tax year $ _____ × 10% (.10) | **11f** |

g   Kilowatt capacity of property in   f above .   .   . ▶ _____ × $200 | **11g** |

h   Enter the lesser of line 11f or 11g   .   .   .   .   . | **11h** |

Combined heat and power system property (see instructions):

Caution: You cannot claim this credit if the electrical capacity of the property is more than 50 megawatts or 67,000 horsepower.

i   Basis of property installed during the tax year $ _____ × 10% (.10) | **11i** |

j   If the electrical capacity of the property is measured in:

    ● Megawatts, divide 15 by the megawatt capacity. Enter 1.0 if the capacity is 15 megawatts or less   .   .   .   .   .   .

    ● Horsepower, divide 20,000 by the horsepower. Enter 1.0 if the capacity is 20,000 horsepower or less   .   .   .   . | **11j** |

k   Multiply line 11i by 11j   .   .   .   . | **11k** |

Qualified small wind energy property (see instructions):

l   Basis of property installed before 2009   . $ _____ × 30% (.30) | **11l** |

m   Enter the smaller of line 11l or $4,000   .   .   .   .   . | **11m** |

n   Basis of property installed after 2008 $ _____ × 30% (.30) | **11n** |

Geothermal heat pump systems (see instructions):

o   Basis of property installed during the tax year $ _____ × 10% (.10) | **11o** |

Qualified investment credit facility property (see instructions):

p   Basis of property installed after 2008 $ _____ × 30% (.30) | **11p** |

q   Total. Add lines 11a, 11b, 11e, 11h, 11k, 11m, 11n, 11o, and 11p   .   .   .   . | **11q** |

12   Credit from cooperatives. Enter the unused investment credit from cooperatives (see instructions)   .   .   .   . | **12** |

13   Add lines 10e through 10j, 10m, 11q, and 12   .   .   .   .   . | **13** |

14   Rehabilitation and energy credits included on line 13 from passive activities   .   .   .   . | **14** |

15   Subtract line 14 from line 13   .   .   .   . | **15** |

16   Rehabilitation and energy credits allowed for 2008 from a passive activity   .   .   . | **16** |

17   Carryback of rehabilitation and energy credits from 2009   .   .   .   .   . | **17** |

18   Add lines 15 through 17. Report this amount on Form 3800, line 29a   .   .   .   .   . | **18** |

Form **3468** (2008)

181. Form 1120 U.S. Corporation Income Tax Return

Form 1120
Department of the Treasury
Internal Revenue Service

U.S. Corporation Income Tax Return

For calendar year 2009 or tax year beginning _____ , 2009, ending _____ , 20 _____

▶ See separate instructions.

OMB No. 1545-0123

20 09

A Check if:
1a Consolidated return (attach Form 851) ☐
  b Life/nonlife consolidated return . . ☐
2 Personal holding co. (attach Sch. PH) . ☐
3 Personal service corp. (see instructions) . ☐
4 Schedule M-3 attached ☐

Use IRS label. Otherwise, print or type.

Name	
Number, street, and room or suite no. If a P.O. box, see instructions.	
City or town, state, and ZIP code	

B Employer identification number

C Date incorporated

D Total assets (see instructions)
$

E Check if: (1) ☐ Initial return (2) ☐ Final return (3) ☐ Name change (4) ☐ Address change

Income

1a	Gross receipts or sales	b Less returns and allowances	c Bal ▶	1c	
2	Cost of goods sold (Schedule A, line 8)	2	
3	Gross profit. Subtract line 2 from line 1c	3	
4	Dividends (Schedule C, line 19)	4	
5	Interest	5	
6	Gross rents	6	
7	Gross royalties	7	
8	Capital gain net income (attach Schedule D (Form 1120))	8	
9	Net gain or (loss) from Form 4797, Part II, line 17 (attach Form 4797)	9	
10	Other income (see instructions—attach schedule)	10	
11	Total income. Add lines 3 through 10 ▶	11	

Deductions (See instructions for limitations on deductions.)

12	Compensation of officers (Schedule E, line 4) ▶	12	
13	Salaries and wages (less employment credits)	13	
14	Repairs and maintenance	14	
15	Bad debts	15	
16	Rents	16	
17	Taxes and licenses	17	
18	Interest	18	
19	Charitable contributions	19	
20	Depreciation from Form 4562 not claimed on Schedule A or elsewhere on return (attach Form 4562)	20	
21	Depletion	21	
22	Advertising	22	
23	Pension, profit-sharing, etc., plans	23	
24	Employee benefit programs	24	
25	Domestic production activities deduction (attach Form 8903)	25	
26	Other deductions (attach schedule)	26	
27	Total deductions. Add lines 12 through 26 ▶	27	
28	Taxable income before net operating loss deduction and special deductions. Subtract line 27 from line 11	28	
29	Less: a Net operating loss deduction (see instructions)	29a	
	b Special deductions (Schedule C, line 20)	29b		29c	

Tax, Refundable Credits, and Payments

30	Taxable income. Subtract line 29c from line 28 (see instructions)	30	
31	Total tax (Schedule J, line 10)	31	
32a	2008 overpayment credited to 2009	32a	
b	2009 estimated tax payments	32b	
c	2009 refund applied for on Form 4466	32c ( ) d Bal ▶	32d	
e	Tax deposited with Form 7004	32e	
f	Credits: (1) Form 2439 (2) Form 4136	32f	
g	Refundable credits from Form 3800, line 19c, and Form 8827, line 8c	32g		32h	
33	Estimated tax penalty (see instructions). Check if Form 2220 is attached ▶ ☐	33	
34	Amount owed. If line 32h is smaller than the total of lines 31 and 33, enter amount owed	34	
35	Overpayment. If line 32h is larger than the total of lines 31 and 33, enter amount overpaid	35	
36	Enter amount from line 35 you want: Credited to 2010 estimated tax ▶ Refunded ▶	36	

Sign Here

Under penalties of perjury, I declare that I have examined this return, including accompanying schedules and statements, and to the best of my knowledge and belief, it is true, correct, and complete. Declaration of preparer (other than taxpayer) is based on all information of which preparer has any knowledge.

▶ _____ _____ ▶ _____
Signature of officer Date Title

May the IRS discuss this return with the preparer shown below (see instructions)? ☐ Yes ☐ No

Paid Preparer's Use Only

Preparer's signature		Date	Check if self-employed ☐	Preparer's SSN or PTIN
Firm's name (or yours if self-employed), address, and ZIP code			EIN	
			Phone no.	

For Privacy Act and Paperwork Reduction Act Notice, see separate instructions.

Cat. No. 11450Q

Form **1120** (2009)

Form 1120 (2009) Page **2**

Schedule A — Cost of Goods Sold   (see instructions)

1	Inventory at beginning of year	1	
2	Purchases	2	
3	Cost of labor	3	
4	Additional section 263A costs (attach schedule)	4	
5	Other costs (attach schedule)	5	
6	Total. Add lines 1 through 5	6	
7	Inventory at end of year	7	
8	Cost of goods sold. Subtract line 7 from line 6. Enter here and on page 1, line 2	8	

9a Check all methods used for valuing closing inventory:

    (i) ☐ Cost

    (ii) ☐ Lower of cost or market

    (iii) ☐ Other (Specify method used and attach explanation.) ▶ _____

  b Check if there was a writedown of subnormal goods   ▶ ☐

  c Check if the LIFO inventory method was adopted this tax year for any goods (if checked, attach Form 970)   ▶ ☐

  d If the LIFO inventory method was used for this tax year, enter percentage (or amounts) of closing inventory computed under LIFO | 9d | |

  e If property is produced or acquired for resale, do the rules of section 263A apply to the corporation?   ☐ Yes   ☐ No

  f Was there any change in determining quantities, cost, or valuations between opening and closing inventory? If "Yes," attach explanation   ☐ Yes   ☐ No

Schedule C — Dividends and Special Deductions   (see instructions)

		(a) Dividends received	(b) %	(c) Special deductions (a) × (b)
1	Dividends from less-than-20%-owned domestic corporations (other than debt-financed stock)		70	
2	Dividends from 20%-or-more-owned domestic corporations (other than debt-financed stock)		80	
3	Dividends on debt-financed stock of domestic and foreign corporations		see instructions	
4	Dividends on certain preferred stock of less-than-20%-owned public utilities		42	
5	Dividends on certain preferred stock of 20%-or-more-owned public utilities		48	
6	Dividends from less-than-20%-owned foreign corporations and certain FSCs		70	
7	Dividends from 20%-or-more-owned foreign corporations and certain FSCs		80	
8	Dividends from wholly owned foreign subsidiaries		100	
9	Total. Add lines 1 through 8. See instructions for limitation			
10	Dividends from domestic corporations received by a small business investment company operating under the Small Business Investment Act of 1958		100	
11	Dividends from affiliated group members		100	
12	Dividends from certain FSCs		100	
13	Dividends from foreign corporations not included on lines 3, 6, 7, 8, 11, or 12			
14	Income from controlled foreign corporations under subpart F (attach Form(s) 5471)			
15	Foreign dividend gross-up			
16	IC-DISC and former DISC dividends not included on lines 1, 2, or 3			
17	Other dividends			
18	Deduction for dividends paid on certain preferred stock of public utilities			
19	Total dividends. Add lines 1 through 17. Enter here and on page 1, line 4 ▶			
20	Total special deductions. Add lines 9, 10, 11, 12, and 18. Enter here and on page 1, line 29b ▶			

Schedule E — Compensation of Officers   (see instructions for page 1, line 12)

Note: Complete Schedule E only if total receipts (line 1a plus lines 4 through 10 on page 1) are $500,000 or more.

(a) Name of officer	(b) Social security number	(c) Percent of time devoted to business	Percent of corporation stock owned		(f) Amount of compensation
			(d) Common	(e) Preferred	
1		%	%	%	
		%	%	%	
		%	%	%	
		%	%	%	
		%	%	%	

2	Total compensation of officers	
3	Compensation of officers claimed on Schedule A and elsewhere on return	
4	Subtract line 3 from line 2. Enter the result here and on page 1, line 12	

Form **1120** (2009)

Form 1120 (2009)   Page **3**

Schedule J   Tax Computation   (see instructions)

1. Check if the corporation is a member of a controlled group (attach Schedule O (Form 1120)) . . . ▶ ☐
2. Income tax. Check if a qualified personal service corporation (see instructions) . . . . ▶ ☐   **2**
3. Alternative minimum tax (attach Form 4626) **3**
4. Add lines 2 and 3 . . . . **4**

5a. Foreign tax credit (attach Form 1118) **5a**
  b. Credit from Form 8834, line 29 . . . . **5b**
  c. General business credit (attach Form 3800) **5c**
  d. Credit for prior year minimum tax (attach Form 8827) **5d**
  e. Bond credits from Form 8912 . . . . **5e**
6. Total credits.   Add lines 5a through 5e **6**
7. Subtract line 6 from line 4 . . . . **7**
8. Personal holding company tax (attach Schedule PH (Form 1120)) **8**
9. Other taxes. Check if from: ☐ Form 4255   ☐ Form 8611   ☐ Form 8697
                        ☐ Form 8866   ☐ Form 8902   ☐ Other (attach schedule) **9**
10. Total tax.   Add lines 7 through 9. Enter here and on page 1, line 31 . . . . **10**

Schedule K   Other Information   (see instructions)

				Yes	No
1	Check accounting method: a ☐ Cash b ☐ Accrual c ☐ Other (specify) ▶ _____				
2	See the instructions and enter the:				
a	Business activity code no. ▶ _____				
b	Business activity ▶ _____				
c	Product or service ▶ _____				
3	Is the corporation a subsidiary in an affiliated group or a parent-subsidiary controlled group?				
	If "Yes," enter name and EIN of the parent corporation ▶ _____				
	_____				
4	At the end of the tax year:				
a	Did any foreign or domestic corporation, partnership (including any entity treated as a partnership), trust, or tax-exempt organization own directly 20% or more, or own, directly or indirectly, 50% or more of the total voting power of all classes of the corporation's stock entitled to vote? If "Yes," complete Part I of Schedule G (Form 1120) (attach Schedule G)				
b	Did any individual or estate own directly 20% or more, or own, directly or indirectly, 50% or more of the total voting power of all classes of the corporation's stock entitled to vote? If "Yes," complete Part II of Schedule G (Form 1120) (attach Schedule G) .				

				Yes	No
5	At the end of the tax year, did the corporation:				
a	Own directly 20% or more, or own, directly or indirectly, 50% or more of the total voting power of all classes of stock entitled to vote of any foreign or domestic corporation not included on Form 851, Affiliations Schedule? For rules of constructive ownership, see instructions If "Yes," complete (i) through (iv).				

(i) Name of Corporation	(ii) Employer Identification Number (if any)	(iii) Country of Incorporation	(iv) Percentage Owned in Voting Stock

                                                                           Form **1120** (2009)

Form 1120 (2009)   Page **4**

Schedule K	Continued

b Own directly an interest of 20% or more, or own, directly or indirectly, an interest of 50% or more in any foreign or domestic partnership (including an entity treated as a partnership) or in the beneficial interest of a trust? For rules of constructive ownership, see instructions
If "Yes," complete (i) through (iv).

(i) Name of Entity	(ii) Employer Identification Number (if any)	(iii) Country of Organization	(iv) Maximum Percentage Owned in Profit, Loss, or Capital

6 During this tax year, did the corporation pay dividends (other than stock dividends and distributions in exchange for stock) in excess of the corporation's current and accumulated earnings and profits? (See sections 301 and 316.) . . . .
If "Yes," file Form 5452, Corporate Report of Nondividend Distributions.
If this is a consolidated return, answer here for the parent corporation and on Form 851 for each subsidiary.

7 At any time during the tax year, did one foreign person own, directly or indirectly, at least 25% of (a) the total voting power of all classes of the corporation's stock entitled to vote or   (b) the total value of all classes of the corporation's stock? . . . .
For rules of attribution, see section 318. If "Yes," enter:
(i) Percentage owned ▶ _____ and (ii) Owner's country ▶ _____
(c) The corporation may have to file Form 5472, Information Return of a 25% Foreign-Owned U.S. Corporation or a Foreign Corporation Engaged in a U.S. Trade or Business. Enter the number of Forms 5472 attached   ▶ _____

8 Check this box if the corporation issued publicly offered debt instruments with original issue discount . . . . ▶ ☐
If checked, the corporation may have to file Form 8281, Information Return for Publicly Offered Original Issue Discount Instruments.

9 Enter the amount of tax-exempt interest received or accrued during the tax year   ▶ $ _____

10 Enter the number of shareholders at the end of the tax year (if 100 or fewer)   ▶ _____

11 If the corporation has an NOL for the tax year and is electing to forego the carryback period, check here . . . . . . ▶ ☐
If the corporation is filing a consolidated return, the statement required by Regulations section 1.1502-21(b)(3) must be attached or the election will not be valid.

12 Enter the available NOL carryover from prior tax years (do not reduce it by any deduction on line 29a.)   ▶ $ _____

13 Are the corporation's total receipts (line 1a plus lines 4 through 10 on page 1) for the tax year and its total assets at the end of the tax year less than $250,000? . . . .
If "Yes," the corporation is not required to complete Schedules L, M-1, and M-2 on page 5. Instead, enter the total amount of cash distributions and the book value of property distributions (other than cash) made during the tax year.   ▶ $ _____

Form **1120** (2009)

Form 1120 (2009)   Page **5**

Schedule L	Balance Sheets per Books	Beginning of tax year		End of tax year	
	Assets	(a)	(b)	(c)	(d)
1	Cash				
2a	Trade notes and accounts receivable				
b	Less allowance for bad debts	( )		( )	
3	Inventories				
4	U.S. government obligations				
5	Tax-exempt securities (see instructions)				
6	Other current assets (attach schedule)				
7	Loans to shareholders				
8	Mortgage and real estate loans				
9	Other investments (attach schedule)				
10a	Buildings and other depreciable assets				
b	Less accumulated depreciation	( )		( )	
11a	Depletable assets				
b	Less accumulated depletion	( )		( )	
12	Land (net of any amortization)				
13a	Intangible assets (amortizable only)				
b	Less accumulated amortization	( )		( )	
14	Other assets (attach schedule)				
15	Total assets				
	Liabilities and Shareholders' Equity				
16	Accounts payable				
17	Mortgages, notes, bonds payable in less than 1 year				
18	Other current liabilities (attach schedule)				
19	Loans from shareholders				
20	Mortgages, notes, bonds payable in 1 year or more				
21	Other liabilities (attach schedule)				
22	Capital stock: a Preferred stock				
	b Common stock				
23	Additional paid-in capital				
24	Retained earnings—Appropriated (attach schedule)				
25	Retained earnings—Unappropriated				
26	Adjustments to shareholders' equity (attach schedule)				
27	Less cost of treasury stock		( )		( )
28	Total liabilities and shareholders' equity				

Schedule M-1	Reconciliation of Income (Loss) per Books With Income per Return

Note: Schedule M-3 required instead of Schedule M-1 if total assets are $10 million or more—see instructions

1	Net income (loss) per books		7	Income recorded on books this year not included on this return (itemize):	
2	Federal income tax per books			Tax-exempt interest $ _____	
3	Excess of capital losses over capital gains			_____	
4	Income subject to tax not recorded on books this year (itemize): _____			_____	
	_____		8	Deductions on this return not charged against book income this year (itemize):	
5	Expenses recorded on books this year not deducted on this return (itemize):		a	Depreciation $ _____	
a	Depreciation $ _____		b	Charitable contributions $ _____	
b	Charitable contributions $ _____			_____	
c	Travel and entertainment $ _____			_____	
	_____		9	Add lines 7 and 8	
6	Add lines 1 through 5		10	Income (page 1, line 28)—line 6 less line 9	

Schedule M-2	Analysis of Unappropriated Retained Earnings per Books (Line 25, Schedule L)

1	Balance at beginning of year		5	Distributions: a Cash	
2	Net income (loss) per books			b Stock	
3	Other increases (itemize): _____			c Property	
	_____		6	Other decreases (itemize): _____	
	_____		7	Add lines 5 and 6	
4	Add lines 1, 2, and 3		8	Balance at end of year (line 4 less line 7)	

Form **1120** (2009)

182. Form 8910 Alternative Motor Vehicle Credit

Form **8910** Department of the Treasury Internal Revenue Service	**Alternative Motor Vehicle Credit** ▶ Attach to your tax return. ▶ See separate instructions.	OMB No. 1545-1998 20**08** Attachment Sequence No. 152

Name(s) shown on return | Identifying number

Part I — Tentative Credit

Use a separate column for each vehicle. If you need more columns, use additional Forms 8910 and include the totals on lines 8 and 12.		(a)	(b)	(c)
1 Year, make, and model of vehicle	1			
2 Enter date vehicle was placed in service (MM/DD/YYYY) .	2	/ /	/ /	/ /
3 Maximum credit allowable (see instructions)	3			
4 Phaseout percentage (see instructions)	4	%	%	%
5 Tentative credit. Multiply line 3 by line 4	5			

Part II — Credit for Business/Investment Use Part of Vehicle

6 Business/investment use percentage (see instructions) . . .	6	%	%	%
7 Multiply line 5 by line 6	7			
8 Add columns (a) through (c) on line 7			8	
9 Alternative motor vehicle credit from partnerships and S corporations			9	
10 Business/investment use part of credit. Add lines 8 and 9. Partnerships and S corporations, report this amount on Schedule K; all others, report this amount on Form 3800, line 1r			10	

Part III — Credit for Personal Use Part of Vehicle

11 Subtract line 7 from line 5	11			
12 Add columns (a) through (c) on line 11		12		
13 Regular tax before credits: • Individuals. Enter the amount from Form 1040, line 44 (or Form 1040NR, line 41) • Other filers. Enter the regular tax before credits from your return .		13		
14 Credits that reduce regular tax before the alternative motor vehicle credit: a Personal credits from Form 1040 or Form 1040NR (see instructions) .	14a			
b Foreign tax credit	14b			
c Credit from Form 8834	14c			
d Add lines 14a through 14c		14d		
15 Net regular tax. Subtract line 14d from line 13. If zero or less, stop here; do not file this form unless you are claiming a credit on line 10		15		
16 Tentative minimum tax (see instructions): • Individuals. Enter the amount from Form 6251, line 34 . . . . • Other filers. Enter the tentative minimum tax from your alternative minimum tax form or schedule		16		
17 Subtract line 16 from line 15. If zero or less, stop here; do not file this form unless you are claiming a credit on line 10		17		
18 Personal use part of credit. Enter the smaller of line 12 or 17 here and on Form 1040, line 54; Form 1040NR, line 49; or the appropriate line of your return. If line 17 is smaller than line 12, see instructions		18		

For Paperwork Reduction Act Notice, see separate instructions. | Cat. No. 37720F | Form **8910** (2008)

183. Application–New Mexico Alternative Energy Product Manufacturers Tax

RPD-41330
Int. 04/2008

State of New Mexico - Taxation and Revenue Department
APPLICATION FOR
ALTERNATIVE ENERGY PRODUCT MANUFACTURERS TAX CREDIT

Name of business

Address

City	State	ZIP code

New Mexico CRS identification number

Name of contact person	Telephone number ( )

I. QUALIFYING INFORMATION

1. Calendar year in which the qualified expenditures were made: _____
   (Purchase must be made after July 1, 2006 to qualify.)
2. Attach a detailed schedule showing the types of manufacturing equipment purchased, the date of purchase and the amount expended.
3. Description of the alternative energy product that is being manufactured by the applicant:

   _____

   _____

4. a. Number of new full-time employees hired: (Itemize on Form RPD-41330, Schedule A) _____

   b. Number of full-time employees employed one year prior to the date of this application: _____

II. CALCULATION OF CREDIT CLAIMED

A. Total qualified expenditures on which credit is claimed: $ _____

B. Alternative Energy Product Manufacturers Tax Credit claimed: (Line A x 5%) $ _____

III. I CERTIFY THAT:

☐ The equipment on which credit is claimed on this application was used directly and exclusively in the taxpayer's manufacturing operation and does not include a vehicle that leaves the site of a manufacturing operation.

☐ The equipment on which credit is claimed on this application does not include any property for which the taxpayer claims a credit against compensating tax pursuant to Section 7-9-79 NMSA 1978.

I declare I have examined this application, including accompanying invoices, schedules and/or statements, and to the best of my knowledge and belief this application is true, correct and complete.

Authorized signature	Title	Date

FOR DIVISION USE ONLY

This application for Alternative Energy Product Manufacturers Tax Credit was reviewed by the Taxation and Revenue Department and was:

☐ Approved in the amount of $ _____

☐ Adjusted and Approved in the amount of $ _____

☐ Disapproved

Reason for Adjustment/ Disapproval_____

Signature of Director or Delegate	Date	Approval Number

184. Oregon Business Energy Tax Credit Application

Business Energy Tax Credit

Application for Final Certification for Pass-through Projects

For office use only
Application #:
Date received:
Final certified cost:

Application must be complete

1. Project information

Application #: (See Preliminary Certificate):

Project owner name:
(Must be the same as the Preliminary Certificate)

Contact person: Title:

Mailing address:

City/state/zip

Phone: E-mail:

Site address of project:

City: County: Zip:

2. Date project completed:
(The specific date the project is operational and all contractors, vendors, etc. have been paid in full.)

3. Permits and licenses (Check one)

☐ I have submitted copies of all applicable permits and licenses required for my facility under local and state laws

☐ My facility did not require any permits or licenses under local and state laws

4. Compliance with land use laws of city and/or county (Check one)

☐ I have submitted copies of documents demonstrating that this facility complies with or has a variance from the land use laws of the city/county where the facility is located

☐ Compliance with land use laws was not applicable to my facility

5. Facility property taxes (Required)

☐ I have submitted documentation from the county where the facility is located that the facility property taxes are current

3   11/09 ODOE-088

6. Business plan

As project owner, I intend to maintain and operate this business for at least 5 years?
☐ Yes ☐ No

Have you received or applied for other Business Energy Tax Credits for this facility or other facilities? ☐ Yes ☐ No

If YES, please list the BETC application numbers:_____

Number of jobs created by project? _____

Number of jobs eliminated by project? _____

7. Project cost

Final project costs (Regardless if these costs are eligible costs for the Business Energy Tax Credit)	☐ I have enclosed a CPA letter if final project costs are $50,000 or more	$
Subtract any federal grants Is this part of the 2009 federal stimulus package? ☐ Yes ☐ No		$
Total final project costs		$

Other incentives: Please list any utility, Energy Trust of Oregon, or other organization rebates or incentives (not loans) or any federal tax credits that you received (or expect to receive) for this project. List the name of the group and the amount received. If there are none, state "none." (**This is a required field**.) These financial incentives and any federal tax credits will not be deducted from your final eligible project costs, however, the sum of all financial incentives and a federal tax credit and the Business Energy Tax Credit may <u>not</u> exceed 100 percent of the final eligible project costs.

$

$

$

Loan contracts or binding agreements: If your project was paid for with loan agreements or binding contracts, you must provide documentation from the lender that your loan/contract is not in default. Please check one.

☐ Yes – I have a loan agreement or binding contract to pay for this project. I have included **required** documentation from the lender that my loan/contract is current and not in default.

Amount of loan: _____

Lender: _____

☐ No – I do not have a loan agreement or binding contract to pay for this project.

4   11/09 ODOE-088

8. Project Owner Statement (All fields must be completed)

1. I certify that the information in this application is correct and I am the owner of this energy project. I have complied with all conditions of the Preliminary Certificate: ORS 469.185-225, 315.354, 315.356, and OAR 330-090-0105 to 330-090-0150. I grant to the Oregon Department of Energy permission to inspect the project for compliance with tax credit requirements either before issuing Final Certification or during the years in which a tax credit is being claimed.

2. I understand that Oregon Department of Energy approval and certification of my project is for tax credit purposes only. The Oregon Department of Energy does not guarantee or in any way ensure the performance of any equipment, the quality of any system or the reliability of any dealer.

3. I will comply with the provision that the facility must operate in accordance with the representation made in the Application for Preliminary Certification. I understand that I must inform the Oregon Department of Energy in writing within 60 days and before any additional tax credits are claimed if the facility is sold, traded or disposed of in some way, or if the term of a leased facility has ended and that the Director will revoke the Final Certification.

4. I certify that the project complies with all local, state and federal requirements and I obtained all necessary permits.

5. I understand that this tax credit application is a public record and that Oregon Department of Energy may be required by law to disclose information in this tax credit application to the public on request. I have marked any information that I request be kept confidential. I understand that marking information does not guarantee that it will be kept confidential and that the Director of the Oregon Department of Energy will make any decisions regarding public disclosure of information contained in this application in accordance with the Oregon Public Records Law.

6. I understand that the Oregon Department of Energy does not endorse any company that requests information on this application and does not sell information as a mailing list.

7. I hereby (a) release the State of Oregon and its commissions, agencies, officers, employees, contractors, and agents, and agree to defend and indemnify the foregoing from and against any claims, demands, or costs (including attorney and expert witness fees at trial and on appeal) arising from or in any way related to claims made by applicant or any parent or subsidiary of applicant and which are related in any way to the Oregon Department of Energy's issuance or failure to issue any pre-certification or final certification to applicant for a Business Energy Tax Credit, or the inability to obtain a Business Energy Tax Credit; and (b) agree to reimburse the State of Oregon for any damages, costs and expenses, including, but not limited to attorney fees and reasonable expenses for agency staff and in-house legal counsel incurred as a result of, or arising from or in any way related to the applicant obtaining certification for a Business Energy Tax Credit by fraud or misrepresentation or failing to construct or operate the facility in compliance with the plans, specifications and procedures in any certification to applicant for a Business Energy Tax Credit. Agreement to the terms of this paragraph by applicants that are agencies of the State of Oregon is subject to the limitations of Article XI, section 7 of the Oregon Constitution and the Oregon Tort Claims Act (ORS 30.260 through 30.300).

8. I understand that the sum of all financial incentives for this project and the tax credit amount can not exceed the total eligible project cost.

9. I verify that the project owner does not restrict membership, sales, or services on the basis of race, color, creed, religion, national origin, sexual preference or gender.

Project Owner Name:
(Must be the same as the Preliminary Certificate)

SSN or Tax ID#:	Application #

By signing this Statement, I acknowledge that I have read and agree with the terms and conditions of the Project Owner Statement and have not altered it in any way. I certify that I am the owner, partner, member, officer or shareholder of the project owner.

Signature:_____ Date:_____

Printed Name: _____ Title: _____

All fields must be filled or application will be returned.

11/09 ODOE-088

9. Tax Credit Recipient Statement Please photocopy for each tax credit recipient

1. I understand that OAR 330-090-0130 authorizes the Oregon Department of Energy to use my federal tax identification or social security number as an identification number in maintaining internal records and may be shared with the Oregon Department of Revenue to establish the identity of an individual in order to administer state tax law.

2. I understand that the tax credit recipient must comply with Oregon Department of Revenue requirements to document that the credit has been appropriately assigned, allocated or transferred, and claimed, and that compliance is subject to audit.

3. I understand that this tax credit application is a public record and that Oregon Department of Energy may be required by law to disclose information in this tax credit application to the public on request. I have marked any information that I request be kept confidential. I understand that marking information does not guarantee that it will be kept confidential and that the Director of the Oregon Department of Energy will make any decisions regarding public disclosure of information contained in this application in accordance with the Oregon Public Records Law.

4. I understand that the Oregon Department of Energy does not endorse any company that requests information on this application and does not sell information as a mailing list.

5. The undersigned Tax Credit Recipient hereby releases the State of Oregon and its commissions, agencies, officers, employees, contractors, and agents, and agrees to defend and indemnify the foregoing from and against any claims, demands, or costs (including attorney and expert witness fees at trial and on appeal) arising from or in any way related to claims made by Tax Credit Recipient or any parent or subsidiary of Tax Credit Recipient and which are related in any way to the Oregon Department of Energy's issuance or failure to issue any pre-certification or final certification to applicant for a Business Energy Tax Credit, or the inability to obtain a Business Energy Tax Credit. This release and indemnification does not affect the right of the undersigned to claim a Business Energy Tax Credit on an Oregon tax return under a final certification issued by the Oregon Department of Energy and in accordance with applicable law.

6. I verify that the tax credit recipient does not restrict membership, sales, or services on the basis of race, color, creed, religion, national origin, sexual preference or gender.

7. I have completed this form to the best of my knowledge.

Tax Credit Recipient (All fields must be completed. Please print)	Application #
Tax credit recipient name:	
Recipient SSN or Tax I.D. #:	Tax credit share: %
By signing this statement, I certify that I am an individual or corporation that has an Oregon tax liability. * (A pass-through tax credit may **not** be issued to a partnership, an LLC, or an LLP filing taxes as a partnership.)	
Recipient mailing address:	
City/state/zip:	
Recipient phone:	Recipient E-mail:
By signing this statement, I acknowledge that I have read and agree with the terms and conditions of the Tax Credit Recipient Statement above and have not altered it in any way.	
Signature of tax credit recipient:	Date:

* **Information will be shared with the Oregon Department of Revenue to administer state tax law. Please contact the Oregon Department of Revenue for more information 1-800-356-4222. All fields must be filled or application will be returned.**

6   11/09 ODOE-088

CHAPTER 17

Forms for Keeping Track of Web Metrics

VEN IF YOUR BUSINESS DOESN'T HAVE A website (which it should), it's going to be visible on the Web whether you like it or not. Conduct a search on the major search engines (Google, Bing, and Yahoo!) to see where your business appears. The results may surprise you as it's likely even the most remote sole proprietor who sells lumber to locals in the northern outposts of Maine has been mentioned in a blog, a popular social media site, an online merchant circle, and even local online newspaper publications. Case in point—your business is online and you can extract quantifiable figures using the right forms and metrics. In addition, many small business owners have already conducted one or several online marketing campaigns.

Do you generate customers online? If so, use the sample *Behavior Metrics for Online Customers* spreadsheet to analyze your online reach. Assess the impact your online audience has on your bottom line by monitoring activity on your site.

If you email to a list of current subscribers or use outsourced lists to reach new audiences, it's important to keep track of your e-mail marketing campaigns. Refer to the sample *E-Mail Marketing Campaign Analysis* form as an example of how to monitor your own campaigns and determine if they're effective.

Connecting with customers online can be a difficult task considering the lack of face-to-face time. If a portion (or all) of your customer base exists online, use the *Month by Month Online Revenue Trends* form to assess online orders, transaction trends, and ultimately the customers' impact on your business.

Your total online marketing efforts may consist of multiple online marketing strategies. Email, display ads, contextual ads, and paid search campaigns are the general ingredients of an online marketing plan.

Social media networks have rivaled "veteran" search engines and become viable sources of income for many start-ups and established business alike. This chapter includes social media forms to help you keep track of that online buzz essential to marketing metrics. It's important to separate the qualitative and quantitative metrics and identify campaign goals before launch.

Social sites have proliferated in the last few years. Tweets, Friends, Diggs, and the like have all become part of business' vernacular. And while as a business owner the last thing you want your employees doing is spending time on social media sites, the metrics may convince you otherwise. To start, use the simple *Online Viral Campaign Metrics* form to track your buzz-worthy reach. Use the sample *Widget and Social Media Application Monitoring* form to track the number of people who install and use widgets and applications created by your company. The sample *Monthly Twitter Campaign Monitoring* form can be duplicated to track if Twitter is an effective marketing tool for your company.

185. Behavior Metrics for Online Customers by Month

Site:	Jan	Feb	Mar	Apr	May	Jun	Jul	Aug	Sep	Oct	Nov	Dec
Number of visits												
Number of unique visitors during the month												
Total unique visitors acquired by the site												
Frequency (Total Visits / Total Unique Visits)												
Total time spent on all pages												
Duration (Total Time / Total # of Visits)												

186. E-mail Marketing Campaign Analysis

Campaign	Campaign Dates	Size of List	Inbox (delivered)	# of Opened E-mails	click Through Rate (# of clicks / # of opens)	Total Cost of Campaign (marketing + media costs)	Total Aqcuisitions	Cost per Aqcuisition (total advertising costs / # of acquisitions)
List 1								
List 2								
List 3								
List 4								
List 5								

187. Month by Month Online Revenue Trends

Year:	Jan	Feb	Mar	Apr	May	Jun	Jul	Aug	Sep	Oct	Nov	Dec
Unique Visits to Entire Site												
Total Site Page Views												
Acquisitions (customers)												
Conversions												
Revenues												
Revenue Growth												
Revenue per 1000 page views [1000 (Total Revenue / Total Unique Visits)]												
Revenue per Unique Visitors [1000 (total revenue / total pageviews)]												
Revenue per Customer (total revenue / total # of customers)												
Revenue per Order (total revenue / amount of total sales)												

188. Online Viral Campaign Metrics

Campaign:	Campaign Dates	Digg: Total # of Diggs	Mixx: Total # of Votes	Reddit: Total # of Points	Delicious: Total # Saved	StumbleUpon: Total # Reviews	Facebook: Total # Fanned	Twitter: Total # Tetweets

189. Widget and Social Media Application Monitoring

Widget/Application Name:	Week 1	Week 2	Week 3	Week 4	
Launch Date					Total Growth +/-%
End Date					
Installs					Total Installs:
Active Users					Total Users:

Audience Profile	Location	Age	Gender	Ethnicity	Income	Education Levels	Single/ Married	Kids/ No Kids

190. Monthly Twitter Campaign Monitoring

Campaign/Account Name:						
Start Date:						
Objective:						
	January	February	March	April	May	June
Followers						
ReTweets						
Click-Throughs						
Direct Messages						
Follower Mentions						
List Followers						
Totals						